ABOUT THE AUTHOR

Professor Carlos M Correa is Director of the University of Buenos Aires' Masters Programme on Science and Technology Policy and Management. Trained originally both as a lawyer and as an economist, he has made a speciality of technology and intellectual property rights. A former public servant (he was Undersecretary of State for Informatics and Development, 1984-89, and the Argentinian Government's official delegate to GATT and WIPO during the negotiations on intellectual property rights), he has also acted as a consultant to many international and regional organizations, including UNCTAD, UNIDO, WHO, FAO, ECLAC, the Inter-American Development Bank, and the Secretariat of the Convention on Biological Diversity. He has also been a Visiting Professor at various universities in Latin America, and is the author of several books and articles in international journals on issues of technology and intellectual property.

D0113597

Intellectual Property Rights, the WTO and Developing Countries
The TRIPS Agreement and Policy Options

CARLOS M CORREA

Zed Books Ltd.
London and New York

TWN
Third World Network
Penang, Malaysia

Intellectual Property Rights, the WTO and Developing Countries:
The TRIPS Agreement and Policy Options
is published by:
Zed Books Ltd.,
7 Cynthia Street,
London, N1 9JF, and
Room 400, 175 Fifth Avenue,
New York, 10010
and
Third World Network,
228 Macalister Road,
10400 Penang, Malaysia.

Copyright © Carlos M Correa 2000

First Printing: 2000
Second Printing: 2000

Printed by Jutaprint, 2 Solok Sungai Pinang 3,
11600 Penang, Malaysia.

ISBN 1 85649 736 4 Hb
ISBN 1 85649 737 2 Pb

CIP data is available from the British Library.

To Liliana for her permanent support,
and to Julia, Carlos, Laura, Juan Ignacio,
Elisa and Carolina for their encouragement

Contents

CHAPTER VII

UPCOMING REVIEW OF THE TRIPS AGREEMENT

ANNEX

OPTIONS FOR IMPLEMENTING THE TRIPS AGREEMENT IN DEVELOPING COUNTRIES

ACRONYMS AND ABBREVIATIONS

ASTA	American Seed Trade Association
BIOS	Basic Input-Output System
CAD/CAM	computer-aided design/computer-aided manufacturing
CBD	Convention on Biological Diversity
CFCs	chlorofluorocarbons
CGIAR	Consultative Group on International Agricultural Research
CITED	Copyright in Transmitted Electronic Documents
DSU	Dispute Settlement Understanding
EMRs	exclusive marketing rights
EPO	European Patent Office
EST	environmentally sound technology
EU	European Union
FAO	Food and Agriculture Organization
FDA	Food and Drug Administration (US)
FDI	foreign direct investment
FTC	Federal Trade Commission (US)
G7	Group of 7 (leading industrial nations)
GATS	General Agreement on Trade in Services
GATT	General Agreement on Tariffs and Trade
GSP	Generalized System of Preferences
IPRs	intellectual property rights
ITs	Information Technologies
IU	International Undertaking on Plant Genetic Resources
MEAs	multilateral environment agreements
MERCOSUR	Southern Cone Common Market
MNEs	multinational enterprises
NAFTA	North American Free Trade Agreement
NGOs	non-governmental organizations
NICs	newly industrializing countries
NIEs	newly industrializing economies
NWIC	National Wheat Improvement Committee (US)
OECD	Organization for Economic Cooperation and Development
PBRs	plant breeders' rights
PGRs	plant genetic resources
PTO	Patent and Trademark Office (US)
R&B	research and breeding

R&D	research and development
SCPA	Semiconductor Chip Protection Act
SPC	supplementary protection certificate
TNCs	transnational corporations
TPA	tissue plasminogen activator
TRIPS	Trade-Related Aspects of Intellectual Property Rights
UNCTAD	United Nations Conference on Trade and Development
UNESCO	United Nations Educational, Scientific and Cultural Organization
UPOV	Union for the Protection of New Varieties of Plants
USTR	United States Trade Representative
WHO	World Health Organization
WIPO	World Intellectual Property Organization
WTO	World Trade Organization

Foreword

THIS book is the result of research undertaken by the author at the Masters Programme on Science and Technology and the Center for Interdisciplinary Studies on Law and Economics (CEIDIE) of the University of Buenos Aires. Some of the material that went into producing this book had earlier been published in the *Journal of World Intellectual Property*, the *European Intellectual Property Review* and *Science and Public Policy*, as well as by the Third World Network. These have, however, been revised and updated for this publication.

The book also includes the Report of an Expert Group on the TRIPS Agreement and Developing Countries, which provides guidance to developing countries on ways of implementing said Agreement in a manner consistent with development needs.

There is no intention to cover all issues raised by the adoption and implementation of the new rules on intellectual property adopted as a result of the Uruguay Round of multilateral trade negotiations. Rather, this book aims at succinctly addressing the main issues, providing bibliographic sources for further research and stimulating independent thinking on the implications of the TRIPS Agreement in developing countries.

The author thanks the Third World Network for the support given to the research, and his colleagues at the University of Buenos Aires for their cooperation.

Chapter I

General Context

WHAT IS TRIPS?

THE Uruguay Round introduced, for the first time in the history of the General Agreement on Tariffs and Trade (GATT), multilateral negotiations on "trade-related intellectual property rights". Under strong pressure by the industrialized countries, a specific agreement on the availability and enforcement of such rights became part of the Final Act of the Round: the Agreement on Trade-Related Aspects of Intellectual Property Rights (hereinafter the "TRIPS Agreement").

The TRIPS Agreement is, by its coverage, the most comprehensive international instrument on intellectual property rights (IPRs), dealing with all types of IPRs, with the sole exceptions of breeders' rights (only incidentally referred to) and utility models (or "petty patents").

The Agreement establishes minimum standards on

- copyright and related rights, including computer programs and databases
- trademarks
- geographical indications
- industrial designs
- patents
- integrated circuits, and
- undisclosed information (trade secrets).

The Agreement is based on and supplements, with additional obligations[1], the Paris, Berne, Rome and Washington[2] conventions in their respective fields. In other words, the Agreement does not constitute a fully independent convention, but rather an integrative instrument which provides "convention-plus" protection for IPRs[3]. The standards of protection set forth relate both to the availability of rights as well as to their enforcement. This means that Member countries cannot, in the specific areas and issues covered by the Agreement, confer a lower level of protection than provided under the Agreement. At the same time, Members cannot be obliged to provide "more extensive" protection (Article 1.1).

The development of detailed provisions on "enforcement" in the TRIPS Agreement is a major departure from preexisting conventions on IPRs. The Agreement stipulates specific obligations related to administrative and judicial procedures including, *inter alia*, provisions on evidence, injunctions, damages, measures at the border against counterfeiting, and penalties in case of infringement.

Another innovation is that, with the approval of the TRIPS Agreement, any controversy as to compliance with the minimum standards should be subject to a multilateral procedure in accordance with the Dispute Settlement Understanding (DSU). Once the existence of a violation has been determined, the affected country can apply cross-retaliations to the non-complying country, in any area covered by the World Trade Organization (WTO) Agreement (for instance, it may apply quotas to exports from the non-complying country).

The described mechanism provides an institutionalized, multilateral means to address disputes relating to IPRs. It is aimed at

---

[1] The provisions of the international conventions which are supplemented become compulsory even for countries that have not ratified them, except in the case of the Rome Convention (relating to producers of phonograms, performing artists and broadcasting organizations) which continues to be binding only on States that have joined it.

[2] The provisions of the Washington Convention on the protection of layout designs of integrated circuits (1989), which has never entered into force, became, however, enforceable through the TRIPS Agreement.

[3] There are some cases, however, where "convention-minus" protection is granted, such as in the case of moral rights provided for by the Berne Convention (see Correa, 1994a).

preventing unilateral actions, such as those undertaken by the United States under Section 301 of its Trade Act.

THE CONTEXT

Industrialized countries forced developing countries to initiate negotiation of an agreement on TRIPS with the clear objective of universalizing the standards of IPRs protection that the former had incorporated in their legislation, once they had attained a high level of technological and industrial capability. The evolution of IPRs standards, following changes in the relative strength of different industries, has been particularly tangible in the patent field, as illustrated by the late introduction of pharmaceutical product patents by France, Switzerland, Japan, Spain and other developed countries (Bercovitz, 1990).

Developing countries reluctantly negotiated increased standards of protection for IPRs in GATT, and finally acquiesced in making important concessions in terms of reforms of their intellectual property legislation, without obtaining any compensating concession from industrialized countries.

A number of factors that converged during the last decade explain the priority given by some countries, notably the United States, to a far-reaching reform of the intellectual property system worldwide (Correa, 1994b).

Firstly, technology became a factor of growing importance in international competition, particularly for the production of technology-intensive goods and services, which account for the most dynamic segments of international trade. This trend was reflected in the steady increase of research and development (R&D) expenditures in industrialized countries since the 1970s, with growing participation of the private sector in total R&D. In many of these countries, half or more of R&D expenditures are funded by the private sector, particularly by big companies in science-intensive sectors.

Secondly, high externalities in the production of knowledge associated with new technologies limited the appropriability of R&D results and prompted reforms in the IPRs regimes in order to create or reinforce exclusive rights. The United States pioneered the extension of IPRs protection in the field of new technologies. Based on their domestic developments, US firms and government actively pursued the internationalization of the new standards of protection via unilateral action and initiatives in various multilateral fora, including the World Intellectual Property Organization (WIPO) and GATT. This process was clearly shown with regard to computer programs (after the amendment of the copyright law in the United States in 1980, which recognized computer programs as a copyrightable work), semiconductors (protected in 1984 under a *sui generis* regime in accordance with the Semiconductor Chip Protection Act) and biotechnology (after the US Supreme Court's decision in *re Chakrabarty* in 1980 that admitted the patentability of living forms *per se*).

Thirdly, the elimination or reduction of trade barriers in developing countries increased the opportunities for direct exports to those countries. It also led to increased pressure by multinational enterprises to get unrestricted access to those markets and to be freed from the obligation to exploit patented inventions locally or to transfer technology to local firms.

Fourthly, during the 1980s US supremacy in manufacturing and technology had been eroded by catching-up processes in Japan, first, and in Asian newly industrializing countries (NICs) later. These countries emerged as aggressive competitors in consumer electronics, microelectronics, robotics, computers and peripherals, as well as in various services (e.g., engineering and construction). The erosion of the technological leadership of US firms in certain high-tech areas, coupled with the high US trade deficit, was partially attributed to a too-open technological and scientific system which allowed foreign countries to imitate and profit from US innovations. Thus, a major source of declining American competitiveness was conceived to be the losses from overseas piracy and counterfeiting activities (de Koning, 1997, p. 65).

This perception was astutely and effectively promoted by industrial lobbies (particularly the pharmaceutical, software and phonogram industries), which convinced the US government about the need to link trade and IPRs in order to increase the returns on R&D and to prevent imitation. The monopoly rights granted by IPRs were regarded as an instrument to avoid further catching-up based on imitative paths of industrialization, that is, as a tool to freeze the comparative advantages that had so far ensured US technological supremacy.

THE NORTH-SOUTH ASYMMETRIES

It is in the context described in the previous section that the United States launched an initiative to negotiate IPRs standards within GATT. The TRIPS Agreement was not merely conceived as an instrument to combat counterfeiting and piracy, an objective that most developing countries would have shared. The Agreement was also regarded as a component of a policy of "technological protectionism" aimed at consolidating an international division of labour whereunder Northern countries generate innovations and Southern countries constitute the market for the resulting products and services. It was also an expression of an aggressive action by the US industries to establish international rules that counter their declining competitive position in world markets.

The new emerging framework on IPRs basically universalizes standards of protection that are suitable for industrialized countries or, more precisely, for certain industrial sectors in which firms based in such countries dominate. Though the TRIPS Agreement leaves a certain room for manoeuvre at the national level, it restricts the options available and ignores the profound differences in economic and technological capabilities between the North and the South.

The developing countries' share in world R&D expenditures is negligible. It declined over the past decade from nearly 6% in 1980 to about 4% in 1990, despite the steady increase of R&D outlays in Asian NICs, particularly South Korea and Taiwan. Developing countries are, hence, overwhelmingly dependent upon innovations made in the North.

This dependence is also reflected in patent statistics. Thus, 95% of 1,650,800 patents granted in the United States between 1977 and 1996 were conferred on applicants from 10 industrialized countries. In that period, developing countries accounted for less than 2% (Kumar, 1997, pp. 5-9).

The share of developing countries in the trade of medium- and high-tech goods also indicates that industrialized countries will benefit the most from the new rules on IPRs. Of the exports of the Group of 7 (G7) leading industrial countries to OECD (Organization for Economic Cooperation and Development) countries, 56.7%

consist of medium- and high-technology goods[4], a proportion similar to that of the Asian "Tigers" (53.3%). The degree of Latin American specialization in those goods is significantly lower (26.5%). But Asian Tigers and Latin American countries together only account for about 11% of total exports of such goods to OECD countries, against 50.6% for G7 countries (Alcorta and Peres, 1995).

Not surprisingly, a study by the University of Delaware has shown, by applying a Helpman-Krugman model, that a positive correlation existed between an increase in exports from the United States in 1992 and the strengthening of patent protection in the importing countries (Smith, 1995).

THE LIMITS OF THE TRIPS AGREEMENT

Despite the origins of and main forces behind the TRIPS Agreement, as described earlier, this Agreement still contains elements that, duly applied, may permit a certain balance in its implementation.

In accordance with the Preamble, the main goal of the Agreement is "to reduce distortions and impediments to international trade". Though it is recognized that IPRs are "private rights", "the underlying public policy objectives of national systems for the protection of intellectual property, including developmental and technological objectives", are recognized as well.

More specifically, Articles 7 ("Objectives") and 8 ("Principles") provide a framework for the interpretation and implementation of IPRs. In accordance with Article 7, the protection of IPRs is not only intended to promote "technological innovation", but the "transfer and dissemination" of technology, which are of particular importance to developing countries. In addition, the concepts of Article 7 mean that the recognition and enforcement of IPRs are not ends in themselves, but are meant to enable each country – within the limits defined by the Agreement – to define a balanced regime of protection, to the mutual

---

[4] IPRs are of definite relevance in relation to goods of "high" and "medium" R&D intensity (such as automobiles, electronics, capital goods and pharmaceuticals) in that, except for trademarks and other signs, they are of greater importance to such goods than to those of "low" R&D intensity (such as textiles and food).

advantage of producers and users of technological knowledge and in a manner conducive to social and economic welfare. Article 8.1, on its side, stipulates that "Members may, in formulating or amending their national laws and regulations, adopt measures necessary to protect public health and nutrition, and to promote the public interest in sectors of vital importance to their socio-economic and technological development, provided that such measures are consistent with the provisions of this Agreement". Though a "consistency test" is to be applied, this principle stresses that no Member country can be prevented from taking into account its own public interests in its IPRs legislation in the post-TRIPS Agreement environment.

Another important "principle" is that "appropriate measures, provided that they are consistent with the provisions of this Agreement, may be needed to prevent the abuse of IPRs by rights-holders or the resort to practices which unreasonably restrain trade or adversely affect the international transfer of technology" (Article 8.2).

These are important provisions for framing national IPRs laws that respond to particular public health and other public interests and, particularly, for the interpretation of the provisions of the TRIPS Agreement. They leave room for adopting different solutions at the national level. They also make clear that measures may be adopted in order to prevent or remedy abuses of IPRs, in the light of Article 7 and of the Preamble, that is, taking social and economic welfare into account.

Under those provisions, national legislation can provide for a variety of measures that promote competition and balance, to some extent, the rights of the title-holders with those of the users of the technology. Such measures may include the following:

• Admissibility of parallel imports, under the principle of international exhaustion of rights (Article 6 of the TRIPS Agreement)

• Non-patentability of substances existing in nature and of animals and plants[5]

---

[5] Article 27.3(b), which allows for this exception, is to be reviewed in 1999.

- Exceptions to exclusive rights, such as experimentation under patent law, and "fair" or "private" use under copyright

- Compulsory licences of various types in the patent field

- Reverse engineering of computer programs and other copyrightable works.

In sum, while implementing the obligations imposed by the TRIPS Agreement, developing countries may take advantage of the room left in many areas to design legislation that is compatible with their own level of development and with their economic and techno-logical policies. The extent of that room and possible options for developing countries are further elaborated in the following chapters and in the annex ("Options for Implementing the TRIPS Agreement in Developing Countries"), particularly with respect to patents and undisclosed information in connection with new technologies.

THE TRIPS AGREEMENT AS A CEILING

The TRIPS Agreement sets forth the *minimum* standards to be applied by all Members of the WTO. Such standards are, at the same time, the upper limit that many countries are prepared to accept.

In accordance with Article 1 of the TRIPS Agreement,

"Members shall give effect to the provisions of this Agreement. Members may, but shall not be obliged to, implement in their law more extensive protection than is required by this Agreement, provided that such protection does not contravene the provisions of this Agreement. Members shall be free to determine the appropriate method of implementing the provisions of this Agreement within their own legal system and practice."

This provision provides a defence against demands for higher levels of protection or for ignoring the transitional terms provided for by the Agreement. At the same time, it explicitly allows a country, if it so wishes, to expand the protection to new areas not covered by the

Agreement, such as knowledge in possession of local and indigenous communities.

Non-compliance with the obligations stipulated by the TRIPS Agreement may only lead to action by other States and not by affected private parties. In addition, if a WTO Member does not observe certain minimum standards, no other Member can unilaterally apply trade sanctions against the former. Any complaint brought up should be dealt with under the multilateral procedures established by the Dispute Settlement Understanding. This clearly outlaws unilateral retaliations as applied by the United States under Section 301 of the US Trade Act.

TRANSITIONAL ARRANGEMENTS

All WTO Members had one year after the date of entry into force of the WTO Agreement to apply the obligations relating to intellectual property protection (Article 65.1). Developing countries have an additional period of four years, except for obligations concerning national and most-favoured-nation treatment, which become applicable after the expiry of the aforementioned one-year period (Article 65.2).

In addition to the general transitional period referred to above, a further period of five years is contemplated for countries which are bound to introduce product patent protection in areas of technology not so protected in their territory on the general date of application of the Agreement for these countries (Article 65.4). This applies to pharmaceutical products in countries such as Argentina, India, Egypt and other Arab countries.

The application of these transitional periods does not require any specific declaration or reservation by the concerned country: they are automatically applicable.

The establishment of these periods was not a generous concession by industrialized countries. It was the result of hard negotiations in which the latter obtained, in exchange, long transitional periods for complying with their obligations in agriculture and textiles. In other words, the transitional periods in TRIPS had a "price" – and a high one at that – for developing countries, in terms of export losses in such sectors.

On the other hand, transitional periods are essential for many developing countries, which need to introduce new legislation and adapt the affected economic sectors to the new regulatory framework. Studies made in some developing countries reveal that significant direct costs will have to be incurred to implement the new regulations, which imply changes not only in the administration of IPRs, but also in customs regulations and judicial procedures. In implementing the TRIPS Agreement, least developed countries will be confronted, according to the United Nations Conference on Trade and Development (UNCTAD), with "severe financial and administrative constraints" (UNCTAD, 1996, pp. 2-3).

The application of the transitional periods established by the TRIPS Agreement may provide the necessary time – but not the resources[6] – to introduce changes in legislation, develop the infrastructure for administration of IPRs, and introduce other measures required to reduce any eventual economic losses derived from the new framework.

However, the United States is threatening several developing countries with sanctions under Section 301 of its Trade Act. It requests, among other things, not only the immediate introduction of the TRIPS standards for patents but its retroactive application (under the so-called "pipeline" solution).

Such a request is completely illegitimate under the TRIPS Agreement. It disregards international binding rules, and deprives developing countries of their right to take the necessary time to introduce legal reforms and adopt measures that mitigate their eventual negative economic and social impact.

The US pressures are exerted principally with regard to pharmaceutical products, under the direct influence of the powerful US pharmaceutical industry. The US government has not shown interest in accelerating conformity with the TRIPS Agreement in other areas, such as geographical indications, breeders' rights or industrial designs.

---

[6] Developed country Members committed themselves to providing technical and financial cooperation to developing and least-developed country Members "to facilitate the implementation" of the TRIPS Agreement (Article 67). The text is, however, too general and subject, in any case, to "mutually agreed terms".

UNILATERAL OR MULTILATERAL?

An important trade-off sought by developing countries from the negotiation of the TRIPS Agreement was the establishment of a multilateral mechanism for dispute settlement that would avoid unilateral actions by developed countries. As a result of this concern, one of the explicit aims of the Agreement has been to reduce "tensions by reaching strengthened commitments to resolve disputes on trade-related intellectual property issues through multilateral procedures" (Preamble).

After the entry into force of the TRIPS Agreement, any controversy should be subject to a multilateral procedure of dispute settlement, and only after the completion of the procedure may retaliatory measures be adopted[7]. Unilateral actions undertaken by a Member to force another Member to adopt the Agreement's minimum standards are illegal under the new rules governing the WTO. *A fortiori*, no WTO Member may seek from another Member levels of protection which are beyond the standards accepted under the TRIPS Agreement.

The TRIPS Agreement does not exhaustively indicate the conditions that should be met for a Member State to initiate an action against another Member State for non-compliance under the WTO rules. It is reasonable to expect the application of the principle of "exhaustion of local remedies", that is, the parties that are supposedly affected should have to have previously exhausted the available local remedies before the Member State to which they belong initiates any action under the DSU.

The expectations created by the Agreement, as an instrument to eliminate tensions and institutionalize conflicts, have been undermined by actions against some developing countries to amend IPRs laws before the expiration of the transitional periods, and to provide protection beyond the requirements of the TRIPS Agreement.

---

[7] Thus, President Clinton's submission (of 15 December 1993) to the US Congress of the Final Act of the Uruguay Round states that "if Members of the Dispute Settlement Understanding (DSU) do not comply with their obligations *at the end of the dispute settlement process*, trade action under section 301 of the Trade Act of 1984 will be legitimized and there will be no risk of counter-retaliation" (emphasis added).

Illustrative of this situation is the case of Argentina, where the Parliament approved a new patent law in May 1995. During the legislative process, the US government repeatedly threatened Argentina with unilateral trade retaliations. Its main claim has been the lack of retroactive ("pipeline") protection for pharmaceutical patents, ignoring the transitional period that Argentina can apply in accordance with Article 65 of the Agreement[8]. A law on "confidential information" was approved in December 1996. In January 1997, the US government announced the partial withdrawal of Argentina's benefits under the Generalized System of Preferences (GSP) as a sanction based on Argentina's failure to protect IPRs in accordance with "international standards".

MAIN SUBSTANTIVE PROVISIONS[9]

This section covers these areas: copyright and related rights, trademarks, geographical indications, industrial designs, patents, layout designs of integrated circuits, and undisclosed information.

In the area of **copyright and related rights**, the TRIPS Agreement enhanced the market position of the software, database and phonogram industries, in which US firms play a dominant role worldwide. Though the phonogram industry was one of the industries that benefited most from the outcome of the negotiations on TRIPS, a dispute between Europe and the United States on the sharing of royalties arising from the performing of audio works in Europe remained unresolved. To a large extent, copyright was an area of North-North controversy[10].

---

[8] This attitude contrasts with the more respectful approach of the European Union with regard to the agreed transitional periods. For instance, in accordance with Decision No. 1/95 of the EU-Turkey Association Council, the EU accepted Turkey's delay in conferring patent protection on pharmaceuticals till 1 January 1999.

[9] This section is partially based on Correa (1997).

[10] The negotiations did not involve, however, new and hot issues such as copyright in cyberspace, which were dealt with in 1996 in the framework of the negotiation of new international agreements on copyright and related rights, under the auspices of the World Intellectual Property Organization (WIPO).

A. Main provisions on copyright and related rights

- Protection of works covered by the Berne Convention, excluding moral rights, with respect to the expression and not the ideas, procedures, methods of operation or mathematical concepts as such.
- Protection of computer programs as literary works and of compilations of data.
- Recognition of rental rights, at least for phonograms, computer programs, and for cinematographic works (except if rental has not led to widespread copying that impairs the reproduction right).
- Exceptions to exclusive rights must be limited to special cases which do not conflict with a normal exploitation of the work and do not unreasonably prejudice the legitimate interests of the rights-holder.
- Recognition of a 50-year minimum term for works (other than photographic or applied artworks) owned by juridical persons, and for performers and phonogram producers.
- Recognition of rights of performers, producers of phonograms and broadcasting organizations (Article 14).

Trademark protection was reinforced by a comprehensive definition of signs that can constitute trademarks, and by putting on an equal footing trademarks for goods and for services. The Agreement allows Members to keep existing differences between the anglo-american and continental legal systems, for instance, with regard to the use of a trademark as a means of acquisition of rights.

A major achievement for multinational corporations in the negotiation of the TRIPS Agreement related to the protection of "well-known" trademarks, which should be given protection even if they became known on the basis of publicity and not of effective use in a country. Trademark owners may also significantly benefit from new measures against counterfeiting, particularly those that should be taken at the border.

The issue of **geographical indications** had been given a high priority in the TRIPS negotiations by European countries, particularly those that produce wines and spirits. Unlike the case of other

B. Main provisions on trademarks

- Definition of protectable signs, which should be capable of distinguishing the goods or services of one undertaking from those of other undertakings. Service marks shall receive protection equivalent to that for marks for goods.
- Registrability, but not filing of an application, can be dependent on use.
- Protection of well-known trademarks for goods and services, including if knowledge thereon is acquired through their promotion.
- Exceptions to exclusive rights must be limited and take into account the legitimate interest of the trademark owner and of third parties.
- The minimum term of protection is seven years, indefinitely renewable.
- Requirements for use are to be limited in terms of both the minimum period of non-use and the admissibility of reasons for non-use.
- Special requirements for use are limited, as well as the conditions of licensing and assignment of trademarks. A trademark can be assigned without the transfer of the business to which it belongs.
- Measures to combat trade in counterfeiting products should be available at the border.

issues, notably patents, the United States did not show enthusiasm, but rather reluctance, to expand protection in this field (Neff and Smallson, 1994). The Agreement permits exceptions for indications which have become a term "customary in the common language" (Article 24.6) or which had been continuously used for given periods.

The provisions on **industrial designs** leave considerable freedom for national legislation, since very few elements are actually harmonized by the Agreement. National legislation may opt for protection based either on novelty or on originality (Article 25). Since designs essentially dictated by technical or functional considerations need not be protected under the Agreement, Member countries may, at their discretion, develop legislation on utility models or "petty patents".

C. Main provisions on geographical indications

• Geographical indications are indications that identify goods as originating in the territory of a Member, or a region or locality in that territory, where a given quality, reputation or other characteristic of the good is essentially attributable to their geographical origin.

• Legal means shall be provided to prevent use of an indication in a manner that misleads the public or when it constitutes unfair competition, and to invalidate a trademark if the public is misled as to the true place of origin.

• Additional protection is conferred on geographical indications for wines and spirits, including ways of protecting homonymous indications.

• Negotiations shall be undertaken to establish a multilateral system of notification and registration, aimed at increasing the protection of indications for wines and spirits.

• Exceptions to the required protection may be based on prior and continuous use of an indication, prior application or registration in good faith of a trademark, or on the customary use of the indication.

• Obligations only relate to geographical indications that are protected in their country of origin.

In the area of industrial designs, the main controversy during the negotiations was between Europe and the United States, since the latter had so far conferred weak protection on designs. An internal controversy between the US car industry and spare-part producers was also reflected during the negotiations (Neff and Smallson, 1994).

A crucial chapter of the Agreement relates to **patents**. It includes, *inter alia*, standards relating to patentability and its exceptions, compulsory licences and the duration of protection (at least 20 years). The US pharmaceutical industry was one of the most active and strong lobbies arguing for the need for an expansion and strengthening of patent protection, and is certainly a major beneficiary of the outcome of the Uruguay Round (Smith, 1995).

Patents are to be granted and the conferred rights to be exercised

D. Main substantive provisions on industrial designs

• Protection should be conferred on designs which are new or original.

• Requirements for protection of textile designs should not impair the opportunity to seek and obtain such protection.

• Exclusive rights can be exercised against acts for commercial purposes, including importation.

• Ten years is the minimum term of protection.

without discrimination as to the place of invention, the field of technology or whether the protected product is locally produced or imported[11]. For biotechnological inventions, however – and as a reflection of the complexity of and still unresolved differences on the issue[12] – the Agreement only provides for a transitional solution which allows for non-patenting of plants and animals, and of essentially biological processes for their obtention.

The TRIPS Agreement specifies the contents of the exclusive rights to be conferred under a patent, including the protection of a product directly made with a patented process. As mentioned in Box E, Article 6 allows Member countries to adopt the principle of international exhaustion of rights and, therefore, to admit parallel imports. The reversal of burden of proof is stipulated for civil procedures relating to process patents in order to strengthen a patentee's position in cases of infringement, leaving each Member the option to apply this principle only with respect to "new" products.

Additionally, detailed norms recognize the Members' rights to permit "other use without authorization of the right-holder", i.e., to grant compulsory licences under the conditions specified in Article 31 of the Agreement. Compulsory licences should be non-exclusive and terminate when the circumstances that originated their granting cease

---

[11] This limitation is a clear expression of the internationalization of the patent system, and of the search by industrialized countries for a legal system that facilitates international trade rather than the local working of inventions (see Bercovitz, 1990).

[12] Unlike the United States and Japan, in Europe patents for plant varieties and animal races are not admitted.

E. Main provisions on patents

Section 5, Part II of the TRIPS Agreement contains minimum standards on the following aspects:

- Patents shall be granted for any inventions, whether products or processes, provided they are new, involve an inventive step and are capable of industrial application.
- Patents shall be granted in all fields of technology. No discrimination is allowed with respect to the place of the invention, or based on whether the products are locally produced or imported.
- Member countries can exclude from patentability diagnostic, therapeutic and surgical methods of treatment for humans or animals, as well as plants and animals and essentially biological processes for the production thereof.
- Plant varieties shall be protected by patents, an effective *sui generis* regime or a combination of both.
- Exclusive rights conferred in the case of product and process patents are defined, subject in the case of imports to the principle of exhaustion (Article 6).
- Inventions shall be disclosed in a manner which is sufficiently clear and complete for a skilled person in the art to carry out the invention. Indication of the best mode of carrying out the invention, as well as information concerning corresponding patent applications and grants, may be required.
- Limited exceptions to the exclusive rights can be defined by national laws (Article 30).
- Conditions for granting other uses without the authorization of the patent-holder (compulsory licences) are set forth; Member countries can determine the grounds to allow such uses.
- Revocation/forfeiture is subject to judicial review.
- The term of protection shall be at least 20 years from the date of application.
- Reversal of the burden of proof in civil proceedings relating to infringement of process patents is to be established in certain cases.

to exist.

The **layout designs (topographies) of integrated circuits** shall be basically protected in accordance with the provisions of the Washington Treaty of 1989, which never entered into force. The TRIPS Agreement excludes provisions of the Treaty (notably on compulsory licences) that had been rejected by the United States and Japan during the negotiations of the Treaty, and supplements the latter with provisions that those countries had failed to obtain at the Diplomatic Conference in Washington (Correa, 1990).

In the area of **undisclosed information**, trade secrets are deemed protectable under the rules of unfair competition and Article 6 *bis* of the Paris Convention. This type of protection does not confer exclusive rights but the right to prevent practices contrary to honest commercial practices with respect to the disclosure and acquisition of undisclosed information.

The TRIPS Agreement is the first multilateral agreement ever adopted on "trade secrets". Negotiations in this area reflected substantial differences between the anglo-american and the continental European law traditions. Most delegations rejected a US proposal aiming at recognizing "proprietary" rights over undisclosed information, which is only protected under the Agreement against unfair commercial practices.

In addition, obligations are recognized in the Agreement in relation to test results and other data submitted to governments to obtain approval of pharmaceutical and agrochemical products. This provision is another victory for the pharmaceutical industry, though it obtained less in GATT than under the North American Free Trade Agreement (NAFTA) or European regulations.

TRANSFER OF TECHNOLOGY

One of the main concerns of developing countries with the adoption of the TRIPS Agreement has been the extent to which the new rules will affect the transfer of technology, a vital element to foster economic development.

Though it is too early to provide conclusive evidence, the strengthening and expansion of IPRs are likely to adversely affect the conditions for access to and use of technology, and thereby the

F. Layout designs of integrated circuits

* The layout designs (topographies) of integrated circuits shall be protected according to the provisions of the Washington Treaty of 1989, except those specifically excluded by the Agreement (e.g., provisions on compulsory licences).
* Protection shall extend to layout designs as such and to the industrial articles that incorporate them.
* *Bona fide* purchasers of products involving infringing layout designs shall be liable to pay a compensation to the rights-holder after notification.
* The term of protection shall be a minimum of 10 years.

G. Main provisions on undisclosed information

* Undisclosed information is to be protected against unfair commercial practices, if the information is secret, has commercial value and is subject to steps to keep it secret.
* Secret data submitted for the approval of new chemical entities for pharmaceutical and agrochemical products should be protected against unfair commercial use and disclosure by governments.

prospects for industrial and technological development in developing countries. Strengthened IPRs may increase royalty payments required by technology-holders, as well as the imposition of restrictive practices on licensees. Moreover, technology-holders, unless an effective system of compulsory licences is established, may simply refuse to transfer their technology and block industrial initiatives by third parties.

Under the TRIPS Agreement, reverse engineering and other methods of imitative innovation – that industrialized countries extensively used during their own processes of industrialization – shall be increasingly restricted, thereby making technological catching-up more difficult than before.

Developing countries may, within the framework of the TRIPS Agreement, provide for two kinds of measures aimed at fostering technology transfer and avoiding abusive conditions in licensing agreements. As mentioned before, they can establish different types of compulsory licences. No specification is made in the Agreement on the grounds under which such licences can be granted. The cases of national emergency or extreme urgency, dependency of patents, licences for governmental non-commercial use, and licences to remedy anti-competitive practices are specifically mentioned, to illustrate the type of grounds that may be applied.

National laws can also provide for the granting of such compulsory licences whenever the title-holder refuses to grant a voluntary licence "on reasonable commercial terms" (Article 31.a) (see WTO, 1995) and for other reasons, such as public health or public interests at large. The text of the Agreement is also open with respect to the rights that can be exercised by the licensee, including production or importation.

In addition, Section 8 (Part I) of the Agreement establishes certain conditions for the control of anti-competitive practices in contractual licences relating to IPRs. Practices that may be prevented are those that "constitute an abuse of intellectual property rights having an adverse effect on competition in the relevant market" (Article 40.1). In other words, the control of such practices should be subject to a "competition test", as requested by industrialized countries during the failed negotiations of a Code of Conduct on Transfer of Technology (Roffe, 1985).

Section 8 sets forth the rules within which the transfer of technology by means of licensing agreements may be regulated at the national level. Many developing (and a few developed) countries have in the past enacted laws on technology transfer that limit the parties' contractual freedom in certain respects. The aim of the TRIPS Agreement is to put such laws under the framework of competition law, and thus avoid the use of other criteria (e.g., impact on development) to judge and condemn restrictive practices.

CONCLUSION

The adoption of the TRIPS Agreement represented a major victory for industrialized countries and for their most active industrial lobbies. It mirrors the standards of IPRs protection that are suitable for industrialized countries at their current level of development. Such an agreement, however, allows flexibility – under certain limits – in the development of domestic legislation consistent with social and economic needs.

In order to use the margin of manoeuvre left by the Agreement and to avoid or reduce eventual negative effects, developing countries need the time, expertise and the political determination to implement the Agreement in conformity with their own conditions and needs.

Their main guiding criterion for the reform of national laws for that purpose should lie in striking a proper balance between the interests of title-holders and those of the public at large and, particularly, between the protection of technology on the one hand and the promotion of its transfer and dissemination on the other.

The following chapters explore how such a balance can be achieved using said margin of manoeuvre.

References

Alcorta, L. and Peres, W. (1995), *Innovation Systems and Technological Specialization in Latin America and the Caribbean*, UNU/INTECH, Maastricht.

Bercovitz, Alberto (1990), "Evolución histórica de la protección de la tecnología en los países desarrollados y su relación con la protección en los países en desarrollo", *Revista del Derecho Industrial*, Vol. 12, No. 35.

Correa, Carlos (1990), "Intellectual Property in the Field of Integrated Circuits: Implications for Developing Countries", *World Competition*, Vol. 14, No. 2.

Correa, Carlos (1994a), "TRIPS Agreement: Copyright and related rights", *IIC*, No. 4.

Correa, Carlos (1994b), "Trends in technology transfer: Implications for developing countries", *Science and Public Policy*, Vol. 21, No. 6.

Correa, Carlos (1996), "The TRIPS Agreement and Information Technologies: Implications for developing countries", *Information & Communications Technology Law*, Vol. 5, No. 2.

Correa, Carlos (1997), "The TRIPS Agreement. New international standards for intellectual property: Impact on technology flows and innovation in developing countries", *Science and Public Policy*, Vol. 24, No. 2.

de Koning, Martine (1997), "Why the Coercion-based GATT Approach is Not the Only Answer to International Piracy in the Asia-Pacific Region", *EIPR*, No. 2.

Kumar, Nagesh (1997), *Technology Generation and Technology Transfers in the World Economy: Recent trends and implications for developing countries*, The United Nations University/INTECH, Maastricht.

Neff, R. and Smallson, F. (1994), *NAFTA. Protecting and Enforcing Intellectual Property Rights in North America*, Shepard's/McGraw-Hill, Colorado Springs.

Roffe, Pedro (1985), "Transfer of technology: UNCTAD's draft international code of conduct", *International Lawyer*, Vol. 19, No. 2.

Smith, Pamela (1995), "International patent protection and United States exports: Evidence in the data", paper submitted to the Conference on International Relations of Intellectual Property: Challenges at the Turn of the Century, The American University, April, Washington, D.C.

UNCTAD (1996), *The TRIPS Agreement and Developing Countries*, New York and Geneva.

WTO (1995), *Environment and TRIPS*, WT/CTE/W/8, Geneva.

Chapter II

Implications for Developing Countries

INTRODUCTION

THIS Chapter deals with the implications of the TRIPS Agreement on different areas of crucial importance for development, such as foreign direct investment (FDI), technology transfer and innovation. Given their particular importance, the cases of information technology and genetic resources are separately dealt with in Chapters V and VI respectively.

Among their main arguments, developed countries affirmed that enhanced and global protection of IPRs would foster technology and investment flows to developing countries, thus promoting their participation in trade and economic development. Developed countries also offered the multilateral way as a means to reduce trade tensions and avoid the use of unilateral retaliation.

As evidence shows, these promises are not materializing. In fact, the new multilateral disciplines are contributing to increased exports from developed countries, while welfare losses in developing countries are starting to appear. In addition, unilateral pressures and trade retaliations continue to be applied, even against countries that comply with the WTO standards.

The negotiation on TRIPS was presented by developed countries as a necessary condition to promote innovation and to stimulate technology and capital flows to developing countries. The assumption was that people from developed and developing countries will benefit alike from IPRs.

It remains unproven, however, that reinforced and expanded protection of IPRs worldwide shall increase the flows of capital and technology to developing countries.

Given the wide coverage of the TRIPS Agreement and the disparities existing among developing countries, it is very difficult to make a quantitative assessment of its likely economic impact. It is evident that the impact of the Agreement will significantly vary in accordance with the levels of economic and technological development of the countries concerned.

An important problem is that IPRs only constitute one of the elements that may influence FDI, innovation and technology transfer; it is difficult to isolate their impact from the effects of other factors, such as market size, macroeconomic policies, availability of personnel, etc. Paradoxically perhaps, once all WTO Member countries adopt the TRIPS Agreement standards and provide more uniform protection, IPRs – being a standardized element – will become a less important factor for FDI and technology transfer flows. IPRs being almost equal, other factors will primarily determine the nature and volume of such flows.

Changes in IPRs are most relevant for countries which are more advanced in their industrialization process. Though many of them have already amended, to a considerable extent, their IPRs regimes (as the cases of South Korea, China, Mexico, Argentina and Brazil illustrate), further changes may be required. The impact of reinforced IPRs is likely to be felt not only in terms of market prices of protected products, but also with regard to the conditions for access to foreign technology, as well as the viability of productive activities based on imitation. In those countries, hence, the effects of changes in IPRs will go well beyond trade, and involve access to technology and the patterns of industrial development.

In the case of developing countries with a low level of industrial development, the main impact of the TRIPS Agreement in the short and medium terms will be on market prices of products that become protected, or for which protection is enhanced and made actually enforceable.

The following sections explore, with the aforementioned reservations, the possible impact of the TRIPS Agreement on different development-related areas.

WELFARE EFFECTS

Many authors have investigated the likely impact of the strengthening or introduction of IPRs in developing countries. Most of the studies are, however, limited to the patent field. They include Chin and Grossman (1988), Primo Braga (1989, 1992, 1995), Primo Braga and Fink (1995), Deardoff (1990, 1992), Evenson (1990), Subramanian (1990, 1995a, 1995b), and Diwan and Rodrik (1991), among others. It is difficult to draw general conclusions from these studies, given their different scope, assumptions and methodologies.

Chin and Grossman (1988), for instance, examined the "welfare economics of patent protection" in a trading environment. They concluded that IPRs do enhance global efficiency at least for substantial innovations, but the South would incur losses which the North should be willing and able to compensate.

Some studies distinguished the impact of patents in accordance with the levels of development of the countries where they are applied. Deardoff (1992) explored the welfare effects of extending patent protection and found that, since at least the poorest countries could not be expected to gain from it, they should be exempted from any new agreement that is made to extend patent protection under GATT[1].

The "small-country" case was also investigated by Subramanian, who found that in welfare terms the individual country will be worse off, because there are no dynamic benefits (such as an appreciable effect on R&D) to offset the static efficiency losses (Subramanian, 1995b, p. 25).

Evenson argued, however, that stronger IPRs "can aid poor countries to move forward in the technology draft" and that the case for these countries is "actually stronger than for the drafting (pirating) countries". He stressed the need to "address the balance between IPR protection for mainline and derivative inventions" and that "utility model protection and possible design patent protection could be used to stimulate adaptive invention" (Evenson, 1990, p. 325).

---

[1] It should be recalled that the TRIPS Agreement provides a special transitional period for least developed countries, as well as special measures to facilitate the adoption by those countries of the Agreement's standards.

The case of large countries, particularly newly industrializing economies (NIEs), has also been addressed. Primo Braga (1992, p. 6) argued that there is a "development threshold" beyond which protection of IPRs generates net welfare gains (see also Frischtak, 1989, p. 1). Diwan and Rodrik (1991) showed that when the R&D inducement effect of IPRs is sufficiently strong, higher IPRs protection could lead to global gains as well as gains for individual countries (see also Subramanian, 1995b, p. 26).

More generally, Nogués found that low productivity of R&D in developing countries suggests that "patent protection should not necessarily be as strong as in high productivity competitive economies". He concluded that "patents should be strengthened once economies have stabilized and restructured" (Nogués, 1990, p. 27).

FOREIGN DIRECT INVESTMENTS

Available evidence on the economic impact of IPRs on different activities (investments, technology transfer, innovation, etc.) and sectors, as well as on countries with diverging levels of development, is scant and elusive[2]. Any analysis of the impact of IPRs confronts several methodological difficulties.

Firstly, as mentioned, it is very problematic to isolate IPRs in order to identify the effects that are exclusively attributable to them, as distinct from those deriving from other economic or institutional factors.

Secondly, intellectual property is not an homogeneous set. It includes titles relating to inventions, minor innovations, designs, literary or artistic works as well as to means for the identification of products and services (trademarks and geographical indications). Therefore, any reference to the "impact of intellectual property" in general is likely to constitute an oversimplification that would hardly be useful to understand present reality and anticipate future trends.

Thirdly, even when one particular type of intellectual property is considered, its actual importance significantly varies in accordance with the sector and the type of activities or products involved.

---

[2] For a review of economic literature on intellectual property issues, see Siebeck *et al.* (1990).

One of the basic questions to be addressed is whether enhanced protection of IPRs – in accordance with the standards of the TRIPS Agreement – shall increase or otherwise affect the volume or composition of FDI to developing countries. Many countries had already changed their IPRs regimes before 1995 and, therefore, the impact of the said Agreement may not be substantial. Could the adoption of such standards affect the situation of countries which are not yet major recipients of FDI and which have not yet increased their levels of IPRs protection?

Some theoretical analyses suggest, while recognizing that IPRs are only a component of a broader set of important factors, that strengthening IPRs can be an effective means of inducing additional inward FDI (Maskus, 1997a).

Available evidence on the nature of the FDI/IPRs relationship, however, is very inconclusive. Data on FDI flows to countries with allegedly low levels of IPRs protection show that the perceived inadequacies of intellectual property protection did not hinder FDI inflows in global terms. Thus, FDI increased substantially in Brazil since 1970 until the debt crisis exploded in 1985, while in Thailand FDI boomed during the eighties (United Nations, 1993). In contrast, many developing countries that have long ago adopted standards of protection comparable to those in force in industrialized countries have not received significant FDI flows.

Nogués (1991, p. 351) explored the relationship between FDI and intellectual property, and found no definite reason to expect an increase in FDI in general as a result of the introduction or strengthening of patent protection in developing countries. Similarly, since in the area of copyright, protection abroad is usually not necessary nor intended to guarantee FDI, US support of copyright protection is just "a matter of propping up profits and stemming losses in one of the US's strongest export sectors" (Callan, 1996).

The United Nations (1993) concluded that innovative companies in the North are likely to opt growingly, in the new post-Uruguay scenario, to sell directly the products or services that incorporate the innovations, rather than transfer the technology through FDI and licensing agreements. The likely result: more exports by developed countries and less opportunities for transfer of technology to developing countries.

Thus, a report by the US Council on Foreign Relations points out that "the intellectual property-dependent industries are important because they export. Copyright industries exported $45.8 billion in 1993, second only to the automotive industry. Chemical products, which includes pharmaceuticals and other goods heavily reliant on patent protection, exported $45.1 billion that same year. In general, 'high technology' goods are increasingly important to trade, accounting, in the US, for more than 52% of all merchandise trade, and growing 17% faster than trade in all goods (from 1985 to 1993)" (Callan, 1996, p. 4).

On the other side, a study by the University of Delaware has shown, applying a model developed by Helpman and Krugman, a positive correlation between an increase in exports from the US in 1992 and the strengthening of intellectual property in importing countries (Smith, 1995).

The inconclusiveness of data is also present when particular sectors are considered. FDI in the pharmaceutical industry outpaced FDI in most other sectors in Brazil after patent protection for medicines was abolished in that country. Similarly, FDI in that sector was the largest among all other manufacturing industries with foreign participation in Turkey, which had eliminated pharmaceutical patent protection in 1961 (United Nations, 1993). In contrast, recent data suggested an increase in FDI in Italy after the introduction of such patent protection for pharmaceutical products in 1978 (Challú, 1992).

The "economic environment" of a country (including skills and natural resource availability, market size and characteristics, etc.) has an overriding effect on FDI decisions[3]. The importance of IPRs for FDI is likely to vary in accordance with the sector involved and, in particular, with the intensity of R&D and the propensity to centralize/decentralize it, the role of "tacit" *vis-à-vis* formalized knowledge, the type of producer/user relationship, and the degree of market concentration, among other factors. Thus, different industries rely more or less heavily on different types of IPRs. Industrial designs are critical for the clothing industry, trade secrets for chemicals, copyright for software producers and patents and trademarks for pharmaceuticals.

---

[3] For a review of econometric studies on the determinants of FDI, see United Nations (1992). The availability and scope of IPRs is not mentioned among the most relevant determinants for FDI in this study.

In a survey comprising 94 major US firms in six industries (chemicals, including drugs, transportation equipment, electrical equipment, machinery, food and metals), Mansfield found that the perceived effects of IPRs on FDI were heavily dependent on the type of investments involved: "For investment in sales and distribution, only about a fifth of the firms reported that intellectual property rights protection was of importance. For investment in rudimentary production and assembly facilities, less than a third said that such protection was important. But for investment in facilities to manufacture components or complete products, about half said it was important. And for investment in research and development facilities, about four-fifths said it was important".

"Based on the results," Mansfield concludes, "it seems likely that, to the extent that foreign direct investment by US firms is largely devoted to sales and distribution outlets and rudimentary production and assembly facilities, a country's intellectual property rights protection will have little effect on the total amount invested by US firms in that country. However, it is likely to have a considerable effect on how much is invested in facilities to manufacture components and complete products as well as R&D facilities" (Mansfield, 1994).

Other studies show empirically, however, that IPRs are a significant determinant of neither FDI flows (Ferrantino, 1993) nor the location of R&D facilities by multinational enterprises (Kumar, 1996). This latter type of activity is likely to be undertaken only in some developing countries, notably the new industrializing economies in East Asia (see below).

The impact of the implementation of the TRIPS Agreement on FDI is also likely to vary substantially across countries.

Inflows of FDI in Asia and the Pacific have been strongly concentrated so far in a few countries: China, Singapore, Malaysia, Thailand, Hong Kong and Indonesia, which accounted for about 90% of such inflows to the region in 1992 (UNCTAD, 1994). These countries have become major recipients of FDI before changes in IPRs, even under legislation with a considerable degree of inconsistency with the standards of protection now deemed the minimum acceptable under the TRIPS Agreement. No significant changes in those flows can be expected as a direct result of the reinforcement of IPRs in those countries.

The same will apply at the other extreme, i.e., with respect to the least developed countries, which have historically received an insignificant amount of FDI[4]. There are no reasons to think that higher IPRs standards may by themselves change this situation in any substantial manner.

It should be recalled, finally, that the adoption of minimum standards on IPRs will put all developing countries on an equal footing in these matters. Therefore, whatever the current importance of IPRs as determinants of FDI flows may be, once the Agreement becomes fully applicable, other factors (availability of skills, R&D infrastructure, macroeconomic policies, etc.) will have an overriding influence as determinants of such flows and activities. In other words, compliance with the TRIPS Agreement will not ensure by itself greater attractiveness of a particular country *vis-à-vis* other countries competing for the same investment.

TRANSFER OF TECHNOLOGY

Evidence on the implications of the levels of IPRs on transfer of technology is as limited and elusive as in the case of FDI. Countries with "weak" IPRs protection (in terms of the standards adopted by the TRIPS Agreement) have been among the major technology borrowers. The reverse situation can also be found, i.e., countries with high standards of protection but "low" performance as technology importers.

A few studies which have attempted to assess the weight of IPRs (in general) in transfer-of-technology decisions indicate that they generally are of medium importance[5].

---

[4] All least developed countries participated with a meagre 2.1% (US$0.3 billion) of FDI flows to developing countries (UNCTAD, 1994).

[5] Thus, an OECD survey on international technology licensing named limited or unsatisfactory protection of industrial property rights as one of the three main problems and disincentives associated with licensing in less developed countries (rank 3, cited by 75% of respondents) after foreign exchange controls and government regulations on transfer-of-technology agreements (OECD, 1987). Another OECD study on the computer software industry found that the lack of legal protection was considered by firms to be of "medium importance" (20-38% of respondents) (OECD, 1989).

It is arguable that IPRs protection will constitute a precondition for innovators to license their technology. It is unclear, however, whether the introduction of such protection would increase the net flows of technology (Nogués, 1991), since the patent-holder may prefer the direct exploitation of the invention through exports or subsidiaries (United Nations, 1993, p. 20).

Arguments on the relevance of adequate intellectual property protection in connection with transfer of technology are particularly strong where high, easily imitable technology is at stake, such as in the case of biotechnology and computer software. It is also possible to argue that in cases where "tacit", non-codified knowledge is essential to put a technology into operation, the transfer is more likely to take place if it is bundled with the authorization to use patents and other IPRs. If protection of such rights and of trade secrets in the potential borrowing country is weak, the originating firms are unlikely to enter into transfer-of-technology contracts.

Technology transfer has been, and will continue to be, one of the main mechanisms through which developing countries may advance in their industrialization processes.

Stronger (or expanded) IPRs may certainly imply higher costs in terms of royalties and other payments, which may in turn reduce the resources available for local R&D. Changes in intellectual property legislation may also affect the bargaining position of potential contracting parties and can make access to technology more problematic (Skolnikoff, 1993); but, at the same time, the lack of or insufficient protection may actually pose a barrier to obtaining the required knowledge.

In fact, a number of factors suggest that innovative firms are growingly reluctant to transfer their technology in an unpackaged form under licences and similar contractual arrangements. Those factors (see United Nations, 1992, pp. 154-155; and Correa, 1994a, p. 378) include the following:

• Developments in information technologies tend to increase the internationalization advantages of transnational corporations (TNCs). These developments facilitate and cheapen the cost of intra-firm communication, coordination and control.

- Recent policy changes in developing countries to attract FDI tend to reduce the cost and risk of internationalization through FDI.

- The high costs of development and rapid obsolescence of technologies in some fields are likely to reinforce efforts of innovative firms to secure a quicker pay-back through internationalization of the R&D expenditure.

- The fear of creating competitors on a global scale may deter the transfer of technology.

If technology is transferred, the improved bargaining position of the rights-holder is likely to lead to an increase in royalty rates and other costs[6]. Borrowing firms will find it more difficult to compete, particularly in an open, globalized, international market. Higher levels of IPRs protection could also deepen negotiating imbalances and lead to the imposition of abusive practices that restrain competition. As stated by Maskus, "economists cannot be entirely optimistic about the implications of stronger IPRs for technology transfer" (Maskus, 1997a, p.16).

Appropriate measures in this latter respect should be implemented at the national or regional level[7] in line with Section 8, Part II of the TRIPS Agreement ("Control of anti-competitive practices in contractual licences"). Though many developing countries have adopted transfer-of-technology regulations, there may be a need to revise them in the light of the TRIPS Agreement and the new patterns of technology transfer under strengthened IPRs.

It should be noted, in addition, that access to scientific knowledge is also becoming more problematic. The growing economic

---

[6]   This effect will be strongly dependent, however, on the modalities under which patents are granted and, particularly, on the availability of measures to combat restrictive practices in licensing agreements (Section 8, Part II of the TRIPS Agreement), and of uses without the authorization of the rights-holder, for instance, in cases of refusal to deal (Article 31 of the TRIPS Agreement).

[7]   An example of regional regulations on this subject is the "Block exemption" regulation adopted by the EC on know-how and patent licences (CE No. 240/96).

relevance of scientific research "increases pressures to limit the free dissemination of research results and to constrain the traditional openness of university laboratories where most basic research is performed in Western countries" (Skolnikoff, 1993, p. 118). This scientific and technological protectionism is likely to reduce the possibility of a successful and rapid "catching-up" process by developing countries, and the prospects of improving their social and economic conditions.

A topic of particular importance is the impact of the WTO rules on the transfer of environmentally sound technology (EST). Chapter 34 of Agenda 21[8] recognized the need for favourable access to and transfer of EST, in particular to developing countries, including on concessional and preferential terms. That Chapter also incorporated a detailed provision on actions to be undertaken to support and promote the access to and use of EST.

Despite the clear justification and purposes of these provisions, little has been done to implement them. Moreover, the strengthening of IPRs in accordance with the TRIPS Agreement has reinforced the power of private parties to control the use and eventual transfer of EST.

The said Agreement has set high standards of protection for patents and "undisclosed information" whereunder title-holders may retain their technologies or charge high royalties for allowing access to them.

A good example is provided by the case of a substitute to chlorofluorocarbons (CFCs). India has encountered difficulties in getting access to technology for HFC 134 A, which is considered the best available replacement for certain CFCs. That technology is covered by patents and trade secrets, and the companies that possess them are unwilling to transfer it without majority control over the ownership of the Indian company.

The paradox with regard to EST is that under multilateral environment agreements (MEAs), obligations have been adopted in order to phase out the use of certain substances or technologies.

---

[8] "Agenda 21", a Programme of Action for Sustainable Development, was approved at the United Nations Conference on Environment and Development, also known as the "Earth Summit", held in Rio de Janeiro from 3 to 14 June 1992.

Despite some measures to support developing countries in that process, the crucial issue is that technologies remain under the monopolistic power of patent-holders. Similarly, there are standards adopted at the national level that ban imports if they do not comply with certain environmental requirements. Here, again, the lack of access to alternative ESTs poses an additional barrier to exports from developing countries.

The TRIPS Agreement contains some provisions that may be applied to deal with environmental concerns, notably:

•   the possible exclusion from patentability of inventions which may cause serious prejudice to the environment;

•   the possible exclusion from patentability of plants and animals;

•   the right to confer compulsory licences on grounds determined by national legislation.

These provisions are important and should be explicitly incorporated into national laws. For instance, all kinds of plants and animals, including those genetically altered, may be excluded from patentability[9]. Such an exclusion can also be applied to all substances as they exist in nature, since the TRIPS Agreement does not define "invention" nor does it oblige Members to grant patents on nature.

As recommended by Agenda 21, compulsory licences grounded on the protection of the environment should also be specified in national legislation.

These measures, however, may be insufficient to ensure the transfer of EST as needed by developing countries. In line with proposals made by India during discussions at the WTO Committee on Trade and Environment, the TRIPS Agreement requires changes in order to actually promote the transfer and use of EST. It also needs to incorporate provisions to protect the knowledge of local and indigenous communities, in order to promote the conservation and adequate use of such knowledge.

---

[9]   For a discussion on the patentability of plants, see The Crucible Group (1994).

Box 1: Impact of patents on prices of medicines

According to a World Bank economist, the minimum welfare loss to a sample of developing countries (Argentina, Brazil, India, Mexico, Korea and Taiwan) would amount to a minimum of US$3.5 billion and a maximum of US$10.8 billion, while the income gains by foreign patent owners would be between US$2.1 billion and US$14.4 billion (Nogués, 1990).

A "national health disaster" has been anticipated by the Indian Drug Manufacturers' Association as a result of the implementation of the TRIPS Agreement in the country, where only 30% of the population can afford modern medicines in spite of the fact that drug prices in India are one of the lowest in the world. Comparisons of prices of drugs between India and countries where patent protection exists indicate that in some cases they are up to 41 times costlier in countries with patent protection (National Working Group on Patent Laws, 1993).

Similarly, the IMF economist A. Subramanian noted that drug prices in Malaysia, where patent protection existed, were from 20% to 760% higher than in India, which reflected a profit-maximizing behaviour based on "what the market can bear" (Subramanian, 1990). In more recent studies, the same author developed different scenarios to estimate the likely impact of pharmaceutical product patents in small and large countries, in cases where either a perfectly competitive market or a Nash-Cournot duopolistic market becomes a monopoly under patents. Welfare and price effects were found to be negative for a number of Asian countries. Price increases estimated for patented drugs ranged from 5% to 67%. Annual welfare losses for India (the biggest market) ranged between US$162 million and US$1,261 million, and annual profit transfer to foreign firms between US$101 million and US$839 million (Subramanian, 1995a and 1995b).

Price increases of drugs resulting from the introduction of product patents in Egypt were estimated at five- to six-fold as compared to non-patented products (El Shinnawy et al., 1997).

A study conducted in Argentina (Challú, 1991) estimated that the introduction of pharmaceutical product patents in the country would imply an annual additional expenditure of US$194 million with a reduction of 45.5% in the consumption of medicines, as a result of a price increase of around 270%. The increase in remittances of foreign firms abroad would reach US$367 million. Fiscal expenditures would have to increase by around US$200 million annually in order not to affect the current public health level.

Another study for Argentina – based on Subramanian's methodology – concluded that significant price increases (71%) and fall in consumption (50%) will take place in the case where monopoly follows a competitive situation, while a 16% price increase and 25% decline in consumption would follow a duopolistic-monopoly scenario (Chambouleyron, 1995, pp. 163-164).

The implementation of the TRIPS Agreement standards, in sum, is likely to affect transfer of technology in an ambivalent way, by, on the one hand, creating favourable conditions for such transfer to take place but, on the other, eventually impairing the bargaining position of recipients in developing countries. This shall not necessarily apply, however, in cases where mature or relatively simple technologies, which are not covered under exclusive IPRs, are transferred, such as in the case of technical assistance or technologies for assembly operations. The possible use of compulsory licences, as allowed by the TRIPS Agreement, should also be considered, particularly in connection with EST.

IMPACT ON DOMESTIC MARKETS

It is in the logic of monopoly to charge as high a price as the market can bear, with the purpose of maximizing profits. Price increases shall be a regular feature, and not an accident, with the introduction and/or strengthening of patent protection in developing countries.

One outstanding example is the case of pharmaceuticals. There is an uncontested and solid set of studies, undertaken in developed and developing countries, and in institutions such as the World Bank and the International Monetary Fund, that consistently indicate (see Box 1) that developing countries are going to suffer from substantial price increases and other costs.

Other studies, however, predict a less significant impact on prices of pharmaceuticals (Redwood, 1994 and 1995; Watal, 1996; Lanjouw, 1997), based, among other considerations, on estimates of a relatively low participation of patented drugs in the pharmaceutical market, or no increases at all (Rozek and Berkowitz, 1998)[10].

The immediate introduction of pharmaceutical patents in developing countries that did not recognize them on the date of entry into force of the Marrakesh WTO Agreement may lead, without the appropriate policy measures and transitional periods, to the elimination of many small and medium local firms, and to growing imports and increased prices. A study on the Jordanian pharmaceutical

---

[10] The methodology applied in this latter study is particularly questionable since, among other flaws, it includes countries where product patent protection is still non-existent or where price controls apply.

industry, for instance, indicates that "the local industry shall suffer in terms of investment and production" (IDB, 1995) (see Box 2).

In sum, an impact on prices may be expected in those sectors, such as pharmaceuticals, in which product patent protection did not exist before. Since the existence of a patent allows, by the very nature of the rights conferred, isolation of a product from price-based competition, the question at stake is the **quantum** rather than the possible existence or not of that increase.

INNOVATION

i) General

The role of technology in economic growth and the factors that explain the acquisition and development of technological capabilities, have been the subject of a growing body of research (see OECD, 1992).

Box 2: Expected effects of introducing patent protection in Jordan

- The production of medicaments shall decrease, accounting for the presently produced patent medicaments, in addition to the indirect negative effect on sales of other products produced by the same manufacturer.

- The opportunities for R&D in finding new processes to manufacture patented final products, which is presently practised, shall be narrowed or even eliminated.

- The prices of medicaments in general shall increase remarkably due to the monopolistic nature of supply by the patentee.

- The imports of medicaments shall increase to substitute the decrease in local production. In addition, exports of locally produced patent medicaments shall decrease, thus affecting negatively the Jordanian balance of trade.

- The employment level shall decrease due to the decrease in medicaments production by local manufacturers.

Source: IDB (1995)

It is well established today that there are no clear frontiers between innovation and diffusion. While diffusing, technologies are subject to continuous improvements. Incremental innovations are the basis of further technological progress. The traditional distinction between developed countries, on the one side, as the place where invention and innovation take place, and developing countries, on the other, as the place of imitation and diffusion, constitutes an insufficient basis to address policy problems, particularly in the field of intellectual property (David, 1992).

Industrialization in developing countries has relied extensively on the adaptation and improvement of imported technologies. Although adopting very different strategies, those countries have followed an imitative path in their industrialization, and have selectively used various sources of foreign technology and FDI (see Chamarik and Goonatilake (Editors), 1994). Some of them reached technological levels that were further enhanced by more significant R&D efforts, mainly led by the private sector[11]. Others developed a myriad of "minor" product and process innovations in order to meet local conditions in terms of scales of production, available raw materials and components, and users' demands. Finally, many of them have also contributed through formal and informal innovations to the development and improvement of plant varieties of considerable commercial value.

The impact of strengthened IPRs on domestic innovation in developing countries will depend strongly on the available scientific and technological capabilities. With the exception of a few developing countries which have been able to build up a reasonable R&D infrastructure (such as the East Asian "Tigers", India and Brazil), most developing countries are unlikely to substantially improve their innovative performance just on the basis of an expanded and stronger IPRs regime.

Developing countries only account for about 6% of world R&D expenditures (see Table 1), and given current fiscal constraints, many are reducing their budgets on R&D.

---

[11] See, for instance, the cases of South Korea and Taiwan (OECD, 1992).

Table 1: Distribution of world R&D (%)	
Region	**% world R&D**
Africa	0.4
Latin America	1.5
Asia, including Middle East and China	4.1
NICs and LDCs	6.0
Former USSR and Eastern Europe	20.0
OECD	74.0

Source: Hagerdoorn and Schakenraad (1994) (based on figures of the National Science Foundation, 1989)

From an economic point of view, it is not possible to demonstrate conclusively that the implementation of new IPRs standards, as embodied in the TRIPS Agreement, "will encourage additional innovation and international dissemination of technologies and products" (Maskus, 1997b, p. 27).

Intellectual property systems in developing countries have been very weakly linked to the innovative process taking place there, notwithstanding the diversity of IPRs that may be applied to knowledge not falling within the classical category of "invention". The patent system is related, by definition, to technological developments which are novel and result from an "inventive activity". As reflected by world patent statistics, developing countries only originate a minor part of all applications. Evenson found, in this regard, that IPRs could play a significant role in promoting "adaptive" innovations rather than major innovations, such as in the case of agriculture (Evenson, 1990, p. 354).

This does not mean, however, that patents may not stimulate R&D, if other enabling conditions are met. It rather indicates that in most cases, patents will be simply out of reach for least developed countries and many other developing countries, because of the high standards to be complied with. The patent system as an incentive to local innovations is unlikely to work, except in those countries where there already exist a significant scientific and technological infrastructure and firms of considerable size.

The mismatch between the type of incremental, minor innovations and the current IPRs system does not only affect developing countries. Foray has rightly pointed out that the requirements of protection have become increasingly inconsistent with the main patterns of contemporary innovation, which is mainly based on incremental changes, particularly in high-tech areas such as computers and electronics (Foray, 1995). An area that deserves particular attention relates to know-how or technical "undisclosed information", i.e., innovations and knowledge developed at the shop-floor and in engineering departments, which, by its very nature, is generally non-patentable and often tacit (non-codified or formalized). It refers to processes and product innovations. When the latter entail new configurations and are at least original or novel, utility models may be granted.

The chemical industry, where trade secrets are of particular importance, provides a good example of a sector that is often under the threat of knowledge leaks through mobility of personnel or free-riding. In the engineering field, similarly, improvements introduced to various tools, devices and products which are innovative but which do not entail an inventive activity, are unprotectable in many developing countries. Only a few (e.g., South Korea, the Philippines, Vietnam, Uruguay, Costa Rica, Brazil and, more recently, Mexico, Andean Group countries and Argentina) grant utility models. The latter may not only stimulate firms' innovativeness, particularly in small and medium enterprises; they may also contribute to rewarding employees' creativity and to improving work relations and the innovative climate within the enterprise[12].

Likewise, notwithstanding the importance of the discovery and improvement of new crops, most developing countries have not yet adopted any form of IPRs protection for plant varieties[13]. Under the

---

[12] Utility models should be distinguished from "improvement patents". The latter generally require an innovative step and universal novelty, even though their subject matter is based on the modifications of an existing invention. This type of patent may be granted to the title-holder of the improvement invention or to a third party (see Article 31.1 of the TRIPS Agreement which allows the granting of compulsory licences in these cases).

[13] Exceptions include South Korea, Argentina, Uruguay, Chile, Brazil, Mexico and the Andean Group countries. A draft law is under consideration in India.

TRIPS Agreement, they are bound, as referred to above, to adopt legislation, which may adopt the form of a *sui generis* regime. New approaches may be developed with respect to the protection of plant varieties. Breeders' rights may prove useful as a source of additional funding for public research on plant varieties, as well as to stimulate private research. The so-called "breeders' exemption" authorizes any interested party to develop a variety using as a basis a protected variety belonging to a third party. Though cases of mere "cosmetic" derivation should be prevented[14], the referred exemption is likely to stimulate new-variety developments and enhance competition.

On the other side, breeders' rights, as traditionally conceived, allow the re-use by the farmer, in its own exploitation, of the seeds obtained while employing protected varieties. This "farmers' privilege" is also a source of flexibility and equitable distribution of the costs and benefits of the system of protection. Finally, the recognition of farmers' rights (as defined in the UN Food and Agriculture Organization (FAO) International Undertaking on Plant Genetic Resources and its Annexes) should also be considered (Correa, 1994b).

It may be argued, finally, that TRIPS disciplines may increase R&D undertaken by multinational corporations in developing countries.

A trend towards a gradual "globalization" of R&D activities has been observed in several reports and studies (Dunning, 1993; OTA, 1994). This trend is, however, limited in several respects, notably:

- Fully integrated foreign affiliates of multinational enterprises (MNEs) that conduct independent product R&D are rare.

- R&D moves overseas much more slowly than production, sourcing and other business opportunities.

---

[14] To this effect, the UPOV (Union for the Protection of New Varieties of Plants) Convention, as revised in 1991, incorporated the concept of "essentially derived varieties".

• R&D remains highly centralized across the industrialized countries; R&D activities by foreign firms in developing countries are very scarce (OTA, 1994, pp. 87-89)[15].

While some evidence exists about R&D conducted by foreign firms in developing countries[16], this phenomenon is very limited and explained by very specific reasons. Overall, foreign ownership is either not significantly or negatively correlated to R&D performance (Dunning, 1993, p. 304). Moreover, in some cases, the R&D intensity of foreign-controlled firms is less than that of their locally controlled counterparts, like in the case of pharmaceuticals in Canada (Dunning, 1993, p. 305).

Rather than a real "globalization" of R&D activities, current trends reveal a modest decentralization of such activities within the developed world, with little direct impact on developing countries (Kumar, 1996).

ii) The case of pharmaceuticals

Though some developing countries have already admitted patent protection for medicines, others will be bound to do it under the provisions of the TRIPS Agreement, when it enters into force for the particular country. The likely implications for national industries and consumers have been dealt with elsewhere (Nogués, 1990). This is one of the important policy issues to be considered with a view to adopting appropriate measures during the transitional period (as applicable) in order to safeguard investments made, facilitate the restructuring of the local industry and ensure access to medicines under affordable conditions[17].

---

[15] According to Dunning, in 1989 some 95% of the foreign R&D expenditure of US firms was concentrated in industrialized countries, whereas only 78% of the output of goods was (Dunning, 1993, p. 304).

[16] Wellcome, for instance, is reported to have set up four laboratories in developing countries to develop new drugs for tropical diseases; and Dutch pharmaceutical MNEs are reported to have undertaken R&D in India.

[17] Another relevant policy issue relates to the conversion of counterfeit production into legitimate activities under a more effective IPRs regime.

The impact on R&D expenditures in pharmaceuticals, both domestic and global, has been examined in a few studies. Nogués (1991, p. 352) analyzed the case of Argentina, and found no reason to expect an increase in domestic R&D in pharmaceuticals due to the recognition of product patents. The main reason is that the development of new chemical entities is outside the reach of local companies in any developing country, since there are no firms in such countries big enough (in terms of total sales) to finance the high costs of pharmaceutical R&D (see also Scherer, 1995, p. 30).

Scherer explored the impact of the extension of patent protection on R&D undertaken by multinational drug companies. According to his analysis, less-developed countries (LDCs) "might be better off if the extra profits conveyed to drug firms led to the development of more new drugs, and hence to a multiplication of consumers' surplus" (Scherer, 1995, p. 29).

Scherer's analysis indicates, however, that low-income nations account for only about one-fifth of world gross national product, and that multinational drug companies already have substantial operations in LDCs – many of which yield profits – despite weak patent protection. Given these conditions, a three-fold increase in the development of new drugs would be required in order to leave LDC citizens as well off after introducing patent protection as before. Scherer's model shows that this is unlikely to happen: the increase in the number of new drugs would be only in the order of 20%, assuming diminishing returns in either the production function or the quasi-rent function or both[18].

The findings of Scherer and Weisburst (1995) with respect to the impact of the granting of patents since 1978 in Italy, are also relevant. They found that drug product patenting exhibited a strong upward trend well before the change in the patent regime, and that after 1978 there was a statistically significant upward jump in the number of Italian patents received per US$ of R&D outlays (due to increased patenting abroad). They also found that "Italy's patent regime change apparently had little or no impact on the trend of inflation-adjusted

---

[18] This conclusion is not substantially altered, according to Scherer, if the assumption of an R&D strategy that maximizes the collective profits of the pharmaceutical companies is relaxed, and a Demsetz-Barzel competition model is employed (*ibid.*, p. 31).

R&D expenditures" (*ibid.*, p. 1020). They did not find an impact on the introduction of new chemical entities either (*ibid.*, pp. 1020-1022). With regard to trends in foreign trade after patents were introduced, Scherer and Weisburst identified a rapid deterioration of the trade balance, which turned negative, attaining substantial negative values during the second half of the 1980s (p. 1022). On the basis of this study, the authors conclude that:

> "...one must remain skeptical whether significantly increased new drug development efforts are likely in the nations required under the Treaty of Marrakesh to offer drug product patents for the first time. Most of those nations are less-developed. Most have scientific infrastructures less conducive to state-of-the-art pharmaceutical research and development than Italy's (India may be an exception). Like their counterparts in industrialized nations, most of their governments impose more or less comprehensive price controls on pharmaceutical products. Thus, the factors that inhibited dramatic changes in the Italian environment are likely to operate even more strongly in the nations whose patent policies must be adapted to satisfy new World Trade Organization mandates" (p. 1024).

In view of these findings and of the little impact that the introduction of patents may have in developing countries to induce R&D, Prof. Scherer has concluded that such countries should apply to the fullest possible extent the transitional periods allowed under the TRIPS Agreement[19].

MAIN CONCLUSIONS

The analysis made indicates that though the implications of the new international rules for IPRs on development and, particularly, on FDI, innovation and technology transfer are difficult to foresee, nothing suggests that, in the absence of other factors, IPRs could automatically and positively influence FDI, innovation, access to foreign technology

---

[19] Contribution to the WHO Electronic Conference on Patents and Medicines, March 1998.

or other development-related activities. Appropriate measures can be adopted at the national level in order to minimize the costs of introducing new rules on IPRs. In particular, the implementation of the TRIPS Agreement should be accompanied by the enactment or improvement of legislation to deal with anti-competitive practices, including abuses of IPRs and restrictive practices in licensing agreements.

IPRs related to incremental innovations in industry should be considered with particular care. The promotion of innovativeness and creativity is certainly essential in any developmental strategy, particularly in order to enhance international competitiveness of firms. The role of IPRs in this regard should not be limited only to "inventions" which may be captured by the patent system.

Sectoral studies and concrete plans of action may be required in order to minimize costs and identify areas where public and/or private action may be required. In some sectors, for instance, a more active role of the government in supporting R&D[20] and diffusion of technology may be called for, in order to prepare local industries for the introduction of more stringent IPRs rules. In some areas where economic and social implications may be significant, as in the cases of pharmaceuticals and the access to and use of genetic resources, specific policies should be developed in due time.

References

Callan, Bénédicte (1996), "Pirates on the high seas: Why we care about global intellectual property rights and what we can do about them", Council on Foreign Relations, New York.
Challú, Pablo (1991), "The Consequences of Pharmaceutical Product Patenting", World Competition, Vol.15, No. 2.
Challú, Pablo (1992), "Patentamiento monopólico en Italia. Consecuencias", Revista del Derecho Industrial, No. 39.
Chamarik, S. and Goonatilake, S. (Eds.) (1994), Technological independence. The Asian experience, UNU, Tokyo.

---

[20] It should be noted that the Agreement on Subsidies and Countervailing Measures, which is also a component of the Final Act of the Uruguay Round, explicitly allows R&D subsidies, under quite broad terms.

Chambouleyron, A. (1995), "La nueva ley de patentes y su efecto sobre los precios de los medicamentos. Análisis y propuestas", *Estudios*, Vol. XVIII, No. 75.

Chin, J. and Grossman, G.M. (1988), *Intellectual Property Rights and North-South Trade*, Research Working Paper Series No. 2769, National Bureau of Economic Research, Cambridge, MA.

Correa, Carlos (1994a), "Trends in technology transfer: Implications for developing countries", *Science and Public Policy*, Vol. 21, No. 6.

Correa, Carlos (1994b), *Sovereign and Property Rights over Plant Genetic Resources*, Background Paper No. 2, FAO, Rome.

Crucible Group, The (1994), *People, Plants and Patents. The Impact of Intellectual Property on Trade, Plant Biodiversity, and Rural Society*, IDRC, Ottawa.

David, Paul (1992), *Knowledge, property and the system dynamics of technological change*, World Bank, Washington, D.C.

Deardoff, A. (1990), "Welfare Effects of Global Patent Protection", The University of Michigan, Ann Arbor.

Deardoff, A. (1992), "Welfare of Global Patent Protection", *Economica*, Vol. 59, pp. 35-51.

Diwan, I. and Rodrik, D. (1991), "Patents, Appropriate Technology And North-South Trade", *Journal of International Economics*, Vol. 30, No. 1/2, pp. 27-47.

Dunning, John (1993), *Multinational Enterprises and the Global Economy*, Addison Wesley, Suffolk.

El Shinnawy, Azza; Salah, Hassan; Hassan, Ibrahim Ali and El Sawy, Tayseer (1997), *The Impact of GATT/TRIPS Agreement on the Egyptian Pharmaceutical Sector* (mimeo), Cairo.

Evenson, R. (1990), "Intellectual Property Rights, R&D, Inventions, Technology Purchase, and Piracy in Economic Development: An International Comparative Study", in R. Evenson and G. Ranis (Eds.), *Science and Technology for Development Policy*, Westview Press, Boulder & San Francisco.

Ferrantino, M. (1993), "The effect of intellectual property rights on international trade and investment", *Weltwirtschaftliches Archiv*, No. 129, pp. 300-31.

Foray, Dominique (1995), "Production and distribution of knowledge in the new systems of innovation: The role of intellectual property rights", *STI*, No. 16.

Frischtak, C.R. (1989), *The Protection of Intellectual Property Rights and Industrial Technology Development in Brazil*, World Bank Industry Series Paper, No. 13, Washington, D.C.

Hagerdoorn, J. and Schakenraad, J. (1994), "The internationalization of the economy, global strategies and strategic technology alliances", in Commission of the European Communities, *The European Community and the Globalization of Technology and the Economy*, Brussels.

IDB (Industrial Development Bank) (1995), *Study for the development of the pharmaceutical industry in Jordan*, Final Report (draft), Amman-New York.

Kumar, Nagesh (1996), "Intellectual property protection, market orientation and location of overseas R&D activities by multinational enterprises", *World Development*, Vol. 24, No. 4.

Lanjouw, Jean (1997), *The introduction of pharmaceutical product patents in India: "heartless exploitation of the poor and suffering"?*, Economic Growth Center, Yale University, Center Discussion Paper No. 75, Connecticut.

Mansfield, Edwin (1994), *Intellectual Property Protection, Foreign Direct Investment, and Technology Transfer*. Discussion Paper No. 19, World Bank, Washington, D.C.

Maskus, Keith (1997a), *The role of intellectual property rights in encouraging foreign direct investment and technology transfer*, prepared for the Conference "Public-Private Initiatives After TRIPS: Designing a Global Agenda", University of Colorado, Boulder.

Maskus, Keith (1997b), *The international regulation of intellectual property*, prepared for the IESG Conference "Regulation of International Trade and Investment", University of Nottingham, Nottingham.

National Working Group on Patent Laws (1993), *Patent regime in TRIPS: Critical analysis*, New Delhi.

Nogués, Julio (1990), "Patents and pharmaceutical drugs: Understanding the pressures on developing countries", *Journal of World Trade Law*, Vol. 24, No. 6.

Nogués, J. (1991), "El rol de las patentes en la industria farmacéutica: el caso de la Argentina", in *El Comercio Exterior Argentino en la Década de 1990*, Ediciones Manantial, Buenos Aires.

OECD (1987), *International licensing: Survey results* (mimeo), Paris.

OECD (1989), *The internationalization of software and computer services*, Paris.

OECD (1992), *Technology and the Economy. The Key Relationships*, Paris.

OTA (1994), *Multinationals and the U.S. Technology Base. Final Report*, Washington, D.C.

Primo Braga, C.A. (1989), "The Economics of Intellectual Property Rights and the GATT: A View from the South", *Vanderbilt Journal of Transnational Law*, Vol. 22, No. 2, pp. 243-264.

Primo Braga, C.A. (1992), *The Newly Industrializing Economies and Intellectual Property Rights*, World Bank, Washington, D.C.

Primo Braga, C.A. (1995), "Trade-Related Intellectual Property Issues: The Uruguay Round Agreement and its Economic Implications", paper presented at World Bank Conference on "The Uruguay Round and the Developing Economies", Washington, D.C. (mimeo).

Primo Braga, C.A. and Fink, Carsten (1995), *The Economic Justification for the Grant of Intellectual Property Rights: Patterns of Convergence and Conflict* (mimeo).

Redwood, Heinz (1994), *New horizons in India: The consequences of pharmaceutical patent protection*, Oldwicks Press, Suffolk.

Redwood, Heinz (1995), *Brazil – The future impact of pharmaceutical patents*, Oldwicks Press, Suffolk.

Rozek, Richard and Berkowitz, Ruth (1998), *The effects of patent protection on the prices of pharmaceutical products. Is intellectual property protection raising the drug bill in developing countries?*, National Economic Research Associates, Washington, D.C.

Scherer, F.M. (1995), *Industry Structure, Strategy and Public Policy*, Harper Collins, New York.

Scherer, F. and Weisburst, S. (1995), "Economic effects of strengthening pharmaceutical patent protection in Italy", *International Review of Industrial Property and Copyright Law*, Vol. 26, No. 6.

Siebeck, Wolfgang *et al.* (1990), *Strengthening protection of intellectual property rights in developing countries. A survey of the literature*, World Bank Discussion Paper, Washington, D.C.

Skolnikoff, E. (1993), "New international trends affecting science and technology", *Science and Public Policy*, Vol. 2, No. 3.

Smith, Pamela (1995), "International patent protection and United States exports: Evidence in the data", paper submitted to the Conference on International Relations of Intellectual Property: Challenges at the Turn of the Century, The American University, April, Washington, D.C.

Subramanian, A. (1990), "TRIPS and the Paradigm of the GATT: A Tropical, Temperate View", *The World Economy*, Vol.13, No. 4, pp. 509-521.

Subramanian, A. (1995a), "Putting some numbers on the TRIPS pharmaceutical debate", *International Journal of Technology Management*, Vol. 10, No. 2/3, pp. 252-268.

Subramanian, A. (1995b), "Trade-Related Intellectual Property Rights and Asian Developing Countries: An Analytical View", paper submitted to the Conference on Emerging Global Trading Environment and Developing Asia, International Monetary Fund, Manila.

UNCTAD (1994), *World Investment Report. Transnational corporations, employment and the workplace*, New York and Geneva.

United Nations (1992), *The determinants of foreign direct investment. A survey of the evidence*, New York.

United Nations (1993), *Intellectual property rights and foreign direct investments*, New York.

Watal, Jayashree (1996), "Introducing Product Patents in the Indian Pharmaceutical Sector. Implications for Prices and Welfare", *World Competition*, Vol. 20, No. 2.

Chapter III

Implementing the TRIPS Agreement in the Patent Field: Options for the Developing Countries

THE TRIPS Agreement has become the most influential international agreement ever agreed on intellectual property rights. Shortly after its adoption, and even before the expiration of the transitional periods that it provides for, many developing countries have initiated the complex process of reform of their IPRs legislation. That is notably the case with many Asian[1] as well as a large number of Latin American countries (see Chapter IV).

The TRIPS Agreement leaves considerable room to deal at the national level with a series of issues, such as the definition of what an invention is, exceptions to exclusive rights (including parallel imports), compulsory licences, and others.

This Chapter examines the extent to which the room for manoeuvre left by the Agreement may be utilized in relation to the patent field[2]. In particular, some legislative options are discussed for tackling a number of substantive aspects that may be relevant for enhancing innovation in and technology transfer to developing countries.

The analysis made is based on the framework provided by Articles 7 and 8 of the Agreement, which establish the "Objectives" and "Principles" of IPRs protection under the Agreement. According to these articles, the protection to be conferred should promote both innovation and the transfer of technology, to the mutual benefit of producers and users of technology.

---

[1] For an analysis of post-TRIPS changes in Asia, see Blakeney (1996) and Heath (1997).

[2] For other areas of intellectual property rights, see Correa and Yusuf (Editors) (1998).

As examined in Chapters I and II, the TRIPS Agreement must be implemented in a context of profound asymmetry in the distribution of scientific and technological capabilities in the world. The industrial development of developing countries is strongly dependent on the access to and capacity to use technologies generated in developed countries. A crucial question – addressed in this Chapter – is, therefore, how the standards set forth by the TRIPS Agreement can be implemented in a manner that is consistent with its provisions and that is, at the same time, "development-friendly".

THE SCOPE OF PATENTABILITY (ARTICLE 27 OF THE TRIPS AGREEMENT)

Article 27.1 of the TRIPS Agreement stipulates that "patents shall be available for any inventions, whether products or processes, in all fields of technology" and that patent rights should be "enjoyable without discrimination as to the field of technology".

These rules clearly indicate that the negotiators of the TRIPS Agreement, despite the strong differences existing on this issue, finally agreed to extend protection to all types of products and processes, thus foreclosing the possibility – open under the Paris Convention – of leaving certain matters out of the scope of protection. This possibility had been extensively taken advantage of by developing (and some developed) countries, particularly with respect to pharmaceutical products. By 1980, 65 countries did not recognize such protection. In addition, some countries (e.g., France, Canada) had provisions on compulsory licences that specifically affected the "enjoyment" of patent rights related to medicines (Correa and Bergel, 1996).

While the intent of Article 27.1 is clear, this provision does not mean that the TRIPS Agreement has introduced a uniform rule on patentability. WTO Member countries still have the option, within certain limits, of defining the scope of patentability in quite a broad way, depending on each country's strengths and weaknesses in different areas, and on the impact that patentability may have on the access to or development of technology.

The room for manoeuvre left in this respect stems from the flexibility existing with regard to the definition of invention, the requirements of protection and the possible exceptions to patentability.

Definition of Invention

The Agreement does not define what an invention is. This is not a loophole or inadvertent omission of the Agreement: it just reflects the lack of a unique concept of invention. An "invention" has been defined on the basis of its subjective elements (i.e., those relating to the inventor or the activity he/she performs), or taking into consideration the characteristics of the results obtained (e.g., the existence of "unexpected" or "surprising" effects)[3], but no single notion has emerged.

Given the difficulty in defining an "invention", most national laws do not include a precise concept thereon, but just limit themselves to establishing the traditional criteria for patentability (novelty, inventive step, industrial applicability) and to determining what is not an invention. This is the case with the US Patent Law for instance, and is also typical in European legislation[4]. Case law in countries whose laws do not define "invention" also indicates that courts have been unwilling to provide a concept of invention (see, for instance, the decision of the US Supreme Court in *McClain vs Ortmayer*, US 141, 419).

Though some recent laws (e.g., Patent Laws of Argentina and Mexico) provide a definition of "invention", the dominant trend is to avoid it in order to leave a certain degree of flexibility in a changing scientific and technological context. This is also the approach followed by the TRIPS Agreement; as a result, WTO Member countries have retained the right to define the concept of invention in their national laws, or through administrative and judicial practice.

One of the main areas where the lack of a uniform definition of invention is relevant, relates to the distinction between "invention" and "discovery". According to the basic principles of patent law, while the former is patentable, the latter is not. The distinction is not based

---

[3] For a general discussion on the concept of invention, see Astudillo Gómez (1995), Chapter I.
[4] The European Patent Convention does not contain a definition of invention, but rather a list of cases that do not constitute an invention (Article 52.2).

on the degree of talent, knowledge or investments needed to obtain a discovery or an invention. In both cases, they may or may not be significant. Many discoveries and inventions have been the outcome of chance rather than of effort. A "discovery" is commonly considered to mean the mere recognition of what already exists; it is the finding of casual relationships, properties or phenomena that objectively exist in nature. An "invention", in contrast, entails developing a solution to a problem by the application of technical means (Fernández de Córdoba, 1996, p. 68). The fact that the concept underlying a claimed subject matter resides in a discovery does not necessarily mean, however, that such subject matter is not patentable, to the extent that the discovery can be applied, i.e., that it has been possible to demonstrate its practical value (Patterson, 1995, p. 119).

Biological materials

Drawing the line between what a discovery and a patentable invention are, is often a difficult task. The dividing line is not identical in all legal systems, and it has substantially changed over time. In particular, the developments in the field of biotechnology and the extension of patents to living matter have raised fundamental questions about the extent to which patents may be conferred with respect to biological materials that preexist in nature.

The concept of invention has been significantly broadened in many developed countries since the 1980s so as to cover biological materials as such. A more restrictive notion, however, has been applied in some developing countries. Both approaches are consistent with the TRIPS Agreement, but they certainly have different implications for the countries that adopt them.

In the United States, the Commissioner of Patents and Trademarks indicated in 1987 (in a notice relating to the decision in *Ex parte Allen*[5]) that:

> "An article of manufacture or composition of matter occurring in nature will not be considered patentable unless given a new form,

[5] Published in the Official Gazette, 1077, O.G 24, of 21 April 1987.

quality, properties or combination not present in the original article existing in nature in accordance with existing law".

An isolated or purified form of a natural product is patentable in the said country according to principles developed for chemical patents. The concept of "new" under the novelty requirement does not mean "not preexisting" but "novel" in a prior art sense, "so that the unknown but natural existence of a product cannot preclude the product from the category of statutory subject matter" (Bent et al., 1991, p. 123). As a result of this interpretation, many patents have been granted on purified or crystallized products obtained from a natural source of impure material[6].

Similarly, according to the European Patent Convention, a patent can be granted when a substance found in nature may be characterized by its structure, its process of obtention or by other criteria, if it is new in the sense that it was not previously available to the public. In accordance with the Guidelines of Examination of the European Patent Office:

"To find a substance freely occurring in nature is also mere discovery and therefore unpatentable. However, if a substance found in nature has first to be isolated from its surroundings and a process for obtaining it is developed, that process is patentable. Moreover, if the substance can be properly characterized either by its structure, by the process by which it is obtained or by other parameters... and it is 'new' in the absolute sense of having no previously recognized existence, then the substance per se may be patentable... An example of such a case is that of a new substance which is discovered as being produced by a microorganism" (Part C (IV), 2.1).

A similar approach has been followed in Japan. According to the Enforcement Standards for Substance Patents, patents can be granted

---

[6] Some examples include purified dextrose, pure carbon black in the form of porous pellets, synthetically produced vitamin B12, prostangladin compounds, interferon and strawberry flavouring compositions.

on chemical substances artificially isolated from natural materials, when the presence of the substance cannot be detected without prior isolation with the aid of physical or chemical methods. As mentioned, a different trend with regard to the protection of substances existing in nature can be observed in some developing countries. Since the concept of "invention" is not defined in the TRIPS Agreement and there is no "universal" concept thereof, developing countries can legitimately follow a definition of invention that broadly excludes materials preexisting in nature.

For instance, Decision 344 of the Andean Group[7] provides that substances which exist in nature and their replication are not "inventions" (Article 6.b). Similarly, the Argentine Patent Law excludes from the concept of invention "any kind of living material or substance already existing in nature" (Article 6.g).

According to the Brazilian Patent Law, no invention can be claimed with respect to "the whole or part of natural living beings and biological materials found in nature, or isolated therefrom, including the genome or germplasm of any natural living being, and any natural biological processes" (Article 10.IX, Law 9,279, 1996).

A number of complex economic, legal and ethical aspects are involved in the decision on whether or not to recognize living materials or certain types thereof as an "invention". The concept may be excluded as a matter of principle (see Shiva, 1995), or based on technical and economic considerations. Thus, some developing countries feel that, though rich in biological materials, they are at a disadvantage *vis-à-vis* developed countries that possess the technology and resources to unveil and extract the value resident in such materials.

In summary, there is no obligation under the TRIPS Agreement to adopt a unique concept of "invention" and, particularly, to follow the expansive approach applied in many developed countries with regard to substances existing in nature, biological or not.

---

[7] Composed of Bolivia, Colombia, Ecuador, Peru and Venezuela.

Computer programs

Another area in which, due to the lack of a uniform definition of invention, WTO Member countries may adopt different approaches, relates to the patentability of computer programs. According to the TRIPS Agreement, computer programs are to be protected "as literary works". Despite the difficulties that the functional aspects of computer programs pose (Office of Technology Assessment, 1992, p. 22), WTO Member countries are bound to protect them under copyright, which only protects the expression of an idea, not the idea as such (Article 9.2 of the TRIPS Agreement)[8]. The issue of patentability of computer programs is specifically examined in Chapter V.

Therapeutical uses and formulations

A large proportion of patents granted annually in the world relates to pharmaceutical products and processes. Litigation relating to those patents is also abundant, particularly in relation to biotechnology-based pharmaceuticals.

Pharmaceutical patents only exceptionally correspond to new chemical entities, that is, to active ingredients that really represent a fresh contribution to the stock of products available for medicinal use. The majority of patents granted in this field protect processes and variants of existing products, including uses and formulations thereof. According to one source, only 433 new chemical entities entered the world market between 1983 and 1992; nevertheless, the number of patents granted in the pharmaceutical field was many times greater (Zaveri, 1998, p. 71).

The registration of patents on formulations and/or on therapeutical uses, close to or after the expiration of the original patent on an active ingredient, allows – at least to some extent – monopoly rights to be extended well beyond the expiration of the original patent. This

---

[8] Due to this basic dichotomy, reverse engineering (i.e., the evaluation of a computer program in order to establish its underlying ideas and the writing of an interoperative or substitute program) is legitimate under copyright principles. See Correa (1993).

practice gives rise to the so-called "evergreening" of pharmaceutical patents (Rhein, 1998, p. 37).

Some developing countries that have not so far recognized pharmaceutical product patents have received in the last four years a large number of applications claiming protection for trivial or generically defined processes, second uses of known products and formulations of products already in the market. If granted, these patents may block the commercialization of products that would otherwise be in the public domain.

Of course, many of these applications would be rejected if the patentability requirements were properly applied. The difficulty is that most patent offices in developing countries lack the capabilities for a serious examination of applications. In addition, in many cases, the laws are not clear enough with respect to the patentability of certain alleged inventions.

Developing countries that shift from a situation of non-patentability of medicines to the recognition of product patents thereon should consider the room for manoeuvre that the TRIPS Agreement leaves to deal with different modalities of inventions in that field. The transition to a full regime of patentability may be made in a progressive manner by carefully defining the scope of protection to be granted.

The TRIPS Agreement obliges WTO Member countries to protect products and processes (Article 27.1) but **not** uses of a known product for pharmaceutical purposes.

Very often, patents in the pharmaceutical field relate to the utilization of a known product. The European Patent Convention contains a specific rule (Article 54.5) recognizing the patentability of such utilization if not comprised in the state of the art. No similar provision is contained in the TRIPS Agreement. Such an invention relating to the use of a product may be deemed as non-patentable because it consists of the discovery of an existing property rather than a new development, or because it falls under the exclusion from patentability (allowed by the Agreement and most national laws) of therapeutical methods.

The non-patentability of uses of an existing substance may avoid some cases of "biopiracy", in which a substance found in nature (generally in a developing country) is patented on the basis of the identification of a certain therapeutic use.

Applications relating to the "second use" of a known pharmaceutical product are also frequent. This type of application can only be accepted on the basis of a legal fiction. Such applications were admitted by the European Patent Office only in 1984 (Decision "Amtsblatt EPA" of 5.12.84) when framed under the "Swiss formula"[9], but they are still rejected in some countries (e.g., France). An "invention" consisting of the second use of a substance is nothing more than a set of instructions to physicians that, as such, do not meet the patentability requirements. The TRIPS Agreement does not oblige WTO Members to confer protection on such uses.

Requirements of Protection

Novelty, inventive step and industrial application are the three generally recognized requirements for granting patent protection.

Article 27.1 of the TRIPS Agreement stipulates that patents shall be granted to protect inventions which are "new, involve an inventive step and are capable of industrial application". The Agreement does not define these three requirements, opening up some room for flexibility at the national level. Moreover, in a footnote, the Agreement allows Member countries to interpret "inventive step" as synonymous with "non-obvious", and "capable of industrial application" as synonymous with "useful".

Novelty

The dominant pattern in patent law is to require that, in order to qualify as an invention, the claimed subject matter should be new in absolute terms. That is, it should not have been part of the "prior art" anywhere in the world before the date of the patent application.

However, there are significant differences in national laws – which are not inconsistent with the TRIPS Agreement – with regard to the concept of prior art. Thus, the US Patent Law, unlike the law in force in most countries, does not consider that the "novelty" requirement has been lost when an invention has been divulged outside the United States by non-written means such as public use and sale. Only

---

[9] "Use of X for the manufacture of a medicine to treat Y".

publications made abroad are deemed to destroy novelty under US law. In contrast, in Europe and most countries in the world, novelty is lost by any divulgation whether oral, written or by other means made in a foreign country.

The "relative" novelty required in the US with respect to divulgation in foreign countries has permitted the granting of patents involving knowledge and materials developed and used for many years by local and indigenous communities in developing countries. Paradigmatic of this situation are patents relating to the neem tree, widely used in India for many purposes (Shiva, 1995).

In the context of the growing clamour by many developing countries, the US Patent and Trademark Office declared a patent on turmeric invalid on 14 August 1997. The patent had been issued to the University of Mississippi Medical Centre in December 1993 and had been challenged by the Indian Council for Scientific and Industrial Research[10].

In order to prevent the "biopiracy" facilitated by this relative-novelty requirement, some institutions have initiated the publication of communities' knowledge, thus destroying its novelty for purposes of patentability[11].

The novelty requirement may be subject to other conditions that are not dealt with by the TRIPS Agreement, and which may expand or restrict the scope of patentability. Some examples of these cases are given below. Any WTO Member may provide for these, but none can be obliged to do so when such provisions represent (such as in cases 1 and 3 below) a possible expansion of the scope of patentability (Article 1 of the TRIPS Agreement).

1) In some countries (the United States, Argentina, Mexico), a publication made by the inventor within one year prior to the date of application for a patent does not destroy novelty. This "grace period" may facilitate the interface between scientific and technological research. It may prove useful for the protection of research results

[10] SUNS (South-North Development Monitor), No. 4050, 8 September 1997.
[11] India's Council for Scientific and Industrial Research is reported to have launched a programme to analyze approximately 500 medicinal plants, in order to place the information on CD-ROM and make it available to patent offices as a reference guide.

obtained in universities and other public institutions, where researchers are usually under pressure to publish their findings promptly . The allowance of this period, however, expands the field of patentability in cases where it would have been excluded by the application of the novelty requirement standard.

2) "Prior art" generally includes any publication of the invention prior to the date of the patent application. This concept may be defined so as to also include precedents that have not been divulged before that date, but which demonstrate that a third party had previously reached the same invention. This approach has been followed in some US decisions, based on *Corona Cord Tire Co. vs Dovan Chem. Corp.* (US Supreme Court, 1928), where a prior invention of another party, not publicly known, was deemed as destructive of novelty for a second invention.

Likewise, novelty may be destroyed by the information contained in previous patent applications, even if not published. This is the solution adopted both in Europe[12] and in the United States (Merges, 1992, p. 504).

3) Some countries have defined a number of situations in which, though novelty would not exist according to the standard rules, it is recognized on the basis of a **legal fiction**. This is the case, for instance, with processes which are not novel but which use or produce a new product. The patentability of such processes, denied by case law in the US (notably in *re Durden*, 1985), has been allowed by an amendment to the US law in order to expand the protection of biotechnological processes (Biotechnology Process Patent Protection Act, 1995).

Another case relates to the first medical use of a "*per se* known product". Such use is deemed patentable, for instance, under Article 54.5 of the European Patent Convention, as mentioned above.

The "second use" of a known medicine has also been considered patentable, despite the lack of novelty of the product concerned. However, decisions on this matter, even within Europe, have diverged (while case law in some countries denied patentability, Germany and Switzerland accepted it). In the United States, patents have been

---

[12] In Europe, however, the information contained in a prior, non-published patent application is not considered for the purpose of considering the existence of an "inventive step".

granted in similar situations, but clearly confined to a particular "method use" and not to the composition as such (Merges, 1992, p. 489).

The identification of new uses of known products may be more accessible than the development of completely new products in countries with limited scientific and technological resources. This is, hence, an option that developing countries may consider. It should be noted, however, that due to the "national treatment" principle, a broadening of the scope of patentability would benefit national as well as foreign inventors, and that the latter would generally be better equipped than the former to take advantage of a broad concept of novelty.

Inventive step/non-obviousness

Though very close in practice, there are differences in the evaluation of the "inventiveness" level of a claimed invention based on "non-obviousness", or on the existence of an "inventive activity" or "inventive step". In the United States, in order to be patentable, an invention needs to be non-obvious for an ordinary scientist or engineer in the art, at the time the invention was made. In other countries, the critical date for assessing inventiveness is the date of the patent application.

Obviousness is judged in the United States on the basis of the determination of: a) the scope and content of the "prior art"; b) the differences between the claimed invention versus the prior art; and c) the level of ordinary skill in the art (Wegner, 1994, p. 224). In Europe and other countries, emphasis is given to the extent to which the invention solves a technical problem. This "problem-and-solution" approach makes the inquiry on inventive step more objective than in the United States (Merges, 1992, p. 505).

Utility/industrial applicability

Similarly, national laws may be more or less demanding with regard to the level of industrial applicability of inventions. In the United States, an invention only needs to be operable and capable of satisfying some function of benefit to humanity (Chisum and Jacobs, 1992, pp. 2-50). This concept is broader than the "industrial applicability" concept required in Europe and other countries, since the former would allow the patentability of purely experimental inventions that cannot be made or used in an industry (including agriculture), or that do not produce a technical effect (Bainbridge, 1992, pp. 270-272).

According to Spanish Patent Law (which has been taken as a model by many Latin American countries) for example, "capable of industrial application" means that the object of the invention "can be manufactured or used in any form of industry, including agriculture" (Article 9, law No. 11/96). In Argentina, moreover, the law requires that "the invention causes an industrial result or product to be obtained" (Article 4.e), and that the methods and processes described for carrying out the invention "be directly applicable in production" (Article 20, Law 24,481, 1996).

One of the main areas where the referred differences in concept arise relates to the patentability of methods of surgical, therapeutical or diagnostic treatment applicable to the human body or animals. These methods are generally not deemed to be inventions in countries where "industrial applicability" is required, while they are patentable, for instance, in the United States. As indicated below, the TRIPS Agreement has specifically authorized WTO Member countries not to confer patents on such methods, but rather than being a case of exclusion from patentability, it should be treated as a case where an invention does not exist.

Exceptions to Patentability

Article 27.2 and 27.3 of the Agreement specify the exclusions from patentability that any country may provide for. Based on this provision, several exclusions that are consistent with the Agreement may be provided for:

- inventions the use of which may be contrary to *ordre public* or morality;

- diagnostic, therapeutic and surgical methods;

- plants and animals.

Ordre public *and morality*

Article 27.2 of the TRIPS Agreement includes among the exclusions from patentability that any country may (but is not obliged to) establish in its domestic law, the hypotheses of *ordre public* or morality. Said article states that:

> "Members may exclude from patentability inventions, the prevention within their territory of the commercial exploitation of which is necessary to protect *ordre public* or morality, including to protect human, animal or plant life or health or to avoid serious prejudice to the environment, provided that such exclusion is not made merely because the exploitation is prohibited by domestic law".

The exception, as drafted, raises several issues relevant to the implementation of this article at the national level. The notions of morality and *ordre public* are vague and evolutive (Pollaud-Dulian, 1997, p. 166), and their content will be dependent on national perceptions by patent offices or judges.

The text of the TRIPS Agreement employs the concept of *ordre public* as one of the grounds for exception. This concept may be interpreted as being narrower than "public order" or "public interest". Under the Guidelines for Examination of the European Patent Office, for instance, *ordre public* is linked to security reasons, such as riots or public disorder, and inventions that may lead to criminal or other generally offensive behaviour (Part C, Chapter IV, 3.1).

However, there is no generally accepted notion of *ordre public*: WTO Member countries have, therefore, considerable flexibility to define which hypotheses are covered, depending upon their own conception of the protection of public values. Article 27.2 itself indicates that the concept is not limited to "security" reasons; it also relates to the protection of "human, animal or plant life or health" and may be applied to inventions that may lead to "serious prejudice to the environment".

The concept of "morality" is also relative to the values prevailing in a society. Such values are not the same in different cultures and countries, and change over time. It is a matter of national public policy to determine when a certain conduct may be deemed contrary to the fundamental values of a society.

Some important decisions relating to patentability may depend upon the judgement about morality. As stated by an author, "it is inadmissible to think that patent offices may grant patents to any kind of invention, without considering ethical issues whatsoever" (Bercovitz, 1996, p. 53). A decision based on this type of consideration cannot be challenged under the WTO dispute settlement process, unless it is clearly beyond the reasonable meaning of the concept.

The application of Article 27.2 is subject to two conditions.

First, non-patentability may only be established if the commercial exploitation of the invention needs to be prevented to protect the interests referred to above. Generally, patent offices have no powers to prevent the commercialization of a product. The refusal of protection does not necessarily lead to the exclusion of commercialization. Article 27.2, therefore, seems to require a judgement by another competent authority about the need to prevent the commercialization of an invention.

It is debatable whether the exception can be applied while at the same time permitting the distribution or sale of the invention, or whether there is a need for an actual ban on commercialization. According to one opinion, an effective ban should exist in order to make the exception viable (Otten, 1996, p.46). It has been held, however, that the TRIPS Agreement "does not require an actual ban on the commercialization as a condition for exclusions; only the necessity of such a ban is required. In order to justify an exclusion under Article 27.2, a member state would therefore have to demonstrate that it is necessary to prevent – by whatever means – the commercial exploitation of the invention. Yet, the member state would not have to prove that under its national laws the commercialization of the invention was or is actually prohibited" (Leskien and Flitner, 1997, p. 15).

Second, the general final proviso ("provided that such exclusion is not made merely because the exploitation is prohibited by domestic law") outlaws exclusions which are not actually based on the specific grounds set forth in Article 27.2 even if they are prescribed by a national law. The existence of a legal prohibition will not be sufficient *per se* to sustain the non-patentability of any invention. This solution is in line with Article 4*quater* of the Paris Convention, which refers not only to the granting of a patent but also to its subsequent invalidation, in cases of restrictions or limitations resulting from domestic law.

The TRIPS Agreement, as indicated, contains specific wording on the possible effects of an invention on the environment, explicitly authorizing a WTO Member to exclude patentability "to avoid serious prejudice to the environment".

There is little by way of national case law on the application of moral or public-order grounds to reject or cancel a patent. The European Patent Office (EPO) has decided – on the basis of Article 53(b) of the European Patent Convention – some cases involving genetically engineered products which may illustrate how such a clause may operate. Under the EPO guidelines for patent examination, the patentability of an invention may be rejected on the basis of morality or public-order grounds in rare and exceptional cases.

The EPO jurisprudence has distinguished between morality and *ordre public* (Decision T.356/93). The former includes the "totality of the accepted norms which are deeply rooted in a particular culture". Under the morality clause, the Office has to establish whether an invention would be so abhorrent for the public that its patenting would be inconceivable. The concept of *ordre public* covers the protection of the public interest and of the physical integrity of individuals. It also encompasses protection of the environment (Pollaud-Dulian, 1997, p. 173).

The analysis of the application of Article 53(b) of the European Patent Convention[13] is made on a case-by-case basis. The EPO has employed two methods therefor: the balancing of interests at stake and the opinion of the vast majority of the public.

The balancing of interests takes into consideration the advantages and disadvantages of an invention, including the possible environmental risks due to the eventual dissemination of genes in nature (Decision T.19/90). In the area of plant technology, the Board of Appeals of the EPO has argued that plant genetic engineering is not a technical domain that, as such, may be deemed contrary to morality or public order. In Decision T.356/93 (Plant Genetic Systems), it rea-

---

[13] A similar provision is contained in the 1998 European Directive on Biotechnological Inventions (Article 9).

soned that it needs to be established in each individual case whether a particular invention relates to an improper use or has destructive effects on plant biotechnology. The Board held that "inventions the exploitation of which is likely to breach public peace or social order (for example, through acts of terrorism) or to seriously prejudice the environment are to be excluded from patentability as being contrary to *ordre public*".

The opinion of the majority of the public was considered by the Opposition Division of the EPO in a decision of 8.12.94 in the case of "Relaxine". The patent related to a DNA fragment codifying for a human protein. The Office examined whether the invention would appear immoral to the vast majority of the public.

In all the cases referred to above, the EPO affirmed the patentability of the inventions at stake:

- In the oncomouse case, the balancing-of-interests approach led to the consideration that the advantages for humanity of a genetically modified animal exceeded its eventual inconveniences (Decision T.19/90). The patentability was deemed to depend mainly on a careful weighing up of the suffering of the animals and possible risks to the environment on the one hand, and the invention's usefulness to mankind on the other. With regard to the ecological risks, the Board held that it was not the task of the EPO to regulate the use of dangerous materials, but a matter subject to the consideration of competent national authorities.

- In the Plant Genetic Systems case, the Board of Appeals considered that the adverse ecological effects were not proven and, hence, it was not possible to balance the advantages and disadvantages of the invention, since one of the terms for comparison was missing.

- In the Relaxine case, finally, it was held that there was nothing immoral in the isolation of mRNA from the tissue of a pregnant woman, and that the majority of the public accept and desire the research on the use of human materials for therapeutical applications. The Office added that the patent in question did not give control over the human being and concluded that DNA is not equal to "life".

These decisions indicate that the morality grounds have been applied by the EPO in a rather restrictive way, only when an invention may be regarded as so abhorrent to the vast majority of the public as to render the granting of a patent inconceivable. Such decisions also show that the effects of an invention on the environment may constitute a valid ground for denying patentability. However, the EPO refused to assume a regulatory role with regard to the introduction of genetic engineering inventions. In dealing with this issue, one of the opposition decisions argued that:

> "A patent does not give a positive right to its proprietor to use the invention but rather only confers the right to exclude others from using the invention for a limited period of time.
>
> "Considering the underlying reasons for the existence of patent law and the nature of patent law in general it appears that patent law is primarily an instrument for promoting research and technical advance associated therewith. It would be an overestimation of the potency of patent law if one considered it an appropriate instrument to regulate research which is dangerous or unacceptable for other reasons to certain groups of mankind. Human curiosity could not be hampered by the fact that patent protection were not available if such research promised an interesting result. If the legislator is of the opinion that certain technical knowledge should be used under limited conditions only it is up to him to enact appropriate legislation outside the framework of patent law".

The arguments developed by the EPO illustrate only how the moral and public-order considerations may affect the granting or validity of patents. The EPO philosophy and criteria may not be followed in other jurisdictions, where other values and social perceptions may prevail. The reviewed cases, however, indicate that ecological risks and, in particular, the unpredictable or undesired dissemination in nature of genes, may be the basis for the exclusion of patentability. One important point to be considered is the extent to which the role of a patent office in judging and eventually denying a patent on the basis of moral or public-order grounds may be sufficient to prevent the harmful effects from taking place. Given the competence of a patent office, non-patentability will only ensure that an invention is not monopolized, but by no means would this be sufficient to prevent the use of the invention by any interested person, since it would remain in the public domain.

Diagnostic, therapeutic and surgical methods

Article 27.3(a) of the TRIPS Agreement authorizes Members to exclude from patentability diagnostic, therapeutic and surgical methods for the treatment of humans and animals.

Most countries in the world recognize this limitation because there is no "invention", or to avoid monopolization in an area that may affect human and animal health. The eventual infringement of patent rights on such methods is usually difficult to establish and, hence, the practical value of patents on such methods (where allowed) is doubtful. Patents on therapeutic methods may, however, become more significant with the development of gene therapies.

The non-patentability allowed by this exception does not extend to the devices or products that may be used to apply one of the referred methods.

Plants and animals

Article 27.3(b) of the TRIPS Agreement allows any Member country to exclude the patentability of "plants and animals".

The ethical, economic and legal implications of allowing the patenting of plants and animals (as well as parts thereof), even if genetically altered, have led many countries to establish broad exceptions. For example, in Brazilian law (1996), the exception refers to all "living beings", except "transgenic microorganisms" (Article 18.III of the Patent Law, 1996). In the majority of countries, however, following the European approach, only "plant varieties" and "animal species" are excluded from patentability.

Under the TRIPS Agreement, all WTO Members are bound to grant patents on **microorganisms** (Article 27.3). This obligation may be interpreted as applicable only to genetically modified or "transgenic"[14] microorganisms, and not to those preexisting in nature. In some jurisdictions, the concept of "microorganism" has been extensively interpreted so as to embrace any cell and sub-cellular elements. However, according to the scientific concept, a narrower notion may be adopted by national legislation that would include only members of any of the following classes: bacteria, fungi, algae, protozoa or viruses (Coombs, 1986, p. 198).

In the United States, for instance, genes that are engineered by mutagenesis or genetic engineering techniques, or even unmodified genes that were not known to exist previously in nature, are patentable (Bent *et al.*, 1991, p. 276). Claims in these cases normally refer to an isolated DNA sequence or DNA constructs, and new transformed materials (e.g., plants) derived from them, though claims often include natural DNA sequences without limitations.

WTO Members are also obliged to provide for the protection of **plant varieties** either by patents, by an effective *sui generis* system or by a combination thereof.

Very few developing countries had adopted a regime for the protection of plant varieties at the time the TRIPS Agreement entered into force. Though the patentability of plant varieties is a possible option, it provides a more restrictive framework than the plant breeders' rights system, particularly since the latter generally allows for the "farmers' privilege" (i.e., the possibility of saving and replanting seed) and for the "breeders' exemption" (i.e., the right to use a protected variety as a source for further research and breeding). Most developing countries that needed to establish protection in this field seem to have opted for the breeders' rights approach[15].

---

[14] According to Brazilian law, "transgenic microorganisms" mean organisms, except for plants or animals in whole or in part, that, due to direct human intervention in their genetic composition, express a characteristic that cannot normally be achieved by the species under natural conditions (Article 18, sole paragraph).

[15] Thus, Paraguay enacted a breeders' rights law in 1994, Mexico in 1996 and Brazil in 1997.

WTO Members may, but are not obliged to, follow the standards set forth by the UPOV (Union for the Protection of New Varieties of Plants) Convention. The 1978 Act of this Convention, which provided a more flexible framework for regulating the matter than the new version of the Convention adopted in 1991 (The Crucible Group, 1994, pp. 63-65), is now closed for further membership. New members have only the UPOV 1991 option.

Given the broad freedom left by the TRIPS Agreement to develop a *sui generis* regime, while legislating on this matter, national laws may establish:

* that the protection conferred should not accumulate with other forms of IPRs, notably patents (such as in Article 2 of UPOV 1978 which forbids the cumulative protection of plant varieties through different regimes);

* the obligation to declare the origin of the materials used and to demonstrate the prior consent of the country of origin and, if applicable, of the particular indigenous or farmer community;

* compensation for the local/indigenous communities that provided the materials used in the development of a new variety, in the form of a general contribution to a fund or specific compensation to the communities concerned.

It is important to note that neither the preexisting international conventions on IPRs nor the TRIPS Agreement prevents the development of new IPRs regimes either in completely new areas or to supplement (in a cumulative way) the protection of subject matter already covered by other forms of IPRs. This is particularly relevant for the possible development of new *sui generis* systems for the protection of indigenous communities' knowledge, such as a system proposed by the Thai government in 1997 to protect the medicinal knowledge of indigenous communities.

Article 27.3(b) of the TRIPS Agreement is to be reviewed in 1999. This is the only provision in the whole Agreement subject to an early revision. The precarious nature of this provision has created considerable uncertainty, since any change introduced into law before this date may become incompatible with the new standards that may be introduced on the occasion of the revision[16].

SCOPE OF CLAIMS

The scope of admitted claims is another issue to be considered when designing national regulations for implementing the TRIPS Agreement. In some developed countries, a trend may be observed of admitting very broad patent claims, particularly in the areas of chemistry and biotechnology. However, the TRIPS Agreement leaves full freedom to Member countries to determine the limits of allowable claims.

Product patent claims may, in general, be drafted in structural terms, that is, in a manner in which the claim describes what the invention is, for instance, based on the chemical composition of a product. Nevertheless, some countries – e.g., the United States – accept **"functional"** claims under which the subject matter is described in terms of the function that the invention performs, that is, what the invention does. Such claims allow an extremely broad coverage, since they confer a monopoly on any means that are appropriate to achieve the claimed function, i.e., all ways of solving a problem are protected.

The European Patent Office has accepted functional claims in several cases, but only when there is no other means to describe the invention in a more precise manner (Amaro, 1996, p. 55).

Some patent offices also accept the so-called **"product-by-process"** claims, where a product is characterized by the process used for its obtention and not by the elements and structure of the product as such. In this hypothesis, however, such claims are generally admitted only if it is impossible to define a product by its structural features[17], and if the obtainable product as such is new and inventive

---

[16] The agenda for the revision has not been settled yet. One of the issues that is likely to arise is the definition of "prior art" for the purposes of determining novelty, in order to include knowledge divulged through use in a foreign country as part thereof, and thereby prevent the patenting of communities' knowledge.

[17] See, for instance, the decision of the Board of Appeals of the European Patent Office T.0150/82 (07.02.84).

(Tian, 1998, p. 140). These kinds of claim are not acceptable in some countries, such as Spain (Gimeno Olcina, 1996, p. 300).

"Generic" claims that cover a family of chemical compounds by showing the common structural nucleus of all members with a variable substituent are also accepted in the United States, where these claims are known as "Markush" claims (Wegner, 1994, p. 396).

Many examples of broad-coverage patents may be found in the field of plant-related patents.

The Hibberd patent (the first patent conferred with regard to a plant in the United States) described an increase in tryptophan content rather than a particular structure or particular genes. In that way, the patentee

> "has, in effect, patented all genes that allow for a higher tryptophan level gained through inheritance. This creates serious implications for continued progress in corn breeding, especially for this trait. Essentially then, we now have a situation in which no other breeder can use the high tryptophan variety as the parent of a new generation except by agreement with the patent holder" (Plowman, 1993, p. 35).

Examples of broad claims coverage are also offered by a patent granted to Plant Genetic Systems, related to the introduction of Bt into most field crops[18], and by an Agracetus patent claim, which referred to any genetic manipulation of cotton regardless of the cotton germplasm in use. The Agracetus US patent No. 5,159,135 (27.10.92), which has been revoked by the US Patent and Trademark Office, covered:

> "a method to achieve genetic transformation of cotton plants and lines. Immature cotton tissues are genetically transformed *in vitro* by Agrobacterium-mediated genetic transformation. The resultant cotton tissues are subjected to a selection agent or agents to screen for transformants. The transformed cultures are then induced to commence somatic embryogenesis. One possible

---

[18] Bt (*Bacillus thuringiensis*) is the most commonly used bacillus to develop insect resistance.

regime for generating such somatic embryos into whole cotton plants is disclosed".

Concerns about claims that can extend to many plant varieties, or even to entire species, have been voiced by many experts and entities in agriculture, including the American Seed Trade Association (ASTA) and the US National Wheat Improvement Committee (NWIC) (Schapaugh, 1989, p. 22).

Broad claims may have a negative impact on research, and create – or consolidate – an oligopolistic and potentially monopolistic situation in certain industries that hinders innovation and access by users to new products at reasonable prices. In addition, broad patents have led to a growing number of conflicts, an actual "patent war" that increases the costs for companies and consumers, and that may block the initiatives of small firms faced with high litigation costs (Barton, 1997, p. 7). At least 26 patents related to Bt have been subject to litigation in the United States (Barton, 1997, pp. 9-10).

Nothing in the TRIPS Agreement obliges Members to admit functional or other types of claims as described above. Any WTO Member may, in effect, require that a product invention be defined precisely in terms of its specific structure[19], particularly in the field of chemical substances, in order to avoid excessively broad claims and ensure the practicability of the invention. A requirement of this type may be particularly useful to foster the role of patent documents as a source of information and to facilitate the negotiation of contractual licences and the actual use of patented inventions.

DISCLOSURE[20] (ARTICLE 29 OF THE TRIPS AGREEMENT)

The full disclosure of the invention is one of the basic principles of patent law. The obligation to disclose the invention is reflected in Article 29, which should be implemented in a manner that ensures that

---

[19] This had been, for instance, the practice followed by Japan till the revision of its patent law in 1994.

[20] This section and the following are partially based on a paper presented by the author to the TWN Meeting of Experts on Options for the Implementation of the TRIPS Agreement in Developing Countries, Geneva, 11-14 July 1997.

the invention can be understood and executed by an expert with average skills in the discipline concerned. This test should be applied at the national level, i.e., the description should be sufficient to teach the invention to a local expert.

WTO Members "may require the applicant to indicate the best mode for carrying out the invention known to the inventor at the filing or... at the priority date of the application" (Article 29). This requirement[21] aims not only at ensuring the reproducibility of the invention by a person of ordinary skill, but also to prevent inventors from obtaining protection while concealing from the public the preferred embodiments of their inventions.

Further, legislation may limit protection to the embodiments of the invention for which the applicant has provided sufficient information to enable its reproduction. If several embodiments are claimed, the enablement requirement should preferably apply to the whole range thereof[22]. This would prevent excessively broad claims, for instance, covering methods or products that have not been described by the applicant in a form that allows their reproduction by a third party.

One important issue – which is not dealt with by the TRIPS Agreement – is the disclosure of inventions relating to microorganisms, since access to the relevant knowledge is only possible through access to the material itself. Such access should be available as early as possible, starting from the publication of the application, as provided under European law.

With regard to the interpretation of patent claims relating to biological materials, it is important to ensure that the scope of protection is limited to the material actually deposited. If there were no full correspondence between the description and the deposited material, the patent (or claim) should be deemed void.

Finally, national laws may require that applicants inform the country of origin of any biological material covered by a patent, and that it is demonstrated that they have complied with the relevant rules

---

[21] The "best-mode" requirement is contained in US law and in the laws of many other countries.

[22] This is what a British High Court decided, in 1995, in re *Medeva vs Biogen* (relating to a product for preventing Hepatitis B).

with regard to access to the said material. This requirement[23] will ensure that the provisions of the Convention on Biological Diversity and of related national implementing legislation are observed and enforced.

CLAIM INTERPRETATION

The TRIPS Agreement does not specify how claims are to be interpreted. This is an important issue left to national legislation, since the actual scope of the rights conferred by a patent is determined by the interpretation of the respective claims under the so-called "theory of equivalents". Legislation should define in which cases inventions that are not literally described in a claim may be deemed "equivalent" and therefore considered to infringe the patent rights.

There are different approaches to deal with this issue. In one approach (followed by the United States), equivalence may be found if the allegedly infringing process or product performs substantially the same function as the invention. In a second approach – as developed in Germany, for instance – the analysis of equivalence should be based not merely on a functional analysis, but on an objective comparison of the elements that constitute the invention. This latter approach permits adequate protection of the inventor's interests, but also leaves room for third parties' improvements and further innovation in the field covered by the patent (Franzosi, 1996, pp. 186-201).

Another aspect with regard to which options are open, is the date at which the equivalence should be considered, whether it is the filing date of the application or the date of the alleged infringement. Evaluation of the equivalence at the time of filing limits the analysis to the "state of the art" existing at that time, and thereby is more favourable to incremental innovation than the other option.

---

[23] An obligation of this type was incorporated in the draft of the European Union Directive relating to patents on biotechnology, as approved by the European Parliament in July 1997. However, the European Commission did not accept this proposal and it was removed from the final text.

EXCEPTIONS TO EXCLUSIVE RIGHTS (ARTICLE 30 OF THE TRIPS AGREEMENT)

Article 30 defines in very general wording the exceptions that Members may allow[24]. Exceptions to exclusive patent rights must meet three conditions:

• they must be limited;

• they should not unreasonably conflict with the normal exploitation of the patent; and

• exceptions should not unreasonably prejudice the legitimate interests of the patent owner.

The above conditions are to be applied, however, taking into account the legitimate interests of third parties.

Under this provision, there is considerable freedom for national laws to define the kind and extent of the possible exceptions to the exclusive rights of patent owners. Based on comparative law, different types of exceptions may be provided for within the scope of Article 30, such as:

• acts done privately and on a non-commercial scale, or for a noncommercial purpose;

• use of the invention for research;

• use of the invention for teaching purposes;

• experimentation on the invention to test or improve on it;

• preparation of medicines under individual prescriptions;

---

[24] During the Uruguay Round negotiations, more specific proposals were made (e.g., the EEC submission contained in MTN.GNG/NG11/W/26 of 7.7.88) but were not included in the final text.

- experiments made for the purpose of seeking regulatory approval for marketing of a product after the expiration of a patent;

- use of the invention by a third party that had used it *bona fide* before the date of application of the patent;

- importation of a patented product that has been marketed in another country with the consent of the patent owner.

These exceptions are consistent with the TRIPS Agreement requirements. Some of them are particularly important from the perspective of technological policies, notably the "experimental" exception, the so-called "Bolar" exception, parallel imports, and limitations to exclusive rights in cases of prior use and of inventions relating to life forms. These possible exceptions are considered below.

Experimental Exception

Exceptions relating to research and experimentation on the invention may be an important tool to create a favourable context for innovation[25]. This exception is admitted in the United States, though in a limited manner, basically for scientific purposes (Wegner, 1994, p. 267).

In European and other countries, experimentation on an invention without the consent of the patent owner is admitted for commercial purposes as well. The Community Patent Convention, for instance, provides that there is no infringement in the case of "acts done for experimental purposes relating to the subject-matter of the patented invention" (Article 27.b).

An equivalent provision has been introduced in patent laws of the European Union countries. Case law in these countries – which in all cases relates to pharmaceutical or agrochemical products – has accepted research done to find out more information about a product and to obtain further information about the uses of a product and its

---

[25] A draft bill in the United States (The Patent Competitiveness and Technological Innovation Act, H.R 5598, 1990) expressly stressed the link between the experimentation exception and competitiveness and innovation.

possible side-effects and other consequences of its use (Cornish, 1998, p.736).

The adoption of an experimental exception may permit innovation based on "inventing around" or improvement on the protected invention, as well as permitting evaluation of an invention in order to request a licence, or for other legitimate purposes, such as to test whether the invention works, its sufficiency and novelty.

"Bolar" Exception[26]

Another important exception, first introduced by the United States, deals with the use of an invention relating to a pharmaceutical product to conduct tests and obtain approval from the health authority, before the expiration of the patent, for commercialization of a generic version just after the expiration of the patent.

The US Drug Price Competition and Patent Term Restoration Act (1984) permits testing to establish the bio-equivalency of generic products before the expiration of the relevant patent. The purpose of this exception is to help generic drug producers to place their products on the market as soon as a patent expires, and thereby allow consumers to obtain medicines at much lower prices immediately thereafter. In exchange for this exception to exclusive patent rights, the patent term of the original drug can be extended up to five years.

According to US case law, the "Bolar" exception extends to the following acts (Coggio and Cerrito, 1998):

• using the drug product to raise capital;

• authorizing publications describing product features;

• circulating study results to potential licensees;

---

[26] This exception is named "Bolar" after a case judged by US courts in *Roche Products Inc. vs Bolar Pharmaceutical Co.*(733 F. 2d. 858, Fed. Cir., cert. denied 469 US 856, 1984), in which the issue of the exception was dealt with. The court denied Bolar the right to begin the FDA (Food and Drug Administration) approval process before the expiration of the patent.

- demonstrating features of the drug product at scientific meetings and trade shows;

- acquiring import approval from a foreign government;

- performing clinical studies for foreign regulatory agency clearance as long as the trials also relate to obtaining FDA (Food and Drug Administration) approval;

- obtaining foreign patents;

- manufacturing a product to generate data and creating stockpiles[27];

- selling a product to clinical investigators at a hospital;

- selling a product to international distributors;

- testing of a product in a foreign country by a clinical investigator;

- testing by a foreign company;

- demonstrating the drug to physicians and non-physicians;

- conducting consumer studies;

- describing clinical trials to investors and journalists;

- promoting a product to customers; and

- shipping a product to a potential commercial partner.

Canada also adopted a "Bolar"-type provision in 1991 explicitly allowing a third party to produce and stockpile the product for release

---

[27] Stockpiling was deemed legitimate in two cases (*Intermedics* and *NeoRx*), but was considered as an infringement in *Biogen Inc. vs Schering AG* (1996).

immediately after the expiration of the patent[28]. However, the regulatory review of a product is linked to the patent status: the generic producer must give notice to the patent-holder about the intended use of the invention, and the patentee is given an automatic injunction. According to the Patented Medicines (Notice of Compliance) Regulations, the approval of a generic version may be delayed for 24 months when there is a patent dispute.

Argentina implemented a "Bolar" exception under Law 24,766 of 1996, allowing for experimentation and application for approval of a generic product before the expiration of the patent (Article 8). This exception is not linked to an extension of the patent term.

Israel introduced in 1998 a law – modelled on that in the US – allowing third parties to experiment – before the expiration of a patent – for obtaining registration for marketing in Israel or in a foreign country with a similar exception. The law permits not only the use of the invention to undertake local trials but also the export of materials in small quantities to initiate approval procedures before the expiry of the patent in the countries that allow it. It also grants an extension of the life of the patent for up to five years (or for 14 years from first registration worldwide or upon expiration of an extension granted elsewhere, whichever terminates the earlier).

In Europe, some court decisions had refused to admit an exception to the patentee's rights when experimentation is done for obtaining marketing approval (Cornish, 1998, pp. 739-742). The refusal was generally linked to the submission of a sample of the product for which registration was sought, which was deemed to be an infringement of the patent rights (Cook, 1997). However, the German Federal Supreme Court accepted a "Bolar"-type exception in *Boehringer Ingelhiem Int. GmbH vs Dr. Rentschler Arzneimittel GmbH and others* (11.7.95). The Court stated that:

> "...it is not contrary to the permissibility of clinical tests that the defendants are carrying out or supporting these with the further aim of licensing under the laws relating to pharmaceuticals".

---

[28] The European Union has requested a panel against Canada under the WTO dispute settlement mechanism in connection with this exception.

In this decision, the Court disregarded its own earlier decision in *Ethofumesat* concerning herbicidal trials, on the basis that this was under the old German law. The Court also disregarded Dutch case law (arguing that Dutch law differs from the Community Patent Convention, since the former "solely" admits an exception for experimental purposes) and British case law (*Monsanto vs Stauffer*, 1985), also concerning herbicidal trials, even though this concerned a provision of UK law equivalent to that under the new German law (Cook, 1995). The German Federal Court of Justice confirmed in 1998 that clinical tests to establish the efficacy and human tolerance of a drug containing a patented active ingredient would not infringe the patent (*Klinishe Versuche II, R.P.C. 423*). A similar decision was taken by the Supreme Court of Japan in April 1999 (*Otsuka Pharmaceutical Co. Ltd. vs Towa Yakuhin K.K.*).

In another recent decision (*Wellcome Foundation Ltd. vs Parexel International and others* (1.1.98)), the Paris Court of Appeal held that neither undertaking tests for obtaining marketing approval nor the latter constituted an infringement as such.

The European Parliament has expressed its opinion in favour of the admission of a "Bolar"-type exception. In its resolution of 16 April 1996, paragraph 17, it stated that:

> "Measures should be introduced which enable pharmaceutical companies to begin, in advance of patent or supplementary protection certificate (SPC) expiry, such laboratory experiments and regulatory preparations as may be required only for the registration of generic pharmaceuticals developed in the EU, to be available on the market immediately, but only after the expiry of a patent or SPC for a proprietary product".

In summary, the admission of an exception for initiating approval procedures for generic pharmaceuticals (and, in some cases, agrochemicals) before the expiration of a patent seems to be gaining growing support in developed countries and in at least one developing country. This exception does not need to be linked to the extension of the life of the respective patents in order to be consistent with the TRIPS Agreement requirements.

Differences of interpretation seem to subsist (as illustrated by the

EU-Canada controversy) with regard to the scope of the exception, particularly in connection to manufacturing and stockpiling acts. Since such acts do not affect the normal exploitation of patent rights (full exclusivity to the market is retained by the patent owner till the expiration of the patent) and are a reasonable requirement for ensuring the immediate availability of generics after the invention falls in the public domain, an exception under Article 30 which includes these acts should be regarded as compatible with the TRIPS Agreement.

Parallel Imports

Parallel imports can be legally justified under the doctrine of exhaustion of intellectual property rights on an international scale.

The doctrine of exhaustion of IPRs was first developed by case law in the United States and Europe as an expression of the free-trade ideas prevailing at the end of the 19th century. This doctrine, as applied to patents, is based on the concept – admitted in most patent laws – that the patentee has no right to control the use or resale of goods which he/she has put on the market or has allowed a licensee to market.

In many countries – particularly those under a common law system – the doctrine is based on the existence of an implied licence under which the buyer (and those claiming rights through him/her) of a patented product is free to deal with the product as if it were not patented. The sale of a patented product, unless notification to the contrary is given, gives to the purchaser licence under the patent to exercise for this product all the normal rights of an owner, including the right to resell (Cornish, 1989, p.200; Omaji, 1997, pp. 565-566).

In other countries, such as in continental Europe, the doctrine of exhaustion of IPRs is not subject to the discretion of the title-holder, but is automatic. The inventor is considered to have been rewarded through the first sale or distribution of the product. The equivalent to this doctrine in the United States is known as the "first-sale doctrine" (Yusuf and Moncayo von Hase, 1992, pp. 117-119).

The doctrine of exhaustion of IPRs was originally limited to the domestic market. In the European Communities (EC), however, it has been extended by decisions of the European Court of Justice to the entire common market, in order to avoid the market fragmentation that the application of import bans in each jurisdiction may create. The EC exhaustion doctrine has been applied with respect to different types of IPRs, including copyrights. In the patent field, the validity of the doctrine has been held even in cases where the exporting EC country did not provide for patent protection (see, in particular, the decision of the European Court of Justice in *Merck vs Stephar*, case 187/80, and the more recent decisions in *Merck vs Primecrown* and *Beecham vs Europharm*).

While the EC adopted a principle of regional exhaustion of rights, other countries moved on to implement the same principle on an international basis. This means that whichever the exporting country may be, the IPR title-holder is not granted the right to prevent the parallel importation of a product that was put on the market in the said country with his/her consent.

The application of the exhaustion of rights doctrine on a domestic scale only, has a protectionist effect since a ban on parallel imports avoids competition from abroad. It may, hence, amount to a trade restriction, contrary to Article XI(1) of GATT (1947), which does not allow the imposition of restrictions "other than duties, taxes or other charges". Given that the title-holder has been rewarded through the first sale of the product in the country of origin, the ban on parallel imports is not necessary to secure IPRs-compliance (Yusuf and Moncayo von Hase, 1992, p. 128).

An international exhaustion of IPRs doctrine is **consistent with the TRIPS Agreement**.

The Preamble and Part I of the TRIPS Agreement provide a framework for its interpretation and implementation at the national level. The main goal of the Agreement is "to reduce distortions and impediments to international trade". Though it is recognized that IPRs are "private rights", "the underlying public policy objectives of national systems for the protection of intellectual property, including developmental and technological objectives", are expressly recognized in the Preamble.

In addition, according to Article 7, the protection of IPRs is intended to promote not only "technological innovation", but also the "transfer and dissemination" of technology, and Article 8.1 stipulates that "Members may, in formulating or amending their national laws and regulations, adopt measures necessary to protect public health and nutrition, and to promote the public interest in sectors of vital importance to their socioeconomic and technological development, provided that such measures are consistent with the provisions of this Agreement".

Furthermore, the "method of implementing" the TRIPS provisions can be freely determined within the "own legal system and practice" of each country (Article 1). This provision makes it clear that the TRIPS Agreement is not a uniform law and that differences may exist in the modes of protection available to title-holders in different countries, as well as in the form of implementation of the Agreement's obligations under national law.

In order to consider the issue of international exhaustion of IPRs, the following provisions of the TRIPS Agreement are particularly relevant.

Article 6

Article 6 leaves each country with the freedom to incorporate the principle of international exhaustion of rights in its national legislation. This issue cannot be the subject matter of a dispute settlement procedure under the Agreement. This means that whatever the solution adopted by a Member, another Member country cannot claim violation of the TRIPS Agreement. In other words, any Member can determine the extent to which the principle of exhaustion of rights is applied in its own jurisdiction, without breaking any obligation under the Agreement.

The main issue at stake in Article 6 is the admissibility of international exhaustion of rights, that is, the possibility of legally importing into a country a product protected by IPRs, after the product has legitimately been put on the market elsewhere.

Article 28

Article 28 states that a patent shall confer on its owner, where the subject matter is a product, the exclusive right to prevent unauthorized third parties from "importing" the product for the purposes of making, using, offering for sale, or selling.

In a footnote, however, it is clarified that the exclusive right of importation, "like all other rights conferred under this Agreement in respect of the use, sale, importation or other distribution of goods, is subject to the provisions of Article 6".

It is clear, therefore, that the Agreement does not oblige Members to confer on the title-holder an exclusive right to import the protected product. The title-holder's legal faculties are limited by the principle of international exhaustion, that is, whenever his/her rights have been exhausted in any country, he/she has lost the right to prevent importation by a non-authorized party.

Article 30

Under Article 30 of the TRIPS Agreement, "Members may provide limited exceptions to the exclusive rights conferred by a patent, provided that such exceptions do not unreasonably conflict with a normal exploitation of the patent and do not unreasonably prejudice the legitimate interests of the patent owner, taking account of the legitimate interests of third parties".

Some countries have contemplated the possibility of including parallel imports in national law as an "exception" to the patentee's exclusive rights. The exhaustion doctrine implies that after the sale of the product by the patentee (or with his/her consent), he/she cannot exercise any further rights in respect of the product. Therefore, one should see it not as an exception to his/her rights, but rather as a situation in which such rights have ceased to exist (since they have been "exhausted").

The TRIPS Agreement has, in fact, exceeded the territoriality principle by allowing extraterritorial effects to the sale (with the title-holder's consent) of a product in a country when this product is parallel-imported in another country. However, given the principle of independence of patents provided under the Paris Convention, it might be argued that the rights that have been exhausted are only those granted under the patent in the country of origin, and not in the importing one. If this argument were admitted, Article 30 may then be a legitimate basis for allowing parallel imports.

Article 30 of the Agreement allows considerable freedom for national laws to define the kind and extent of exceptions to be granted. Parallel imports may be one of those exceptions, as provided for in some national laws (see below).

Article 51

This interpretation is further confirmed by Article 51 ("Suspension of release by customs authorities"). Members are obliged to establish measures at the border to prevent the importation of "counterfeit or pirated copyright goods". Members may also apply the same rules to other infringements of IPRs. In any case, however, a footnote states that:

> "It is understood that there shall be no obligation to apply such procedures to imports of goods put on the market in another country by or with the consent of the right holder...".

This provision confirms that the Agreement recognizes legal effects of the commercialization of a protected product, with the consent of the title-holder, "in another country". In this case, there is no obligation to apply measures at the border.

Articles 6, 28 and 51 of the TRIPS Agreement reflect the trend towards the internationalization of the exhaustion of rights principle. The text of these provisions indicates that the exhaustion comprises not only the rights in the exporting country, but also those in the country of importation.

By allowing Members to adopt the international exhaustion principle, and by conferring effects to sales of the product made in another country, the TRIPS Agreement has made an important step towards the qualification of the territoriality principle – in a manner that is compatible with Article 4*bis* of the Paris Convention. Once patent rights are exhausted in one jurisdiction, they may not be exercised in another jurisdiction where the products are imported, if an international exhaustion of rights principle is applied in the latter jurisdiction.

The Agreement's recognition of the principle of international exhaustion of rights may be seen as a logical result of the process of economic globalization. With progress in transportation and communications, and with the steady reduction of tariff and non-tariff barriers on a worldwide scale, the boundaries of "national" markets are being diluted. From an economic point of view, such a principle may contribute to the competitiveness of local companies, which may otherwise be jeopardized if they are bound to buy exclusively from a local distributor which charges higher prices than elsewhere. Likewise, the consumer's interests are better served if the right to purchase legitimate products from the lowest-price source – national or foreign – is recognized.

The application of this principle in the health sector may be of particular importance. By allowing the importation of a (patented) medicine from a country where it is sold cheaper than in the importing country, access to the product may benefit a larger number of patients, while ensuring that the patent owner receives remuneration for the patented invention in the country where the product was sold. The acceptance of parallel imports may thus be regarded as one of the measures, consistent with the TRIPS Agreement, that Member countries are explicitly authorized to take to protect public health (Article 8.1 of the TRIPS Agreement).

Parallel imports are not a means of ignoring the patentee's right to remuneration (which is received with the first sale of the product), but a means of ensuring that patents work "to the mutual advantage of producers and users of technological knowledge" (Article 7 of the TRIPS Agreement) in a global economy.

The legality of providing for an international exhaustion of rights principle under the TRIPS Agreement has been recognized in numerous studies. Thus, a report by the Secretariat of the United Nations Conference on Trade and Development, prepared at the request of the World Intellectual Property Organization, has stated that:

> "Member countries also have the option (under Article 6 of the TRIPS Agreement) to adopt a worldwide exhaustion doctrine that could build upon the experience of economic integration schemes of industrialized countries" (UNCTAD, 1996, p. 34).

Similarly, a document published by the World Health Organization includes among the possible TRIPS-compatible exceptions "parallel importation of the protected product" (Velásquez and Boulet, 1997, p. 27).

An international exhaustion principle has been adopted by the Andean Group countries in their "Common Regime on Industrial Property", as contained in Decision 344 of 1993. Article 34(d) states that the patent owner cannot exercise his/her exclusive rights in the case of "importation of the patented product that has been marketed in any country with the consent of the owner, a licensee or any other authorized person".

Similarly, the Argentine Patent Law No. 24,481 of 1995 provides that the rights conferred by a patent shall have no effect against "any person who...imports or in any way deals in the product patented or obtained by the patented process once the said product has been lawfully placed on the market in any country; placing on the market shall be considered lawful if it conforms to Section 4 of Part III of the TRIPS Agreement" (Article 36(c)).

The doctrine of exhaustion of IPRs on an international scale has been applied in two important cases by Japanese courts. The High Court of Tokyo held in *Jap Auto Products Kabushiki Kaisha & Anor vs BBS Kraftfahrzeug Technik AG* (1994) that the parallel imports of auto parts purchased in Germany did not violate patents granted to BBS in Japan. And in the Aluminium Wheels case, the Japanese Supreme Court affirmed, in July 1997, that Article 4*bis* of the Paris Convention ("Independence of patents for the same invention in different countries") did not apply and that the issue of parallel imports was a matter of the national policy of each country.

The international exhaustion of IPRs has also been admitted in other countries at least in respect of trademarks and copyrights. This has been the case, for instance, with Australia (Omaji, 1997), New Zealand (in respect of copyrights) and the United States. In this latter country, a decision by the Supreme Court of 9 March 1998 affirmed the exhaustion of rights principle with regard to the importation of copyrighted items sold in the "gray market" (*Quality King Distributors Inc. vs L'Anza Research International Inc.*).

The South African Medicines Act has authorized the Health Minister to prescribe "conditions for the supply of more affordable medicines in certain circumstances so as to protect the health of the public". The Minister "in particular may...determine that the rights with regard to any medicine under a patent granted in the Republic shall not extend to acts in respect of such medicine which has been put onto the market by the owner of the medicine, or with his or her consent" (Article 15C.a).

As indicated by this text, the parallel-import exception in South

Africa is limited to medicines and does not automatically benefit any interested party – as in Argentina or the Andean Group: the law only confers on the Ministry of Health the faculty to admit parallel imports in certain circumstances. Despite these limitations, the South African provision has been challenged by foreign firms and by the US government.

It should be noted, finally, that the European Court of Justice confirmed in December 1996 the interpretation given to the Treaty of Rome in the case *Merck vs Stephar*, according to which the fact that a product is not patented in the exporting country is not sufficient to ban parallel imports into a country where a patent on such a product is in force. The Court again gave primacy to the principle of free movement of goods over the rights of a patent-holder who, the Court determined, could not prevent parallel imports even if the State fixed the sale price in the exporting country. To the extent that the marketing of the product in the exporting country was voluntary, the exhaustion of rights principle should apply (*Merck & Co. Inc. vs Primecrown Ltd*).

In summary, the precedent analysis indicates that the provision of an international exhaustion of IPRs is fully consistent with WTO rules and principles and, specifically, with the TRIPS Agreement.

Prior Use

Another common exception, possible under Article 30, relates to the prior use of an invention. When a person in good faith used the invention prior to the filing of a patent by a third party, he/she can be accorded the right to continue to use the invention despite the granting of a patent.

Given the degree of redundancy that exists in science and technology activities, it is not uncommon for two or more firms or researchers to obtain substantially similar results contemporaneously. In fact, many people look for solutions to the same problems, often racing to be the first to arrive at one.

This exception is provided for in many national laws. It was also proposed in the context of a WIPO draft treaty for the harmonization of patent law (Article 20 of the draft treaty presented at the Diplomatic Conference held in The Hague in 1991).

Patents on Life Forms

If the patentability of plants and/or animals is allowed, national laws may incorporate specific provisions to limit the extent of the exclusive rights, particularly with regard to the multiplication of the protected materials. Thus, in line with the concept of the "farmers' privilege" as allowed under plant breeders' legislation, it would be possible to establish that the patent owner should not be able to prevent the replanting of patented seeds or the exploitation of the progeny of patented animals.

The replanting of patented seeds without remuneration to the patent-holders is allowed, for instance, in the case of small farmers, according to Article 11.1 of the EC Directive on the Legal Protection of Biotechnological Inventions (No. 98/44/EC of 6.7.98). In the case of patents relating to breeding stock or other reproductive material, the farmer can use the protected livestock "for an agricultural purpose", but cannot sell the material "within the framework or for the purpose of a commercial reproduction activity" (Article 11.2)[29].

COMPULSORY LICENCES (ARTICLE 31 OF THE TRIPS AGREEMENT)

Article 31 of the TRIPS Agreement on "Other use without the authorization of the right holder" contains a detailed set of conditions for the granting of compulsory licences. The TRIPS Agreement refers to five specific grounds for the granting of compulsory licences:

• Refusal to deal[30]

• Emergency and extreme urgency

• Anti-competitive practices

---

[29] The extent and conditions of this exception are to be determined by national laws (Article 11.3).
[30] Chinese and Argentine patent laws have established the "refusal to deal" of a patent-holder as a legal ground for a compulsory licence.

- Non-commercial use

- Dependent patents

The TRIPS Agreement does not limit the Members' right to establish compulsory licences on other grounds not explicitly mentioned therein, for instance, to protect the environment (as recommended by Agenda 21), or for reason of "public interest" (as provided for by the German Patent Law). The Agreement only sets out the conditions to be met for such a granting.

The only case in which the Agreement does restrict the freedom to determine the grounds for compulsory licensing, relates to "semiconductor technology", which can only be subject to compulsory licences for public non-commercial use and to remedy anti-competitive practices.

It should be noted that in some cases, for instance, emergency and public non-commercial use, there is no need to have previously requested a voluntary licence, as required by Article 31(b) of the Agreement. Moreover, in the case of public non-commercial use, the patent-holder shall be informed after the use of the invention has taken place, "as soon as reasonably practicable" (Article 31(b)).

Licences to remedy anti-competitive practices are subject to a special treatment with regard to the remuneration to be paid to the patent-holder. Article 31(k) may be interpreted as allowing for reduced remuneration or even for a "royalty-free" licence[31].

The TRIPS Agreement also allows for compulsory licences in cases of lack of or insufficient working. Article 27.1 of the Agreement stipulates that "patent rights shall be enjoyable without discrimination...whether the products are imported or locally produced".

The interpretation of this clause is debatable. Though Article 27.1 has been understood as prohibiting any obligation to execute a patented invention locally , this interpretation is not unanimous[32]. The

---

[31] In the US, many compulsory licences have been granted in order to remedy anti-competitive practices. In some cases, these licences have been granted "royalty-free". See Fugate (1991).
[32] Thus, the Brazilian Patent Law (1996) has included an obligation to exploit patented inventions locally .

Preamble of the Agreement, as well as Articles 7 and 8, make it clear that one of the objectives of the Agreement is to promote technology transfer, which may be ensured in some circumstances by means of compulsory licences for non-working. The interpretation of this article is likely to be finally settled under WTO procedures if a dispute thereon arises between WTO Members.

It should be noted that most countries in the world – including developed countries – provide for different modalities of compulsory licences (Correa and Bergel, 1996). Among them, the United States has an extensive practice in this field (see Box 3).

With regard to the granting of compulsory licences to deal with anti-competitive practices in the United States, Scherer has noted that in the said country, "...compulsory patent licensing has been used as a remedy in more than 100 antitrust case settlements, including cases involving Meprobamate, the antibiotics tetracycline and griseofulvin, synthetic steroids, and most recently, several basic biotechnology patents owned by Ciba-Geigy and Sandoz, which merged to form Novartis. My own statistical analysis of the most important compulsory licensing decrees found that the settlements had no discernible negative effect on the subject companies' subsequent research and development expenditures, although they probably did lead to greater secrecy in lieu of patenting" (Scherer, 1999, p. 12).

The US Government has also made extensive use of compulsory licences for governmental use, in a manner that has led to complaints from the European Union. According to a report:

"Under US law (28 US Code Section 1498) a patent owner may not enjoin or recover damages on the basis of his patent for infringements due to the manufacture or use of goods by or for the US Government Authorities. This practice is particularly frequent in the activities of the Department of Defence but is also extremely widespread in practically all government departments. For obvious reasons this practice is particularly detrimental for foreign rights-holders because they will generally not be able to detect governmental use and are thus very likely to miss the opportunity to initiate an administrative claims procedure.

"Article 31 of the TRIPS Agreement introduces a requirement to inform promptly a rights-holder about government use of his

Box 3: Recent cases of compulsory licensing in the United States

Ciba-Geigy and Sandoz merger

A recent example of a compulsory licence for intellectual property is the US Federal Trade Commission's (FTC) 24 March 1997 Decision and Order concerning the merger between Swiss companies Ciba-Geigy and Sandoz into Novartis. The combined entity would also control Chiron, a biotechnology company. The FTC concluded that the merger would violate US antitrust laws, because the merged companies were current or potential competitors for several products. The FTC required divestiture of several products, and ordered compulsory licences of intellectual property rights for a number of other healthcare inventions. For example, Ciba-Geigy, Sandoz and Chiron were required to license a large portfolio of patents, data and know-how relating to HSV-tk products, haemophilia gene rights and other products to Rhone-Poulenc Rorer. The new merged entity and Chiron were also required to grant non-exclusive licences to all requesters for patent and other rights to Cytokine products.

In the case of non-exclusive Cytokine licences (which involve gene therapy) and the Anderson gene therapy patent, the FTC specified that the royalties can be no greater than 3% of the net sales price.

Acquisition of shares of Rugby-Darby Group Companies by Dow Chemical Co.

The FTC required Dow to license to a potential entrant intangible dicyclomine assets, including "all formulations, patents, trade secrets, technology, know-how, specifications, designs, drawings, processes, quality control data, research materials, technical information, management information systems, software, the Drug Master File, all information relating to the United States Food and Drug Administration Approvals" that are not part of the acquired company's physical facilities or other tangible assets.

Upjohn and Pharmacia Aktiebolag merger

Upjohn was required to divest certain intellectual property (including patents), or the FTC would appoint a trustee to issue an exclusive US licence and a non-exclusive rest-of-the-world licence for Pharmacia's research and development assets related to 9-AC. These requirements would protect consumers from reduced competition and higher prices for topisomerase I inhibitors.

Source: Love (1997)

patent, but no action has been taken by the US so far to bring their legislation into conformity with this provision" (European Commission, 1997).

One of the aspects that developing countries may consider is whether a compulsory licence should be granted for the manufacture and/or importation of a protected product. In many cases (such as where large investments are required, where barriers prevent access to operative technology, or where there is a need to remedy anti-competitive practices or to address emergency situations), the only effective way of using a compulsory licence would be through importation.

Though the TRIPS Agreement does not limit the grounds for the concession of compulsory licences, it contains detailed conditions under which a compulsory licence can be granted. The way in which these conditions are applied will determine the effectiveness of the compulsory licensing system.

The conditions for granting such licences include:

• Case-by-case evaluation and decision

• Prior request to the patentee for a voluntary licence

• Determination of scope and duration of the compulsory licence

• Non-exclusivity

• Non-assignability

• Preferably for the domestic market

• Remuneration

• Possibility of requesting the revision of decisions (on validity and remuneration) and the revocation of the licence.

Considerable room is left for interpretation at the national level of the criteria to determine when remuneration is to be deemed "adequate". It must be determined in each individual case, taking into account the circumstances of the licensee and of the market where it operates, as well as the purpose of the licence. A standard that may be used to determine the applicable royalty rate is the average rate paid in voluntary licences in a given sector.

The possibility of revocation of the licence, if too strictly applied, may defeat the whole system of compulsory licensing, since the more effective a compulsory licence is, the sooner the licensee may lose his rights (Correa, 1994).

REVERSAL OF THE BURDEN OF PROOF (ARTICLE 34 OF THE TRIPS AGREEMENT)

Article 34 provides for the reversal of the burden of proof in civil litigation involving process patents. The Agreement specifies two options for the implementation of this provision:

- when the product obtained by the patented process is "new"; or

- when there is "a substantial likelihood that the identical product was made by the process and the owner of the patent has been unable through reasonable efforts to determine the process actually used".

The first option limits the scope of the reversal of the burden of proof to cases involving "new" products, while the second one applies to cases involving any product independent of its novelty, and is likely to create considerable uncertainty with regard to existing processes and products.

When implementing the TRIPS Agreement, an important consideration to be made is the degree to which different solutions may spur litigation in the patent field. Litigation, especially "strategic litigation" by large firms (Barton, 1995, p.163), may have a negative impact on competition and hinder technological innovation.

In addition, the reversal of the burden of proof should only apply if the plaintiff has previously proven that the allegedly infringing product is identical to the product directly produced by his process (see Article 28 of the TRIPS Agreement).

TRANSITIONAL PERIODS AND PROVISIONS

Developing countries and economies in transition can delay until 1 January 2000 the implementation of the Agreement, except for obligations concerning national treatment and most-favoured-nation treatment. In addition, a further period of five years is allowed for developing countries that did not grant product patent protection in certain areas of technology on the general date of application of the Agreement in those countries (i.e., 1 January 2000).

In the case of least-developed countries, the transitional period is 11 years. An extension of this period can be granted by the WTO Council for TRIPS (Article 66.1).

All these transitional periods are automatically applicable. They do not require any notification or reservation by interested countries.

According to Article 70.7, if there is a patent application for which approval is pending at the time the Agreement is enforceable in a Member country (i.e., 1 January 2000 for developing countries), it will be possible to amend the application to claim "any enhanced protection under the provisions of this Agreement". However, such conversion cannot include "new matter", and hence a process claim cannot be transformed into a product claim.

Despite the transitional periods, Members have been obliged to receive applications for pharmaceutical and agricultural chemical products since the date of entry into force of the Agreement, i.e., 1 January 1995 (Article 70.8). Patents are to be granted after the expiration of the transitional period, and for the remainder of the patent term.

However, "exclusive marketing rights" (EMRs) must be granted during the transitional period under Article 70.9 of the Agreement. Such rights can be claimed if a number of precise conditions are met. The scope and effects of EMRs are not specified in the Agreement, and neither have they been determined in the panel decision in the case brought by the United States against India according to WTO procedures (WT/DS50/R, 5.9.97). Hence, different options for implementing EMRs are open to developing countries.

If EMRs were interpreted as providing a right to exclude third parties from marketing the relevant product, they would not be substantially different from patents. If this were the case, the EMRs should be subject, in any case, to the exceptions that apply to the exclusive rights granted by patents, as well as to compulsory licences[33]. However, it is not logical to consider that EMRs confer the same (or stronger) rights as patents themselves, since this would nullify the transitional period as provided in the Agreement.

A reasonable interpretation of EMRs, in the light of the negotiations and the general context of the Agreement, is that they are meant to confer more limited rights than a patent. It is thus clear that EMRs cannot be used to prevent production for export to third countries (since EMRs only refer to "marketing" in the domestic market). Moreover, EMRs may be interpreted as not providing exclusive rights (as patents do) since the patent application may even be rejected.

A possible option is to interpret the EMRs as conferring the right to receive compensation from those that market the invention, rather than the right to forbid their activities. In other words, an infringement of EMRs would allow one to claim only for compensation (that may be equivalent to a reasonable royalty rate or based on actual damages) but not to prevent marketing by third parties.

EMRs have been granted in at least one case. The Argentine Patent Office conferred such rights in favour of a US company in September 1998. Several elements of that administrative act illustrate the contradiction between the provision of a transitional period and the granting of EMRs.

In the referred case, the patent application did not cover a new chemical entity, but just a crystalline form of a product (olanzapine) which was already in the public domain in Argentina. In addition, the claimed form had been disclosed in a previous foreign patent owned by the same company and, therefore, did not meet the patentability requirements.

As one of the bases for the application for EMRs, the US company alluded to a patent granted in Luxembourg after six days of procedures – in Luxembourg, patents are granted without prior examination, and without any guarantee on the existence, novelty, etc. of the invention.

---

[33] This is the approach adopted by the Indian Patents (Amendment) Ordinance 1999, which implemented the granting of EMRs.

Despite such fragile grounds, the US company has attempted to block the marketing by third parties of any product containing the active ingredient. A provisional measure by an Argentine court has prevented the company from doing so, but the final outcome of the case is still unknown. This evident abuse of Article 70.9 of the TRIPS Agreement indicates that developing countries in the transitional period should ensure that EMRs, if granted:

• apply only to new chemical entities, since the rationale of the said article is clearly to provide protection to such entities, and not to a simple new form or formulation of a known product;

• require that a patent obtained in any other WTO Member country that serves as a basis for the EMRs be granted in a country with a serious examination procedure.

CONCLUSIONS

As this Chapter has shown, with respect to the specific area of patents, the TRIPS Agreement does not constitute a uniform law. It provides a number of minimum standards that will substantially increase the degree of harmonization of intellectual property protection on an almost universal scale, but leaving considerable room for national laws to define a number of important aspects.

The room for manoeuvre left by the Agreement derives, in some cases, from the wording of its provisions – such as in the case of Articles 30, 31 and 34 – and, in others, from the absence of any specific rule either in the Agreement itself or in the Paris Convention.

Developing countries were able in the pre-TRIPS era to define patent policies with a great degree of freedom. This has changed dramatically, but it is still possible to design patent laws taking into account broader developmental objectives and, particularly, the creation of a legal environment to promote innovation and technology transfer.

How WTO Members use the flexibility they have to implement the Agreement's obligations is a matter of policy decision. We have argued that developing countries can, in a way that is fully consistent with the TRIPS Agreement, opt for a number of approaches in line with technology policies aimed at fostering access to technology and the promotion of innovation at the national level.

References

Amaro, Alicia (1996), "La reciente evolución de las patentes europeas de medicamentos: de la reivindicación de producto a la reivindicación de uso. Tendencias actuales", in *La Patente Farmacéutica*, Instituto de Derecho y Etica Industrial, Madrid.

Astudillo Gómez, Francisco (1995), *La protección legal de las invenciones. Especial referencia a la biotecnología*, Universidad de Los Andes, Mérida (Venezuela).

Bainbridge, David I. (1992), *Intellectual Property,* Pitman, London.

Barton, John H. (1995), "Adapting the intellectual property system to new technologies", *International Journal of Technology Management*, Special Issue on the Management of International Intellectual Property edited by C. Correa, Vol. 10, Nos. 2/3.

Barton, John H. (1997), *The Impact of Contemporary Patent Law on Plant Biotechnology Research* (mimeo), Stanford.

Bent, S.; Schwab, R.; Conlin, D. and Jeffrey, D. (1991), *Intellectual property rights in biotechnology worldwide*, Stockton Press, New York.

Bercovitz, Alberto (1996), "Panel Discussion on Biotechnology", in Kraih Hill and Laraine Morse (Eds.), *Emergent Technologies and Intellectual Property. Multimedia, Biotechnology & Other Issues*, ATRIP, CASRIP Publications Series No. 2, Seattle.

Blakeney, Michael (1996), "The impact of the TRIPS Agreement in the Asia Pacific region", *EIPR*, Vol. 18, No. 10.

Chisum, Donald S. and Jacobs, Michael A. (1992), *Understanding Intellectual Property Law,* Legal Text series, Matthew Bender, New York.

Coggio, B. and Cerrito, F. (1998), "Immunity for drug approval process", *New York Law Journal,* 9 March.

Cook, Trevor (1995), "Experimental use", *Biosciences Update*, September.

Cook, Trevor (1997), "Pharmaceutical patents and the generic sector in Europe", *Patent World*, February.

Coombs, J. (1986), *Macmillan Dictionary of Biotechnology*, Macmillan, London.

Cornish, W. (1989), *Intellectual Property: Patents, Copyright, Trade Marks and Allied Rights*, Sweet & Maxwell, London.

Cornish, W. (1998), "Experimental Use of Patented Inventions in European Community States", *IIC*, Vol. 29, No. 7.

Correa, Carlos (1993), "Legal protection and innovation in the software industry", *World Competition*, Vol. 17, No. 1, September.

Correa, C.M. (1994), "Trends in technology transfer: Implications for developing countries", *Science and Public Policy*, Vol. 21, No. 6.

Correa, Carlos and Bergel, Salvador (1996), *Patentes y Competencia*, Rubinzal-Culzoni, Santa Fe.

Correa, C. and Yusuf, A. (Eds.) (1998), *Intellectual property and international trade. The TRIPS Agreement*, Kluwer Law Int., London-Cambridge.

Crucible Group, The (1994), *People, Plants and Patents. The Impact of Intellectual Property on Trade, Plant Biodiversity, and Rural Society*, International Development Research Centre, Ottawa.

European Commission (1997), *Report on United States Barriers to Trade and Investment*.

Fernández de Córdoba, Sofía (1996), *Derecho de patentes e investigación científica*, Biblioteca Jurídica Cuatrecasas, Tirant lo Blanch, Valencia.

Franzosi, Mario (1996), *Il Brevetto: Quale Tutela?*, Cuaderni di Giurisprudenza Commerciale, Casa Editrice Giuffré, Milano.

Fugate, W. (1991), *Foreign commerce and antitrust laws*, 4th. ed., Little, Brown and Co.

Gimeno Olcina, Luis (1996), "El alcance de la protección conferida por la patente biotecnológica", in *La Patente Farmacéutica*, Instituto de Derecho y Etica Industrial, Madrid.

Heath, Christopher (1997), "Intellectual Property Rights in Asia – An Overview", *IIC*, Vol. 28, No. 3.

Leskien, Dan and Flitner, Michael (1997), "Intellectual Property Rights and Plant Genetic Resources: Options for a *sui generis* system", *IPGRI*, Issues in Genetic Resources No. 6, Rome.

Love, James (1997), *A Free Trade Area for the Americas. A Consumer Perspective on Proposals as They Relate to Rules Regarding Intellectual Property*, Third Trade Ministerial and Americas Business Forum, (mimeo), Belo Horizonte.

Merges, Robert P. (1992), *Patent law and policy. Cases and materials*, Contemporary Legal Educational Series, Boston.

Office of Technology Assessment (1992), *Finding a Balance: Computer Software, Intellectual Property and the Challenge of Technological Change*, Washington, D.C.

Omaji, Paul (1997), "Infringement by Unauthorised Importation under Australia's Intellectual Property Laws", *EIPR*, Vol. 19, No. 10.

Otten, A. (1996), "Viewpoint of the WTO", in M. Swaminathan (Ed.), *Agrobiodiversity and Farmers' Rights: Proceedings of a Technical Consultation on an Implementation Framework for Farmers' Rights*, M.S. Swaminathan Research Foundation, Madras.

Patterson, Gerald (1995), *A Concise Guide to European Patents: Law and Practice*, Sweet & Maxwell, London.

Plowman, R. (1993), "Intellectual property protection of plants –The agricultural research service perspective", in Crop Science Society of America, American Society of Agronomy, Soil Science Society of America, *Intellectual Property Rights: Protection of Plant Materials*, CSSA Special Publication No. 21, Madison.

Pollaud-Dulian, Frédéric (1997), *La Brevetabilité des inventions. Etude comparative de jurisprudence, France-OEB*, Le Droit des Affaires, No. 16, Paris.

Rhein, Reginald (1998), "Patent passions run high in Canada", *Scrip Magazine*.

Schapaugh, William (1989), "The seed trade's view on proprietary rights", in Crop Science Society of America, American Society of Agronomy, Soil Science Society of America, *Intellectual property rights associated with plants*, ASA Special Publication No. 52, Madison.

Scherer, F. (1999), "The patent system and innovation in pharmaceuticals", paper presented to "Colloque de Toulouse: Brevets pharmaceutiques, innovations et santé publique", Toulouse, 28-30 January.

Shiva, Vandana (1995), *Captive Minds, Captive Lives. Ethics, ecology and patents on life*, Research Foundation for Science, Technology and Natural Resource Policy, Dehra Dun.

Tian, Yin Xin (1998), "Product-by-Process Claims", *IIC*, Vol. 29, No. 2.

UNCTAD (1996), *The TRIPS Agreement and Developing Countries*, New York and Geneva.

Velásquez, Germán and Boulet, Pascale (1997), *Globalization and Access to Drugs. Implications of the WTO/TRIPS Agreement*, World Health Organization, Health Economics and Drugs DAP Series No. 7, Geneva.

Wegner, Harold (1994), *Patent law in biotechnology, chemicals & pharmaceuticals*, Stockton, Chippenham.

Yusuf, Abdulqawi and Moncayo von Hase, Andrés (1992), "Intellectual Property Protection and International Trade-Exhaustion of Rights Revisited", *World Competition*, Vol. 16, No. 1.

Zaveri, N. (1998), *Patents for Medicine. Balanced Patent Law – The need of the hour*, Indian Drug Manufacturers' Association, India.

Chapter IV

Changing National Laws: The Case of Latin America and the Caribbean

INTRODUCTION

THE TRIPS Agreement represents a radical change, a "conceptual leap" in the history of intellectual property (Ricketson, 1995, pp. 881 and 883). It has linked intellectual property and trade disciplines, and provided a mechanism to multilaterally address inter-State disputes on intellectual property.

The new minimum standards of protection are being adopted in the various areas of intellectual property in many developing countries at a very different pace. The most immediate impact has taken place with respect to industrial property, particularly patents. The implementation of the Agreement, as so far made by some developing countries, indicates that they are using to varying extents the room left by the Agreement to legislate on various matters, particularly with regard to the scope of exclusive rights and to measures aimed at facilitating the transfer of technology.

This Chapter describes, first, some aspects relating to the incorporation of the Agreement's provisions into national laws. It further discusses interpretation and instrumental problems that have arisen, and some of the problems faced by developing countries in the process of implementation. In particular, the main changes introduced in Latin American and Caribbean countries to implement the TRIPS Agreement are analyzed.

INCORPORATION INTO NATIONAL LAW

As mentioned in previous chapters, the provisions contained in the TRIPS Agreement constitute **minimum standards** to be adopted by national laws. Members cannot be obliged to grant "more extensive" protection than provided under the Agreement (Article 1). In fact, the Agreement has been regarded by many developing countries as representing both the minimum and the maximum limit of protection to be granted. That is, they consider that the Agreement also sets forth the upper limit of protection that they should confer, in order to ensure a right balance between the producers and users of technology.

An important implication of Article 1 and of Article 64 on dispute settlement is that no Member State can request another Member State to provide standards of protection higher than those established under the Agreement. However, tensions relating to the level of protection have remained after the adoption of the Agreement, as discussed below.

The "method of implementing" the TRIPS provisions can be freely determined within the "own legal system and practice" of each country (Article 1). Two types of differences among legal systems may be relevant with regard to the implementation of the Agreement.

On one side are differences in the modes of protection available to title-holders in certain areas. Such differences are particularly evident between systems based on anglo-american and on continental European law. They are noticeable, for instance, in the fields of copyright and neighbouring rights, and trade secrets protection[1].

A second type of difference may be related to the form of incorporation of the Agreement's obligations into national law. A quite important question is whether or not the Agreement may be deemed "self-executing" and, therefore, whether it may constitute the basis of claims by private parties.

---

[1] Thus, unlike the anglo-american approach, the "Latin" tradition distinguishes the "neighbouring rights" from the "authors' rights", and does not accept the concept of "property" over trade secrets.

The legal status conferred on the Agreement, or on different parts thereof, would ultimately depend on the constitutional law of each country[2] and, in particular, on the treatment conferred on international treaties as a direct source of rights and obligations for private parties, subject, in any case, to the expiration of the transitional periods provided for under Article 65 of the Agreement.

It should be noted, however, that the provisions of the Agreement are addressed to the States. Since the inception of the negotiations, it was clear that the intention of the negotiating States was to develop standards[3] against which national laws were to be judged (UNCTAD, 1989). In addition, in case of non-compliance, it is not a private party which can claim it, but a WTO Member State against another Member.

In fact, the Agreement's provisions only state what the minimum rights should be, but not the precise contents of such rights. The Agreement does not in any manner constitute a uniform law. In many areas, various options are open (e.g., Article 27.3(b) with respect to the protection of plant varieties; Article 34.1 dealing with reversal of the burden of proof)[4].

As indicated by Geller, the TRIPS Agreement creates a regime of "public international law". While the Paris and Berne Conventions, as instruments of "private international law", have given rise to cases

---

[2] In El Salvador, for instance, the Constitution (Article 144) provides that international treaties are to be deemed "laws of the Republic". While the patent term in accordance with the law in force is 15 years, it has been argued that the 20-year patent term of the TRIPS Agreement will be applicable without requiring any amendment to the law, when the Agreement becomes enforceable in El Salvador in the year 2000 (paper submitted by El Salvador to the Workshop on the Implementation of the TRIPS Agreement, SELA/BID, Mexico D.F, 24-26 May 1996). Several court decisions in Argentina and Brazil have also followed this approach.

[3] See, for instance, the US proposal for TRIPS in document MTN.GNG/NG11/W/14, where it was stated that the signatories to the Agreement would agree to adopt new laws and modify the existing ones, where necessary, to reach in the respective legislation the levels of protection established in the Agreement (page 5).

[4] In addition, as mentioned, obligations are subject to transitional periods, before the end of which no Member State can claim non-compliance with the Agreement by another Member State which qualifies as a developing or least-developed country.

between private parties, the TRIPS Agreement applies to "disputes between public entities, that is, WTO Members", since the Agreement obligates them "to undertake measures to protect property interests in intangibles both within and at their national borders" (Geller, 1995). Many developed countries that ratified the Marrakesh Agreement have prepared or already adopted legislation to incorporate the TRIPS Agreement into national law. Thus, while ratifying the former, the EU expressly stated that its provisions were not to be deemed self-executing. The Commission accordingly modified the preexisting Community regulations on geographical indications, trademarks and integrated circuits.

The United States also enacted a special law to incorporate the TRIPS Agreement in 1994. The Trade-Related Aspects of Intellectual Property Rights Implementation Act of 1994 includes rules on rental rights in computer programs, creation and traffic of sound recordings, restoration of copyright protection for certain works, non-registration of misleading geographic indications for wines and spirits, definition of invention and of infringement of patent rights, and extension of patent protection[5].

Implementation of the TRIPS Agreement by national legislation has been made in other developed countries as well, such as Japan, Australia and New Zealand. There are also many examples in the developing world as illustrated below (see also Blakeney, 1996).

In sum, the TRIPS Agreement has not been intended to directly modify the legal situation of private parties and is, in fact, being implemented in most countries through the enactment of domestic legislation.

INTERPRETATION

Interpretation of the Agreement is to be made in accordance with Article 31 of the Vienna Convention on the Law of Treaties (1969). If a Member country disputes the interpretation given by another Member to a certain provision, the former may request the establishment of

---

[5] The application of the new term of protection under the Agreement (20 years) to patents that had not expired on 8 June 1995 (when the referred Act took effect) generated considerable debate and litigation.

a panel under the WTO Dispute Settlement Understanding. The decision by the panel will impose an obligation only on the Member or Members against which the complaint was brought, but may also create a precedent for other Members in a similar situation[6].

A problem will arise if a panel is called upon to fill gaps in the TRIPS Agreement, taking into account that panels "cannot add to or diminish the rights and obligations provided in the covered agreements" (Article 3.2 of the DSU). Minimalist and maximalist views on the powers of TRIPS panels may lead to quite different solutions. Panels may limit themselves, for instance, to ruling on the "exercise" but not the "existence" of rights, along the lines defined by the EC Court of Justice (see Geller, 1995).

There are other cases in which the TRIPS Agreement leaves room to the Member countries to design their legislation within broad parameters. Such is the case, for instance, with the definition of invention, which may or may not include substances existing in nature, the admissibility of reverse engineering for computer programs, the recognition of moral rights under copyright, the determination of exceptions to exclusive rights, the grounds and scope of compulsory licences for patents, and the type and extent of protection of plant varieties.

As discussed in previous chapters, with respect to plant varieties, Member countries are bound to provide protection either by patents, an "effective *sui generis* regime", or a combination of both (Article 27.3(b) of the TRIPS Agreement). This leaves freedom for the development of legislation, with the only requirement being that it should ensure "effective" protection. Breeders' rights, as adopted in many developed and a few developing countries, provide a possible but not unique model of a *sui generis* regime. In view of recent developments in the framework of the Convention on Biological Diversity and the Food and Agriculture Organization (FAO), such a regime may incorporate new features, such as some kind of recognition of the knowl-

---

[6] It should be noted that the TRIPS Council shall "monitor" the "operation" of the Agreement and, in particular, Members' "compliance" with their obligations. The Council has no faculties to provide official interpretations of the Agreement. The latter can only be given by the Ministerial Conference of the WTO or by its General Council (Article IX. 2 of the Marrakesh Agreement).

edge of traditional and indigenous communities and of "Farmers' Rights" (FAO, 1994; Esquinas Alcázar, 1996).

Finally, another category of provisions includes those which are drafted in a manner that allows different, even conflicting, interpretations. Article 27.1 is a good example that illustrates the ambiguity stemming from a last-minute compromise on a controversial issue. That article has been generally interpreted as excluding obligations requiring the industrial exploitation of the invention. The history and background of negotiations makes it clear that the intention of the developed negotiating countries was to exclude under Article 27.1 compulsory licences for non-working.

However, Article 5A of the Paris Convention (which is applicable under the TRIPS Agreement) allows for compulsory licences in cases of non-working[7]. In addition, Article 27.1 of the Agreement is ambiguous with respect to which are the products that are "imported or locally produced"[8]. In at least one country, such licences have been deemed to be consistent with the Agreement[9].

Another example relates to the "exclusive marketing rights" (EMRs) to be conferred under Article 70.9 of the Agreement. This provision also reflects a compromise reached in December 1991. The Agreement does not provide any guidance on the extent of such rights. If they were understood as the right to exclude others from marketing the relevant product, how would they differ from a patent? What would be the benefit of the transitional period if such rights provide, like patents, a *ius excluendi*?

---

[7] It is interesting to note that in the Section related to integrated circuits, the TRIPS Agreement explicitly excludes the application of the Washington Treaty provision relating to compulsory licences (Article 6.3). A similar exclusion is not found with respect to Article 5A of the Paris Convention.

[8] Since a patent (see Article 28) only confers a right to exclude others from certain acts (*ius prohibendi*), it may be interpreted that the "products" referred to by Article 27.1 are those produced or imported by a third party, and not by the patent owner himself.

[9] This is the approach of the recent patent law approved in Brazil in 1996. It incorporated the standards derived from the Agreement, and explicitly provided for compulsory licences in cases of lack of local industrial exploitation (Article 68, Law 9,279).

Given this ambiguity, many questions remain open that will require an interpretation in accordance with WTO rules. What remedies against infringement would be available to the EMRs-holder? To what extent can compulsory licensing provisions be applied? What would be the acts permitted for third parties that wish to use the invention, e.g., for experimentation, tests, manufacture, market approval, etc.?

IMPLEMENTATION PROBLEMS

Developing countries that are Members of the WTO (or which are in the process of accession) are required to introduce massive reforms in their IPRs systems. Several problems have arisen in the implementation of the TRIPS Agreement, in three different dimensions.

Normative Dimension

Developing countries, by agreeing to improve the standards of IPRs protection under the TRIPS Agreement, assumed a wide range of obligations in almost all areas of IPRs: copyright and "related rights", industrial designs, trademarks, geographical indications, patents, plant varieties protection, integrated circuits and undisclosed information.

The countries that have initiated the process of adapting IPRs legislation to the Agreement's minimum standards have advanced to different degrees in this task. Some (e.g., Mexico, Trinidad and Tobago, South Korea) have already enacted legislation that covers all or most areas dealt with by the Agreement. Others (e.g., Argentina, Brazil, Andean Group members) have modified some of the relevant national laws, but many areas still have yet to be adapted to comply with the new standards.

In several of the IPRs areas covered by the Agreement, developing countries had no previous legislation. Most developing countries did not provide for specific protection for geographical indications and plant varieties. Moreover, in the case of integrated circuits and undisclosed information, there were no international instruments in force before the TRIPS Agreement.

Administrative Dimension

Countries that have been able to advance in the reform of IPRs do not just face the task of designing and obtaining parliamentary approval for new legislation.

Even in countries that have introduced amendments to their substantive laws, gaps to be filled often remain with regard to the enforcement of rights. Compliance with the Agreement on this matter requires the alignment of national laws with the Agreement in various fields, such as civil and criminal procedures in courts, administrative procedures, and intervention of police and customs authorities. It also requires increased budgets to face the new tasks.The costs of implementing the TRIPS Agreement standards are substantial, as illustrated by a study made by UNCTAD (UNCTAD, 1996, pp. 2-3).

Developed country Members committed themselves to providing technical and financial cooperation to developing and least-developed country Members "to facilitate the implementation" of the TRIPS Agreement (Article 67). The text is, however, too general and the provision of such cooperation is subject to "mutually agreed terms".

Article 66.2 further established for developed countries the obligation to "provide incentives to enterprises and institutions in their territories for the purpose of promoting and encouraging technology transfer to least-developed country Members in order to enable them to create a sound and viable technological base".

It is unclear how these obligations shall be complied with, given the generality of the texts as well as the absence of a specific time frame for their implementation.

Political Dimension: Facing Trade Retaliation

The TRIPS Agreement provides for transitional periods that allow developing countries (and particularly least developed countries) to delay the implementation of the Agreement's obligations.

The provision of such periods was an important element in the delicate balance reached as an outcome of negotiations. They were included to allow developing countries time to elaborate and adopt the required legislation, and to design any other policies necessary to minimize the possible negative effects of new IPRs rules. This was particularly the case with regard to products which had not been patentable (such as pharmaceuticals, agrochemicals and food), the protection of which may entail important consequences in terms of price increases and the room left for national production, as discussed below.

As mentioned in Chapter I, the transitional periods granted by the Agreement are automatic, i.e., their application is not subject to any reservation, declaration, notification or permission. However, many developing countries have already started to adapt their IPRs laws to the Agreement, particularly in the areas of patents and trademarks. Some of them had even incorporated some of the Agreement's rules before its formal approval in April 1994. Such was the case with the Andean Group countries, whose industrial property and copyright regimes (Decision 344 and Decision 351, 1993) introduced several provisions directly inspired by the draft Agreement, particularly in the area of compulsory licensing of patents and the protection of computer programs.

Despite the existence of the transitional periods and the early compliance with the Agreement by many developing countries, some of them have been under pressure by some developed countries to accelerate the pace of reforms, so as to give immediate application to the TRIPS Agreement standards.

After the entry into force of the Agreement, any controversy should be subject to a multilateral procedure of dispute settlement, and only after the completion of the procedure may retaliatory measures be adopted.

While several complaints have been filed under the TRIPS Agreement, involving alleged infractions by developing and developed countries in the area of IPRs, only one case has been decided after a complaint by the US against India relating to implementation of Article 70.8 of the Agreement.

In this case, India was deemed to be in violation of its obligation to provide for a mechanism of deposit of pharmaceutical patent applications, as stipulated in Article 70.8. The decision held that India had to adopt positive legislation in order to implement the so-called "mail-box" provision, but the panel refused to define the scope of the EMRs, since this was not an issue under dispute.

The United States has continued to "classify" and threaten some developing countries under its Trade Act for reasons related to IPRs. US law determines that a foreign country may be deemed to deny "adequate and effective protection" of IPRs notwithstanding compliance of the said country with the specific obligations stipulated by the TRIPS Agreement[10]. One country (Argentina) was sanctioned in 1997 (see Chapter I) and many others are on the list.

Similar tensions have been reported in other Latin American countries, such as the Andean Group countries, Chile and Brazil. The latter and Mexico were the only countries that accepted in Latin America the "pipeline" protection requested by the US government in order to satisfy the demands of its pharmaceutical industry. The Andean Court of Justice (established by the Cartagena Agreement) declared (Process No. 1-AI-96) on 30 October 1996 that the "pipeline" formula was inherently contradictory to the novelty requirement under patent law, and thus rejected the retroactive registration of patents in the Subregion.

In addition to these political problems in the implementation of the TRIPS Agreement, Latin American and Caribbean countries currently face new negotiations on IPRs in the framework of an initiative to establish a "Free Trade Area of the Americas", before most countries in the region can even consider and implement the reforms required under the TRIPS Agreement. IPRs may also be in the agenda of a new WTO round of negotiations (see Chapter VII).

A final aspect to be mentioned is the demands made by industrialized countries to developing countries seeking accession to the WTO. Several cases have been reported in which the latter are pressured not to apply the transitional periods and to confer levels of protection higher than those required under the Agreement, or to waive the transitional period, as in the case of Ecuador.

This indicates that developing countries that have subscribed the TRIPS Agreement still face political problems in its implementation. In some cases, in addition, new negotiations have been launched with the aim of further harmonizing IPRs legislation, even before most

---

[10] This provision is in clear contradiction to the TRIPS Agreement and the WTO system of dispute settlement.

countries have been able to introduce the reforms required under the TRIPS Agreement.

CHANGES IN LATIN AMERICAN AND CARIBBEAN LEGISLATION

Since 1990, an impressive wave of changes in intellectual property laws has taken place in Latin America and the Caribbean. Many countries have modified or substituted laws in several areas, and/or adhered to international conventions. This section briefly examines the ways in which Latin American and Caribbean countries have modified their legislation on IPRs[11], guided by the TRIPS Agreement's minimum standards[12]. The analysis made is not exhaustive; it only aims at providing an overview of the trends in the implementation of said Agreement, and to identify areas in which further action would be required before the expiration of the transitional periods.

Copyright and Related Rights

Decision 351 (1993) of the Andean Group introduced protection of computer programs and databases, in accordance with Article 10 of the draft TRIPS Agreement. Decision 351 defined the extent of protection (with respect to the "form" of expression) in terms similar to Article 9.2 of the Agreement, and it explicitly incorporated "rental rights"[13].

States Parties to the Southern Cone Common Market (MERCOSUR) drafted a Protocol (not finalized yet) on authors' and

---

[11] This analysis does not consider the adhesion by Latin American and Caribbean countries to international conventions on intellectual property. See in this regard Correa (1997).

[12] It should be noted that Mexico is a member of the North American Free Trade Agreement (NAFTA), which contains a chapter on intellectual property drafted on the basis of the TRIPS Agreement (see Neff and Smallson, 1994). Mexico, Venezuela and Colombia also entered into an integration agreement ("the Group of Three") that reproduced (with the exclusion of the Chapter on patents) the IPRs standards adopted in NAFTA .

[13] Under the "Latin" tradition on authors' rights, rental rights may be considered as one of the components of the "distribution" rights (Antequera Parrilli, 1995). However, as a result of the TRIPS Agreement, many countries in the region are explicitly introducing the latter concept.

related rights whereunder they would commit themselves to respecting the "rules and principles" of the TRIPS Agreement and to applying, as a minimum, the Agreement's rules on enforcement (Article 41 of the Protocol). The direct influence of the Agreement is perceptible in Article 10 of the draft Protocol, which literally reproduces Article 9.2 of the Agreement, in Article 11 (computer programs are protected as "literary works"), and in Article 12 (compilations of data). The principle of exhaustion of rights would be adopted but limited to the Parties to MERCOSUR (Article 8); each Party would have the freedom to decide how moral rights are to be regulated in the case of computer programs (Article 16).

Honduras amended its copyright law (1993) before the formal adoption of the TRIPS Agreement, and incorporated many of the standards of the Agreement with regard, for instance, to computer programs, databases and rental rights.

Costa Rica amended its legislation in 1994 in order to clarify the protection of computer programs under the copyright law. Cuba extended the post-mortem term of protection to 50 years in 1994 and the term of protection for photographic works from 10 to 15 years (Decreto-Ley 156).

In Mexico, a new copyright law was approved in December 1996. Computer programs are protected as literary works and the title-holder can exercise "rental rights" (which are also conferred on phonogram producers). Original databases are protected as "compilations" – as required by the TRIPS Agreement – but non-original databases also receive protection for a five-year period (Article 108).[14]

Trademarks

The impact of the standards on trademarks adopted by the TRIPS Agreement is already apparent in three subregional instruments and in the new industrial property laws enacted by some countries in the region.

---

[14] With this solution, the Mexican law is the first and only one in Latin America to follow an approach on non-original databases similar to the one adopted by the EC Directive on the matter.

Decision 344 of the Andean Group has generally reinforced the protection of trademarks[15], particularly "well-known" trademarks. The latter are protected not only if "confusingly similar without regard to the type of product or service for which registration is sought"[16] (Article 83 e), but also when the mark is a "total or partial reproduction, imitation, translation or transcription of a distinctive sign that is commonly known to the sectors concerned in the country in which registration is sought or in subregional or international business" (Article 83 d). As required by the TRIPS Agreement, the "scale and scope of promotion" is one of the elements to be taken into account (Article 84 b).

The referred Decision also shows how the room for manoeuvre left by the TRIPS Agreement may be used. For instance, the Decision provides for the registration of all "perceptible" signs; therefore audible and other non-visible signs can be protected (Pico Mantilla, 1994), as allowed by Article 15 of Decision 344[17]. The Decision also permits "parallel imports" of legitimately trademarked goods (Article 106); it thereby makes use of the freedom left to Member countries by Article 6 of the Agreement to regulate the "exhaustion of rights".

In the case of MERCOSUR, a Protocol on Harmonization of Rules on Intellectual Property in Relation to Trademarks, Geographical Indications and Denominations of Origin was approved in August 1995. Parties – as provided for under Article 15.1 of the TRIPS Agreement – may require, as a condition for registration, that the signs be visible (Article 5.2 of the Protocol). Well-known trademarks need to be protected taking into account the "knowledge of the sign in the pertinent sector of the market, including as a result of the promotion of the sign"[18] (Article 9.5). Parties also commit themselves to adopting in their respective legislation all measures necessary for the free circula-

---

[15] For instance, protection lasts for 10 years and it can be renewed indefinitely for the same term. The previous regime (Decision 85) only allowed for five years' registration.

[16] This special protection is subject, however, to reciprocity.

[17] Decision 85, which is the most important precedent of Decision 344, allowed for the registration of "visible" signs only.

[18] This provision almost literally reproduces Article 16.2 of the TRIPS Agreement.

tion of legitimately trademarked goods (Article 13).

Another important development has been the revision, in 1994, of the Central American Convention for the Protection of Industrial Property. The revision addressed a number of issues in which the original Convention was inconsistent with the TRIPS Agreement, notably the protection of well-known trademarks, including service marks. The revised treaty also stipulates that the *bona fide* use of a trademark before registration in any Member country confers a preferential right to obtain the title.

Mexico improved the protection of "well-known" trademarks, in line with the provisions of the TRIPS Agreement (including of trademarks known on the basis of their promotion or publicity), in the reform of the industrial property law adopted in 1994. The new law approved in Brazil in 1996 increased the minimum non-use term from two years to five years. It also introduced changes with regard to "well-known" trademarks, an area in which weaknesses had often been noted in the past. Such trademarks are granted "special protection". Trinidad and Tobago amended its trademark law in 1996 in order to comply with the TRIPS Agreement and a bilateral agreement signed with the United States on IPRs. A period of registration of 10 years has been established, and protection for well-known trademarks has been enhanced.

Geographical Indications

Decision 344 of the Andean Group introduced, in 1993, protection, in Chapter VII, of the right to the exclusive use of officially recognized "appellations of origin". Chapter XVIII of the agreement establishing the Group of Three also contains provisions on designations of origin and geographical indications but the conditions for protection are to be defined by the domestic legislation. Within MERCOSUR, the abovementioned Protocol also obliges Parties to protect both categories of indications, but does not specify the extent and scope of protection. The revised Central American Convention for the Protection of Industrial Property (1994) requires the protection of geographical indications where a given quality, reputation or other characteristic of a product is essentially attributable to its geographical origin, as required by Article 22 of the TRIPS Agreement. In Brazil, in accordance with the 1996 law, both "designations of origin" and "geographical indications" are protectable (Articles 176-178), except if they have become the customary name of a product or service (Article 180). Trinidad and Tobago introduced, in 1996, protection of geographical indications for the first time in the country, along the lines of Article 22 of the TRIPS Agreement. Registration creates a presumption of protectability, but is not obligatory. The law recognizes the rights of prior users of geographical indications, provided that the requirements of Article 24 (paras. 4 - 8) of the TRIPS Agreement are met.

Despite the progress made, in most countries of the region further action seems necessary in this area in order to align domestic or subregional regulations with the standards of the TRIPS Agreement, particularly for indications relating to wines and spirits.

Industrial Designs

Decision 344 of the Andean Group protects industrial designs, but it has not followed the TRIPS Agreement as closely as in the case of patents. The duration of protection (though increased with respect to Decision 85 from five to eight years) does not meet the minimum standard of the Agreement. The Andean Group regime, further, excludes from protection "designs relating to clothing" (Article 58, Decision 344), while the Agreement includes a specific provision on "textile designs" (Article 25.1). Trinidad and Tobago introduced new legislation on the matter in 1996, based on the standards of the Agreement. Absolute novelty is required for protection[19], which extends for five years plus two possible renewal periods of five years each.

Patents

An early impact of the then draft TRIPS Agreement is manifested in Decision 344 of the Andean Group, particularly with regard to compulsory licences. The Decision closely followed – in some cases

---

[19] The TRIPS Agreement leaves significant room for determination of the requirements of protection by Member countries. See Correa (1996), p. 119.

literally – Article 31 of the Agreement in Article 46 (cases of "public interest, emergency or national security"), Article 47 (practices that "adversely affect free competition"), Article 48 (cases of dependent patents) and Article 49 (conditions for granting compulsory licences)[20]. Decision 344 also provided for compulsory licences in cases of lack of working (Article 42), but working may be satisfied by importation.

Decision 344 did not accept the so-called "pipeline" solution actively advocated by the US government. The purpose of that proposal was to obtain patent protection of pharmaceutical products which had been patented in the United States before the introduction of patents in the Andean Group countries, but which had not yet been commercialized in the said countries[21]. However, in the framework of a bilateral agreement with the United States, Ecuador (one of the members of the Andean Group) accepted the "pipeline" solution and granted patents with respect to inventions which were not "new" in terms of Decision 344. The Junta del Acuerdo de Cartagena initiated an action against Ecuador for non-compliance with the Andean regime. As mentioned before, the Andean Court of Justice decided (on 30 October 1996) that the novelty requirement was absolute and that the Andean Group had explicitly rejected the "pipeline" principle. The High Court declared that patents granted in accordance with the said principle in Ecuador were void.

Honduras introduced important changes to its patent law in 1993, following to a large extent the standards of the draft TRIPS Agreement. Thus, protection of pharmaceutical and agrochemical products was introduced[22], as well as a number of compulsory licences. The law also incorporated rules for the control of anti-competitive practices in licensing agreements, in line with Section 8 (Part II) of the said Agreement.

---

[20] It should be noted that the TRIPS Agreement does not limit the **grounds** upon which compulsory licences may be granted, but only sets forth the **conditions** to be applied.

[21] This kind of proposal was not accepted during the TRIPS negotiations (McGrath, 1996, p. 403); in fact, the TRIPS Agreement only requires protection of pharmaceutical and agrochemical products for the future, and after the transitional periods have elapsed.

[22] However, the term of protection for pharmaceuticals is 17 years counted from the date of application (while the TRIPS Agreement requires a minimum 20-year period).

The new Argentine patent law (1995) directly draws from provisions of the TRIPS Agreement in the area of compulsory licences, as well as with respect to the criteria for patentability and the exceptions thereto, duration and the reversal of the burden of proof. Among the exceptions, the Argentine law determined the non-patentability of methods of surgical, therapeutic or diagnostic treatment, and of "any kind of material or substances existing in nature" (Article 6 g). Since the TRIPS Agreement does not define the concept of "invention", the said exclusion by the Argentine law is fully compatible with the Agreement. As a result of the application of the transitional periods of Article 65, the patentability of pharmaceuticals and the reversal of the burden of proof will only become enforceable in Argentina in the year 2000. With regard to compulsory licences, the Argentine law incorporated three of the modalities explicitly referred to in Article 31 of the Agreement (national emergency, anti-competitive practices, dependent patents) plus compulsory licences based on non-working and on "refusal to deal"[23]. The conditions set forth by the said article are almost literally reproduced by the law. Argentine law has also exploited the flexibility of the TRIPS Agreement with regard to exceptions to the exclusive rights, particularly with respect to "parallel imports" (Article 36 of the law; Article 6 of the TRIPS Agreement). It also authorized the national patent office to establish "limited exceptions to the conferred rights" in sectors of vital interest to the socioeconomic and technological development of the country (Article 44).

Cuba amended its patent law in 1995 (Decreto-Ley No. 160) to allow the filing of patents for pharmaceutical and agrochemical products, as well as the conversion of applications for "Author's Certificates" to patent applications. This amendment is in line with Article 70.8 of the TRIPS Agreement. Cuba intends to apply the transitional period authorized by Article 65.4 of the Agreement.

The 1996 Brazilian law (No. 9,279) has observed the minimum standards provided for by the Agreement while exploiting the flexibil-

---

[23] Like the Chinese patent law, the Argentine law has considered Article 31 (a) of the TRIPS Agreement both as an autonomous ground for granting compulsory licences and as a condition to be applied to compulsory licences conferred on other grounds. On "refusal to deal" as an autonomous ground, see WTO (1995).

ity left in certain areas. Thus, as explicitly allowed by the latter, diagnostic, surgical and therapeutic methods are not deemed an invention (Article 10.VIII of the law). In addition, the law excludes the patentability of living beings or "biological materials found in nature", even if isolated, including the "genome or germplasm" of any living being. The Brazilian law also provides for several types of compulsory licences, including for lack of local working (meaning industrial use of the invention), dependent patents, national emergency or public interest, and abuses of patent rights. The influence of the TRIPS Agreement is evident in the rules for the determination of the remuneration to the patent-holder (which should take into account the "economic value of the granted licence", Article 73.6 of the law).

Integrated Circuits

Trinidad and Tobago is one of the few countries of the region that have so far implemented the TRIPS Agreement provisions relating to integrated circuits. The Layout Design (Topographies) of Integrated Circuits Act 1996 closely follows the Washington Treaty and the TRIPS Agreement with respect to definition of the subject matter, requirements for protection, reverse engineering (which is expressly allowed by the Treaty), innocent infringement and term of protection (10 years). Mexico has also introduced legislation on the matter.

Undisclosed Information

Special legislation on undisclosed information was first introduced in the region by Mexican law in 1991. The Mexican law in turn largely inspired the Andean Group Decision 344. The referred Decision literally incorporated some articles of the draft TRIPS Agreement on the matter (Article 39.2 and 39.3), but introduced some elements which are not in the Agreement. Like the Mexican law, the Decision requires that in order to be protected, the information must not be "obvious to a person skilled in the art" (Article 76). In addition, the information must be fixed[24]. While these additional requirements may

---

[24] This requirement is also contemplated by NAFTA, but not by the TRIPS Agreement.

limit the scope of protection – as compared to the standards of the Agreement – others clearly set forth levels of protection higher than those of the TRIPS Agreement. This is the case with information submitted to national authorities for the registration of pharmaceutical or agrochemical products involving new chemicals (Article 78 of the Decision). On this point, the Decision, while transcribing Article 39.3 of the TRIPS Agreement, has expanded the protection in a way comparable to the higher standards of Article 1711 of NAFTA[25].

Argentina passed, in December 1996, legislation on "confidential information". It literally reproduces Article 39.2 of the Agreement. Protection is given in the framework of unfair competition. Data submitted for the approval of agrochemical and pharmaceutical products is protected against disclosure, following the Agreement's standards as well (Article 39.3). The Argentine law allows the registration of pharmaceutical products by "similarity", i.e., without requiring the applicant to duplicate preclinical or clinical tests. In Brazil, Article 195 of the new Code on Industrial Property (1996) punishes the unauthorized disclosure or use of confidential information, excluding information publicly known or "evident" for a technical person on the matter. It also condemns, in line with Article 39.3 of the TRIPS Agreement, the disclosure of undisclosed results of tests and other data submitted to government authorities to obtain approval for the commercialization of a product, provided that the production of such data "involved a considerable effort". In Trinidad and Tobago, the protection of undisclosed information is dealt with under a special section ("Trade Secret Misappropriation") of the Protection against Unfair Competition Act 1996.

Breeders' Rights

During the 1990s, several countries have introduced legislation on the matter. This is the case with Paraguay (1994), Chile (1994), the Andean Group countries (Decision 345)[26] and Mexico[27]. Legislation

---

[25] A similar approach has been adopted by the Group of Three (Articles 18-22.2).

[26] This Decision basically follows the UPOV Convention, as revised in 1991.

[27] This latter country was obliged under NAFTA to introduce protection for plant varieties. The law on the matter was finally approved in October 1996.

was also passed in Brazil in 1997. The Brazilian law follows some of the aspects of the UPOV Convention, as revised in 1991, by introducing the concept of "essentially derived variety", although Brazil adhered to the UPOV 1978 Act.

Enforcement

In numerous countries of the region, changes have been introduced either in intellectual property laws (e.g., Argentina, Brazil, Mexico, Trinidad and Tobago) or in other legislation (such as Criminal Codes) in order to better define, incorporate or strengthen sanctions against the violation of IPRs. In many countries (e.g., Guatemala), the penalty of imprisonment has been incorporated or increased in severity to combat such violation. In other countries, civil sanctions have also been better defined and strengthened[28].

In Mexico, new customs regulations (which took effect on 1 April 1996) require customs authorities to detain IPRs-infringing products at the port of entry, at the request of a trademark owner, with a prior order issued by the Mexican industrial property authority or by a court.

MAIN CONCLUSIONS

There have been a number of problems faced in the implementation of the Agreement in developing countries. The broad coverage and complexity of areas to be addressed and the generality or ambiguity of some provisions, create difficulties for implementation as well as generate increased costs of administration. External demands for changes outside and beyond the framework and obligations set forth by the Agreement have not completely ceased.

As the precedent overview indicates, despite the transitional periods that apply to developing countries, the TRIPS Agreement has started to strongly influence intellectual property legislation in those countries. The work still to be done in some areas, however, is

---

[28] In the case of Mexico, for instance, the revision of the industrial property law of 1994 established that damages to be borne in case of infringement should not be less than 40% of the price of the infringing products or services.

significant. The implementation of the TRIPS Agreement shall require, in due time, substantial changes or fully new legislation in some areas (e.g., integrated circuits), and minor or procedural adaptations in others. The changes that have been made so far in Latin America and the Caribbean indicate that, while implementing the Agreement's obligations, governments have used to a considerable extent the room for manoeuvre left by the Agreement in several areas.

Such flexibility has been mainly employed to establish exceptions or other limitations to exclusive rights. This is reflective of a desire to ensure a certain balance between rights and obligations, and particularly to foster the transfer of technologies, in line with Article 7 of the TRIPS Agreement, and to prevent anti-competitive practices, as allowed under Article 8.2 of the Agreement.

Compliance with the Agreement's minimum standards shall ensure a high level of protection in most areas of IPRs. Such standards should also constitute a basis to avoid tensions emerging from discrepancies among WTO Member States on IPRs, thus eliminating the use of unilateral sanctions and contributing to the development of a climate of increased and beneficial international cooperation.

References

Antequera Parrilli, Ricardo (1995), "Tendencias legislativas latinoamericanas en derecho de Autor y derechos Conexos y su adecuación a las modernas tecnologías", in *Nuevas Políticas de Propiedad Intelectual. Arma de Negociación o Instrumento de Desarrollo?*, SELA, Caracas.
Blakeney, Michael (1996), "The impact of the TRIPS Agreement in the Asia Pacific region", *EIPR*, Vol. 18, No. 10.
Correa, Carlos (1996), *Acuerdo TRIPS. Régimen internacional de la propiedad intelectual*, Ciudad Argentina, Buenos Aires.
Correa, Carlos (1997), "Harmonization of intellectual property rights in Latin America. Is there still room for differentiation?", *Journal of International Law and Politics*, Vol. 29, No. 2.
Esquinas Alcázar, José (1996), *Agrobiodiversity and Farmers' Rights*, Swaminathan Research Foundation, Madras.
FAO (1994), *Revision of the International Undertaking. Analysis of some technical, economic and legal aspects for consideration in Stage II*, Commission on Plant Genetic Resources, CPGR.Ext./94/5.Supp., Rome.

Geller, Paul (1995), "Intellectual property in the global marketplace: Impact of TRIPS dispute settlement", *The International Lawyer*, March.

McGrath, Michelle (1996), "The patent provisions in TRIPS: Protecting reasonable remuneration for services rendered – or the latest development in Western Colonialism", *EIPR*, Vol. 18, No. 7.

Neff, Richard and Smallson, Fran (1994), *NAFTA. Protecting and Enforcing Intellectual Property Rights in North America*, Shepard's/McGraw-Hill, Colorado Springs.

Pico Mantilla, Galo (1994), "La Decisión 344 de la Comisión del Acuerdo de Cartagena: Régimen Comnún sobre Propiedad Industrial" (mimeo), Quito.

Ricketson, Sam (1995), "The Future of the Traditional Intellectual Property Conventions in the Brave New World of Trade-Related Intellectual Property Rights", *IIC*, Vol. 26, No. 6.

South Centre (1995), *The Uruguay Round. Intellectual Property Rights Regime. Implications for developing countries*, Geneva.

Ullrich, Hans (1989), "GATT: Industrial property protection, fair trade and development", in F-K. Beier and G. Schricker (Eds.), *GATT or WIPO? New ways in the international protection of intellectual property*, Munich.

UNCTAD (1989), *Trade-related intellectual property rights: Implications of US policy for developing countries and the Uruguay Round of Multilateral Trade Negotiations*, UNCTAD/MTN/INT/CB.19, Geneva.

UNCTAD (1996), *The TRIPS Agreement and Developing Countries*, New York and Geneva.

WTO (World Trade Organization) (1995), *Environment and TRIPS*, WT/CTE/W/8, Geneva.

CHAPTER V

Intellectual Property Rights and Information Technologies

INTRODUCTION

TECHNOLOGY diffusion has been extensively studied by the economic literature (OECD, 1992). Though diffusion literature has considered many factors that may influence the rhythm and modalities of adoption of technologies, the possible impact of legal factors, particularly intellectual property rights, has been only incidentally addressed.

The purpose of this Chapter[1] is to examine recent developments in intellectual property law and the ways in which they may affect the diffusion of Information Technologies (ITs) in developing countries.

The analysis and discussion will be centred around the barriers that IPRs may create for the **access** to and **use** of ITs in such countries. This Chapter also addresses the main issues that arise with regard to the access to information as such, as a result of the digitization of data and the development of large computer networks or "information superhighways".

The problems related to access to and use of ITs are considered here with regard to the application of ITs for **production** of hardware/software as well as with respect to their **use**.

While economic reasons are behind major changes in law, the latter also has a definite influence on the economy. The interaction between law and economics is a complex one. It is often very difficult to isolate the "legal factors" and measure their impact on economic

---

[1] This Chapter is substantially based on a paper prepared at the request of INTECH, University of the United Nations.

decisions. However, rules created by law establish implicit prices for different kinds of behaviour, and the consequences of those rules can be analyzed as the response to those implicit prices (Cooter and Ulen, 1988).

The relationship between IPRs and the economy has been addressed from different perspectives (Correa, 1994a). During the seventies, the impact of IPRs – particularly patents – on developing countries received some attention from scholars. Initiatives to develop new international rules that take into account the interests of those countries were also launched, albeit with little success[2].

More recently, particularly after the launching of the Uruguay Round (1986), economists' interest in IPRs has revived, as illustrated by work done by the World Bank (see Siebeck *et al.*, 1990), David (1993), Mansfield (1993; 1994), UNCTAD (1996) and others[3].

This Chapter considers the new developments in the area of IPRs. The relationship between ITs and IPRs is examined with respect to computer programs, including the trends in the areas of copyright and patents, multimedia products and integrated circuits. Issues related to the protection of and access to databases and digital information in general are dealt with.

The implications of the described trends in access to, and acquisition and use of ITs in developing countries are also considered. Finally, the impact of copyright, patents and integrated circuits protection with regard to the production and use of ITs, as well as to the access to and use of digital information, is analyzed.

NEW DEVELOPMENTS

Several factors contributed to prompting during the last decade a far-reaching reform of the intellectual property system. They relate to the increase in R&D costs, the shortening of the life-cycle of products, difficulties in appropriating the results of R&D, particularly in the field

---

[2]   That was the case with the initiatives to revise the Paris Convention, and to establish an International Code of Conduct on Technology Transfer.
[3]   See also Correa (Ed.) (1995).

of easy-to-copy new technologies (such as computer programs), and the globalization of the economy (Correa, 1994b; David, 1993). The changing framework for the protection of IPRs was reflected in two major developments. On the one side, **new areas of knowledge** are becoming subject to property rights.

One outstanding example is the protection of semiconductors' layout designs under a new, *sui generis* system, which was established for the first time in the United States in 1984. An international obligation (under the TRIPS Agreement) to protect such designs has already been adopted.

Patents have been extended in most countries to living matter, including plants and animals, though this still originates considerable debate (The Crucible Group, 1994). As discussed below, the granting of patents on computer programs is currently admitted in the United States.

Likewise, a new form of *sui generis* right has been developed within the European Union, in order to protect investments made for the development of databases that are otherwise unprotectable under copyright (see section on "Databases" below).

The need to extend IPRs protection to "information products" which are not copyrightable, patentable or subject to other existing IPRs, has also been voiced. Fact and functional materials are the building blocks upon which scientific and technological progress depends. Their content is so closely tied to facts and laws of life and nature that there is little room for creation (Dreyfuss, 1993, pp. 196 and 214). However, it is argued that determining what information the market wants and conveying the information clearly and in appropriate formats can require a high level of ingenuity. In addition, "lead time" allowed in the past for recovery of the investments made for the generation of new knowledge has shortened or vanished. A new, eventually "hybrid" form of protection would be, according to some experts and industry views, required in order to provide the adequate incentives to innovate (Dreyfuss, 1993, pp. 210 and 234; Samuelson *et al.*, 1994).

It has also been noted that the **incremental** nature of innovation in key industries, such as electronics, is not well captured by existing rules. This mismatch may lead to a crisis in the current model of IPRs protection. According to Foray:

"Innovative activity has shifted away from models based on absolute novelty and first improvement towards a model in which innovation is no longer driven by technological breakthroughs but by the routine exploitation of existing technologies. This change has precipitated a crisis in the area of intellectual property rights, particularly in the sectors where the new innovation model is most widespread (biotechnology, software, consumer electronics)" (Foray, 1995, p. 120).

On the other side, a process of **universalization** of minimum standards of protection is taking place. Under the principle of national treatment, each country could in the past frame its intellectual property system in accordance with its own needs and long-term interests, provided that it granted foreigners the same treatment accorded to nationals.

However, the adoption of minimum standards under the TRIPS Agreement (including on aspects such as definition of the protected subject matter, terms of protection, extent of exclusive rights, etc.) has reduced national freedom and increased to an unprecedented level the degree of universal harmonization of IPRs.[4]

This process means, in particular, that developing countries are bound to incorporate standards of protection basically in accordance with those so far in force in industrialized countries.

Even though a new international intellectual property regime could be "Pareto improving", it is likely "to impose institutional arrangements that may be well adapted to the national purposes and legal contexts of one country (or several similar countries) on societies that are quite different in those respects" (David, 1993, p. 55).

ITs AND INTELLECTUAL PROPERTY LAW

The development and rapid diffusion of information technologies has posed major challenges to various aspects of public and private law. The birth of new products and of whole new branches of industry, like semiconductors, computers, computer software, multimedia and

---

[4] On the costs and benefits of this harmonization, see Frischtak (1995).

databases, calls for the adaptation or creation of new legal principles and rules.

Preexisting rules and institutions of intellectual property have been deemed applicable to some of the new areas, with certain adjustments. This is, for instance, the case with computer software: following a number of precedents established by national laws, computer software has become protectable under copyright as literary works. The TRIPS Agreement has explicitly obliged all Member countries to adopt that approach. Though this has proven the adaptability of copyright to new situations, the outcome does not seem to satisfy everybody[5].

In other areas, as in the case of semiconductors, new legal approaches have been developed. Based on the regime adopted by the United States under the Semiconductor Chip Protection Act of 1984, countries that thereafter legislated on the matter have followed the *sui generis* approach first established by that Act, which also influenced the Washington Treaty concluded in 1989.

Though these and other regulations and case law addressed many of the emerging issues, technological developments have continued and posed new, increasingly complex problems to intellectual property law. One of the main directions of such developments has been the convergence of different types of applications, based on the common infrastructure provided by digital technology.

Digitized text, speech, graphics, images (moving or otherwise), music and sound can be combined using appropriate computer software and associated hardware. This combined use gives rise to a wave of new products and services with an expanding market. The products may be either fixed in material form (such as on CD-ROM) or stored and directly accessible online as digital data.

---

[5] Considerable debate is still ongoing due to the functional character of software and its problematic assimilation to literary works. See Samuelson *et al.* (1994).

Protecting Computer Programs

Technologies for software development

Technologies for software development are not proprietary, although the use of certain tools, platforms or interfaces may require the negotiation of a licence and the payment of royalties. Different languages and architectures offer software producers options to develop their products, with different technical (and commercial) advantages and disadvantages.

Technology for software development is largely available at universities and research institutions. The basic knowledge for the creation of computer programs is accessible to individuals of various disciplines (not necessarily software specialists). The nature of software technology permits outsiders to challenge, from time to time, the market position of major software producers, a few of whom dominate the market. "Linux"[6] provides a good example[7].

The knowledge involved in software development, however, constitutes a more complex technology where other skills (e.g., in information systems, hardware architectures, project management, etc.) are required, depending on the type of software to be produced. Besides, as argued elsewhere (Correa, 1996), availability of technology is not enough to overcome the formidable commercial entry barriers prevailing in the software market.

Innovation in software development is typically incremental (Samuelson *et al.*, 1994, p. 2330). Software products are generally developed using previously existing programs and algorithms. Software is a "cumulative systems technology", as opposed to the "discrete invention model". It is a "technology that builds on and interacts with many other features of existing technology to create a new technology" (Nelson, 1994, pp. 2676-2677).

---

[6] This is a Unix-like operating system for PCs, developed at the University of Helsinki in 1991 and freely available. Linux is distributed with its source code under a "general public licence".

[7] Due to these characteristics, software has been deemed a strong candidate for "leapfrogging" by developing countries that possess a good scientific infrastructure (Pérez, 1987).

Though software development is subject to the limits imposed by the particular problem to be solved, there is no unique way of developing a certain product. Software producers can make strategic choices taking the type of products and markets envisaged into account. Considerable room is, hence, left for creativity and ingenuity. Tacit knowledge, based upon experience, plays an important role in software development, which may be described – despite the introduction of software engineering tools – as still being an "amateurship, craft-based discipline" (Cane, 1992, p. 1726) rather than a proper "industrial" activity (Zimmermann, 1993).

Copyright protection

Copyright has been applied to computer programs, with some hesitation at the beginning and with a lot of – still ongoing – controversy over the extent of protection. By pushing the copyright way, the US government and industry strategically opted for a form of protection which is cheaper to obtain than industrial property rights, that does not require disclosure and, above all, that permits almost universal and automatic protection without registration, since the very date of creation of the program.

This latter feature is of utmost importance for an internationalized industry like the software industry. Copyright protection does not require applications and procedures in individual countries. It practically has a global reach as a result of the large membership of the Berne Convention and the WTO.

The recognition of computer programs as a copyrightable work was actively sought by major software producers and the US government. Under Section 301 of the Trade Act, the United States Trade Representative (USTR) initiated several procedures against developed and developing countries that did not, in the USTR's view, adequately protect such programs. The cases of Brazil (Bastos, 1995), Thailand[8] and, more recently, China are illustrative of such actions.

---

[8] In Thailand, a government was forced to step down due to the reaction to its attempt to accept US pressures in the software area (Correa, 1990a).

The pro-copyright campaign also reached GATT. The TRIPS Agreement clearly states that computer programs are to be protected "as literary works". This provision entails the internationalization of a legal framework of protection for computer programs, on the adequacy of which doubts continue to be voiced (Samuelson *et al.*, 1994). The functional aspects of computer programs pose difficult questions that copyright law has so far been unable to resolve (OTA, 1992, p. 22).

Copyright only protects the expression of an idea, not the idea as such. This basic dichotomy – contained in the US copyright law – has been explicitly stated in the TRIPS Agreement (Article 9.2).

As a result of the said dichotomy, the production of an identical copy of a program is prohibited by law, if it is the result of access to the preexisting program. There is no infringement if an identical program is independently created without such access.

Likewise, there is no infringement if a program has the same behaviour but a different expression, even if the new program was created on the basis of access to and reverse engineering of a pre-existing one[9].

It should be noted, finally, that computer programs are not only protectable as copyrightable works. The "source programs" can also be protected as trade secrets or undisclosed information. Such programs contain the most valuable information for software producers that is not made available to the public through the distribution of copies in a magnetic form.

In sum, copyright protection (as supplemented by trade secrets protection) erects barriers against imitation and competition via incremental innovation, but it presents important shortcomings for those looking for stronger means of preventing the development of competitive products via reverse engineering (Correa, 1993).

Different ways have been utilized, particularly by major software producers, in order to neutralize the weaknesses of the existing IPRs protection. They have included extension of the scope and search for new forms of IPRs protection, and strict and aggressive enforcement of available IPRs.

---

[9] There is, however, debate over whether a "substantially similar" imitative program is infringing or not (Kitagawa, 1994, p. 2613).

Extending IPRs protection

a) Beyond expression

A large number of cases (see Box 4) were brought to courts in the United States in order to obtain copyright protection of user interfaces ("look and feel"), a crucial aspect for the development and marketing of competing products.

User interfaces determine the way in which a user interacts with the computer through the use of "menus", certain forms of entering commands, etc. External consistency of a new program with an existing one permits "transfer of learning", and therefore increases the likelihood of adoption by potential users who may be reluctant to invest time in learning how to use new programs.

Protection was recognized for the overall set of command terms and their organization into menus, the menu "structure", the order of

---

Box 4: Limiting competition on expressive elements of computer programs

Suits against competitors due to their copying of expressive elements of computer programs have included the following:

- Placing screen captions at the top centre of the screen
- Using the colour blue as screen background
- Designating which keystrokes a user should press to enter the program function that a given screen menu word designates, by capitalizing and highlighting (making brighter) the letters of the menu word corresponding to the keystrokes
- Labelling the opening menu of a program as "Opening Menu"
- Use of pull-down menu windows in reverse video
- Use of the same command language to operate program functions that the plaintiff's earlier program used for those functions
- Having the same switch patterns on a machine's front panel to actuate the machine's software
- Imitating the plaintiff CADAM's (CADAM is a major CAD/CAM (computer-aided design/computer-aided manufacturing) producer) computer program by being "too CADAM-ish".

Source: Stern (1993), p. 39.

commands in each menu line, the choice of letters, words or "symbolic tokens" (OTA, 1992, p. 143).

Demands for protection of user interfaces in the area of such elements as particular menu styles, the use of pull-down menus, the use of a two-line moving cursor and ways of entering commands, among others, were unsuccessful.

Attempts have also been made to claim protection on computer languages. For instance, Adobe, "a software house that created a popular desktop publishing program, claims that its PostScript language is copyrighted, although it has not sued those who reject this claim" (Warshofsky, 1994, p.152).

b) Limiting reverse engineering

Innovation in the software industry is very dependent, as mentioned before, on the improvement of existing products. Development costs can be significantly reduced by evaluating products on the market and designing new products with enhanced features. A crucial aspect for innovation and competition in the software industry is, therefore, the extent to which the evaluation (reverse engineering) and improvement of computer programs are feasible and legitimate.

In contrast to the tacitness present at the production phase, software products are fully formalized and codified. This affects the appropriability of the results of development work, since much of the embodied know-how is "borne on the face" of the product (Kitagawa, 1994, p. 2615). Other embodied elements of the know-how may be obtained through decompilation and disassembly.

Decompilation and disassembly are technical procedures that permit reverse engineering of software products[10]. Though this is useful for small products, it is not necessarily so for large products, at least under the current state of the art, since decompilation in the latter case is extremely costly and time-consuming (Samuelson *et al.*, 1994, pp. 2336 and 2341). This provides *de facto* protection to innovators against imitation.

---

[10] Decompilation allows one to translate a machine language program into a high-level representation program, i.e., a more understandable form. By disassembly, a machine language program is translated into an assembly language program (OTA, 1992, p. 146).

In principle, under the idea/expression dichotomy, reverse engineering is a legal method of acquiring knowledge on the internal organization and structure of a program, with a view to producing a new program differently expressed. Reverse engineering is also legitimate with regard to trade secrets, except if unfair practices are used to obtain the relevant knowledge (Neff and Smallson, 1994, p.102). The admissibility of reverse engineering of computer programs has, however, originated a heated debate and hesitant case law[11]. Major US firms and the US government have strongly lobbied in order to limit that activity[12].

Thus, when the European Commission decided to clarify, by means of a specific Directive, the scope and extent of protection of computer programs, major software producers – who are able to determine *de facto* market standards – campaigned for the restriction of reverse engineering in this field. They confronted other firms (including from Japan, the United States and Europe[13]) that regarded the prohibition of reverse engineering as a potential insurmountable barrier to competition.

As an outcome, the European Council Directive 91/250 on the Legal Protection of Computer Programs set out a compromise: reverse engineering was deemed legitimate only if it was intended to achieve "interoperability" with the evaluated program. The Directive permitted decompilation when it was "indispensable to obtain the information necessary to achieve the interoperability of an independently created program with other programs" (Article 6).

One important manifestation of the trend towards extending protection of computer programs, even within the framework of copyright law, was US case law holding that such protection could embrace not only the literal code (expression) of a program, but also

---

[11] In *NEC Corp. vs Intel Corp.* (67.434 (N.D. Cal. Feb. 6, 1989)), for instance, a US court did not condemn the disassembling of an Intel microcode (8086/88 microprocessor chips) for the purpose of researching and developing a competitive microcode program.

[12] US action blocked the explicit legalization of reverse engineering in Japan (Kitagawa, 1994, p. 2617).

[13] A group of these firms constituted the European Committee for Interoperable Systems to lobby in favour of decompilation to get access to unprotected elements.

its "structure, sequence and organization" (*Whelan Assoc. vs Jaslow* (1987)). This extended protection was, however, denied in subsequent decisions (*Atari vs Nintendo*; *Sega vs Accolade*, 1992). In *Sega vs Accolade*, the court held that:

> "Where disassembly is the only way to gain access to the ideas and functional elements embodied in a copyrighted computer program and where there is a legitimate reason for seeking such access, disassembly is a fair use of the copyrighted work as a matter of law".

The possible negative impact on innovation of an eventual limitation to reverse engineering has been pointed out by many scholars, who warn that overprotection can not only stifle creativity but also limit developing countries' access to technology (see Mody, 1989, pp. 2 and 34).

c) Applying for patents

Despite the efforts made to extend the rights conferred by copyright protection, major producers remained dissatisfied. The difficulty in appropriating the functional aspects of a program and in preventing reverse engineering prompted a growing use of the patent system, notwithstanding the high inventive standards and the required disclosure of the invention.

Two categories of software-related inventions may be defined: a) computer programs that produce a technical effect within the computer or on other hardware components; and b) computer programs that produce technical effects different from those described in (a), entailing changes in the state of physical matter, such as effects on equipment applied to a specific industrial task (Guglielmetti, 1996, p. 70).

In the United States, the Patent Office and case law have assumed a favourable attitude with regard to the possibility of obtaining patents on computer programs. Since the decision in the leading case *Diamond vs Diehr*, until 1994 more than 3,500 software patents were granted (Warshofsky, 1994, p. 162). In 1997, around 12,000 software patents were issued in that country.[14]

US courts distinguished non-patentable, purely mathematical algorithms from inventions in which such algorithms are "applied". In *Diamond vs Diehr*, a patent on an algorithm used to control a process for curing rubber was upheld. However, patents have also been granted in cases where there is no transformation of physical substances into a different physical state, and where only manipulation of data is involved. Some examples of granted patents (including both categories defined above) are given in Boxes 5 and 6.

The Arrythmia case (958 F.2d 1053 (1992)) is illustrative of current trends in the United States. The invention involves a formula that analyzes heartbeat signals, assigns an arithmetic value to the analysis, and compares that value with a predetermined level. The comparison allows a diagnosis to be made as to whether the individual tested is at risk of heart failure.

While the court reiterated that inventions consisting solely of an abstract mathematical formula or equation are not patentable, it stated that the patent claims did not result in patenting a mathematical formula, but "only foreclosed others from using that formula in conjunction with the diagnostic and computer-run steps of the particular invention" (Fishman, 1994, p.5/32).

Software patents – to the extent that they, unlike copyright, protect ideas – may have significant implications independent of the technical importance of the involved "invention".

Thus, Warshofsky reports that Cadtrak Corporation applied for a patent on a computer screen display and included the exclusive-or statement as one of 15 claims. "They were granted US Patent No. 4,197,590, and as a result, anyone who wants to put a cursor on a computer screen either pays Cadtrak or runs the infringement gauntlet. More than 300 hardware and software companies, including IBM, Texas Instruments, and Fujitsu, chose the easy way and are paying royalties to license that single patent" (Warshofsky, 1994, p.164).

In another case, "Paul Heckel, a California programmer, was granted US Patent No. 4,486,857 and 4,736,308 for a system that displays records or strings of information and then allows the operator

---

[14] *Patent-news*, 19.5.98.

Box 5: Examples of software patents granted in the United States

The patented invention:

* translates between natural languages.
* determines boundaries of graphic regions on a computer screen.
* governs removable menu windows on a computer screen.
* generates and overlays graphic windows for multiple active program storage areas in the computer.
* qualifies and sorts file record data in a computer.
* compresses and manipulates images in a computer.
* handles the data structure and search method for a database management system.
* automates spelling error corrections as in some form of a spell-checker system.
* sets up a securities brokerage cash management system.
* operates a system that values stocks, bonds and other securities.
* automatically makes a two-dimensional portrayal of a three-dimensional object; specifically, it transforms a 2-D drawing of an object into a computer-presentable 3-D drawing.
* allows information to be stored on a hard drive and retrieved by multiple users at different locations.
* measures the performance of a general purpose digital computer.
* determines the behavioural profile of computer users.
* administers a plan for funding investments in education.
* adjusts deposit and loan accounts for inflation.
* operates at least one client financial account.

Source: Fishman (1994), pp.5/22 and 5/23; Union for the Public Domain homepage (1998)

---

to scroll, or browse, through them. Heckel sued Apple Computer, alleging their Hypercard program violated those patents. Despite the fact that scrolling and sub-windows, the techniques incorporated in the patents, were quite well known, using them in a combination may now be considered illegal. Rather than fight what is considered a nuisance suit, Apple simply took out a licence" (Warshofsky, 1994, p. 163).

Box 6: Patenting prime numbers

A troubling case has been identified by the British Parliamentary Office of Science and Technology.

It is a patent on prime numbers: "a patent was issued by the US Patent and Trademark Office (PTO) for a mathematical method (the Partial Modular Reduction Method) which is of use in cryptography and security systems. The claims included the use of two prime numbers (comprising 150 and 320 digits) which have a property that speeds up decryption. Indeed, the claim in the patent extends to using any prime number that allows the short cut to be made. The US PTO agreed that the two prime numbers in the claim represent novel discoveries that have some utility, and can, therefore, be patented under US patent law".

Source: Parliamentary Office of Science and Technology (1996), p. 33

In Europe, patenting of computer programs has been less permissive than in the United States. The European Patent Convention forbids the patenting of computer programs as such. Patents have not been granted in cases where the program only undertakes mathematical operations, analyzes test data (e.g., application by Siemens, 1989) or permits the graphic presentation of data (application by IBM, 1993), among others. In exchange, computer programs that generate a transformation in physical reality by guiding the operation of other means have been deemed patentable, such as a computer-operated radiologic device (Koch & Sertzel, 1987) and a system to automatically manage the order of the supply of services to clients at different sites (Queuing System, 1994) (Guglielmetti, 1996, pp. 78-89).

Enforcing IPRs

Several cases illustrate how aggressively and extensively IPRs may be enforced. One example was the IBM-Fujitsu case relating to the infringement of IBM's software. IBM obtained from Fujitsu a compensation for infringement amounting to US$833 million, plus annual royalties of between US$26 and 51 million. The arbitration process, however, determined that Fujitsu should be allowed continued access to IBM's software (Mody, 1989, p.34).

Further, major software producers have individually or jointly (through the Business Software Alliance) undertaken "anti-piracy" campaigns and brought judicial action against distributors of "pirated" software, as well as against corporate users that did not respect contractual or legal restrictions (particularly those preventing the making of copies other than for back-up purposes).

The piracy levels reported by interested groups are high both in developing as well as in developed countries. Though the basis and mode of calculation of those estimates is unclear, they reflect concern with regard to what seems to be a widespread phenomenon. It is almost impossible to monitor and prevent private copying of computer programs. Litigation costs of prosecuting individual users or small firms are disproportionately high.

In the case of Latin America, legal actions have been initiated against large local (private and public) companies and foreign subsidiaries, as well as against public research institutions[15]. Their aim has mainly been to send signals to major software users in order to discourage illegal copying.

Multimedia Products

The development of multimedia products involves a variety of knowledge and skills, and often the combination of preexisting works developed by different authors. Producers of multimedia integrate multiple technologies and works in a creative form. Producers' skills are required to select the materials and to determine the form in which they are organized and presented in an interactive way.

Multimedia producers may be divided into four categories:

• professional video producers, including TV producers;

• industrial producers, such as corporate graphics and video producers in advertising;

---

[15] In some cases, software suppliers have made global arrangements with universities in order to allow the legal distribution, at low cost, of copies of old versions of computer programs.

- commercial organizations that produce their own multimedia material;

- educational institutions and educators (Buckner, 1995, p. 33).

As a result of the complex nature of multimedia products, a "package" of IPRs, belonging to the same or different title-holders, is involved. Such rights include:

a) Copyright and related rights

Authors of text, computer programs, databases, music, photographs and motion pictures as well as performing artists may claim copyright and related rights with respect to the works partially or totally included in multimedia products.

These rights should be differentiated from those belonging to the multimedia producer as such, i.e., to the person or persons who have combined the various components in an original form. The multimedia producer may develop by himself the different components of the product or may use existing works. The latter is the most common approach. The multimedia producer needs in this case to obtain permission from each author to use their respective works.

Obtaining permission and determining the remuneration to be paid to all possible title-holders involved is one of the outstanding problems in the area of multimedia. It may be extremely difficult to determine authorship and to contact all possible authors, as well as to evaluate the level of the remuneration to be paid. Transaction costs are high.

b) Patents

Patent law may also apply to multimedia products, though in a limited and probably controversial way.

A patent granted to Compton New Media in the United States is an example of the possible extension of patents to the multimedia world. Compton New Media obtained a patent for a computer-controlled system for retrieving text and images from a database and claimed a 1% royalty from companies producing interactive multimedia products. The patent generated widespread concern in industry. It was successfully challenged and finally overturned.

c) Trade secrets

Finally, as in the case of computer programs, trade secrets may also be relevant for multimedia products. The source code of computer programs, as mentioned before, is generally deemed to be protected by trade secrets, in addition to copyright.

The production of multimedia is one of the opportunities that developing countries might try to exploit. However, the legal issues are so intricate and complex that unless a general solution is implemented (e.g., by means of compulsory licensing), the transaction costs for obtaining all required authorizations may be prohibitive and block any possible significant development in this field.

Integrated Circuits[16]

The semiconductor industry is highly concentrated. A few transnational corporations account for an overwhelming share of semiconductor production and trade and for the technologies necessary for state-of-the-art manufacture. Among developing countries, only South Korea has emerged as a world-class competitor. Taiwan has also developed significant capacity in this field. Other developing countries participate as exporters of semiconductors locally assembled by subsidiaries of transnational corporations.

The high investment required for mass chip production and the intensity and cost of R&D in an extremely competitive market constitute formidable barriers for potential new entrants, particularly those from developing countries.

While the production of integrated circuits is beyond the reach of most developing countries, the design, particularly of custom and semicustom chips, has been undertaken in many of them, particularly in the newly industrializing countries (NICs). This has been facilitated, on the one side, by the development of computer-aided design tools that can run on relatively small-size computers; and, on the other,

---

[16] This section is partially based on Correa (1990b).

by the possibility of contracting with various silicon foundries the manufacture of a chip according to independently made designs. Technological advance in the semiconductor industry is an interactive, cumulative process where improvements are directly based on the preexisting stock of knowledge. Studies on the role of IPRs in promoting innovation in this industry have shown that gaining lead time and exploiting learning-curve advantages are the primary methods for appropriating the returns on investments in R&D (Levin *et al.*, 1987, p.788).

The protection of layout designs of integrated circuits as a specific subject matter was born in the United States in 1984, with the approval of the Semiconductor Chip Protection Act (SCPA). The growing concern over the decline of the United States' competitive advantages in chip production and trade during the 1980s prompted Congress to adopt a *sui generis* protection regime. It was assumed, in particular, that the increasing strength of Japanese firms was linked to the copying of American designs.

The *sui generis* regime for integrated circuits established under the SCPA provided for 10-year protection; registration was made compulsory within two years of the first "commercial exploitation" of a mask work; and a special provision allowing for "reverse engineering" was contemplated, following the prevailing practice in the semiconductor industry.

The SCPA, in addition, included stringent reciprocity rules that forced Japan to adopt similar legislation ("Act concerning the circuit lay-out of a semiconductor integrated circuit" (law No. 43)), followed by the European Communities (Council Directive on the legal protection of topographies of semiconductor products 87/54/EEC).

The World Intellectual Property Organization, shortly after the enactment of the SCPA, initiated studies and consultations in order to establish an international treaty on the matter, based on the *sui generis* approach. Negotiations led to the adoption, in 1989, of the Washington Treaty. The United States and Japan, however, did not sign it, due to disagreements with respect to compulsory licences, the treatment of innocent infringement, and the protection of designs when they are incorporated in industrial products.

These perceived shortcomings were expeditiously addressed a few years later. The TRIPS Agreement practically derogated the

Treaty's provisions that had been rejected by the two chip powers, and added those obligations that they felt were missing.

So far, only some developing countries have considered legislation to specifically protect integrated circuits' designs, but all WTO Member countries are obliged to do so.

One of the main reasons for the enactment of the SCPA and its internationalization was the alleged copying of original chip layout designs, particularly by Japanese competitors. However, the very few instances of litigation that took place on the basis of that regime would indicate that the copying of chips' layout designs was not the main bone of contention[17].

The main purpose of the *sui generis* regime on integrated circuits is to prevent copying of original chips' designs, and the commercialization either of the infringing chips or of the products that incorporate them. As mentioned, the *sui generis* regime does not prevent reverse engineering.

The important controversies did not relate to the layout designs, but to the technical ideas underlying them or to their production processes subject to patent protection.

Thus, Texas Instruments was reported to have earned (by 1994) more than US$1.5 billion in royalties from its patent portfolio. Its main source of income was a broad patent originally filed 30 years ago "covering an old-fashioned technology that has been extended by peculiarities unique to the US patent system". Intel also has an aggressive IPRs strategy, with a litigation budget of at least US$100 million, that few companies can match. Based on its patent US 4,338,675, it has attempted to bar competition not only from other major chip producers, but also from small design houses (Warshofsky, 1994, pp. 252 and 256).

Action by Texas Instruments reached competitors worldwide. It sued on the same charges at the same time seven Japanese companies, which have reportedly paid an average of around US$30 million per firm. Samsung was also sued, but it paid over US$90 million. The reason for this different outcome seems to be that the Japanese firms held "several patents of their own and were able to negotiate cross-

---

[17] The SCPA was described, for that reason, as "a solution in search of a problem" (Siegel and Laurie, 1989, p. 14).

licensing agreements and thus lower the amount of royalty payments to Texas Instruments" (Mody, 1989, p. 38).

Digital Information

The current trends in IPRs may, ultimately, affect access to information. As mentioned before, there are attempts to extend protection to factual materials that are unprotectable under existing IPRs. Some authors (Catalá, 1984) advocate property rights over the information as such.

Even if those attempts are rejected, developments with regard to databases and information in "cyberspace" may lead to similar effects, i.e., restraining or excluding the access to and use of information even if unprotectable under IPRs.

Databases

Databases are protectable, under copyright, as compilations. In principle, however, only those databases that meet the copyright originality test are protectable. In other words, simple compilations of data are in the public domain.

This is what the US Supreme Court decided in a case (*Feist Publication Inc. vs Rural Telephone Services*, III S Ct 1282, 1991) where it considered whether an alphabetical arrangement of telephone subscribers' names and numbers was copyrightable. The Court held that information consisting solely of facts arranged in a straightforward manner are not "original works of authorship" within the meaning of the Copyright Act.

This decision was viewed by some authors as "endangering the vitality of our information industries. To a nation that counts information as an important asset and a principal export, the outcome is (or should be) extremely worrisome" (Dreyfuss, 1993, p. 197).

Europe shared this concern. The European Council Directive 96/9/EC developed a new *sui generis* form of protection for any database if it is shown that qualitatively and/or quantitatively a "substantial investment in either obtaining, verification or presentation of the contents" has been made (Article 7).

The EC Directive provides for an "extraction right", i.e., the right to prevent "the extraction or reutilization of the whole or substantial part, evaluated quantitatively or qualitatively, of the contents of the database" (Article 7).

This Directive provides a conspicuous example of the emerging paradigm of IPRs protection, whereunder the main goal is not to protect creativity and ingenuity, but investments. Databases are, in effect, protected under the *sui generis* right without requiring originality in the selection or arrangement of their contents. According to the European Commission, the main feature of the Directive is:

"to create a new economic right to protect the substantial investment by a database maker. Considering the considerable investment of human, technical and financial resources necessary to create a database, and given that those databases can be copied at a much lower cost than that of their development, such legal change is important. Unauthorized access to a database and the extraction of its contents are thus acts which can have grave technical and economic consequences" (EU Commission, 1995, p. 32).

The Directive's sections on the *sui generis* right define two categories of restricted acts: extraction and reutilization. The right applies to the whole or a substantial part of a database, which means that an insubstantial part is not protected. Protection lasts for 15 years, and that period may be renewed if there has been substantial new investment. The Directive defines exceptions to the right which are similar to those existing in the chapter on copyright, but, in view of the volume of information in such databases, the exceptions are generally limited to the right of extraction. The *sui generis* right is conferred in addition to the other existing rights.

The Directive does not prescribe, but only authorizes, the provision by Member countries of exceptions for the cases of extraction for "private purposes", "teaching or scientific research", and "public security or an administration or judicial procedure" (Article 9). Moreover, Member countries may limit the exception relating to teaching and research to "certain categories of teaching and scientific research institutions" (Preamble, No. 52).

The "information industry" has welcomed the Directive, while questioning the US Supreme Court attempt to keep information products in the public domain. A Diplomatic Conference convened by WIPO to develop a Protocol to the Berne Convention that met for the first time in December 1996 may, however, declare the European approach as the universal standard. One of the basic proposals considered by the Conference aims at establishing a treaty for the protection of non-original databases the production of which entailed a "substantial investment"[18].

The "information superhighway"

The digitization of information and the development of computer networks such as the Internet are posing a new and far-reaching challenge to copyright. The way in which it is finally resolved may have important implications with regard to access to information.The main technological change behind this "new revolution" (G-7 Ministerial Conference on the Information Society, 1995) is improvements in data storage, manipulation and transmission.

With digitization, all kinds of data and copyright works may be recorded and compressed in the same, binary, format. While this allows copies to be reproduced without any degradation (every copy is perfect), developments in software permit the manipulation of data, images, etc., "sampling" and alteration of works by interactive techniques (Pearson, 1996).

Data transmission, on the other side, is no longer limited to a one-to-one basis, but can now be effected on a one-to-many or even one-to-all basis. A large computer network, such as the Internet, thus becomes a "broadcasting" system. The growth of the system and the improvement of transmission techniques challenge the market position of several industries and services, including those related to voice transmission (Rowley, 1995), radio broadcasting and phonograms[19],

---

[18] See document WIPO CRNR/DC/6, 30.8.96.
[19] Phonogram producers, who are generally granted an exclusive right of distribution of material copies but only a right to remuneration with regard to sound broadcasts, called for an "exclusive broadcasting" right (Dreier, 1993).

and publishing of literary works (Heker, 1995)[20] as well as of computer programs.

These developments have polarized opinion on the ways in which copyright law should react in order to protect the producers and suppliers of different forms of information.

a) Adapting copyright

On the one side, many authors and industrial groups consider that copyright only requires minor changes in order to adapt to the new technological changes (Holleyman and Steinhardt, 1995, p. 56), particularly with respect to the scope of exploitation rights and the extent of the "fair-use" exception, as conceived under anglo-american law (Dreier, 1993, p. 489; Dessemontet, 1996, p. 287). This is the position held by the US government in its "White Paper on Intellectual Property and the National Information Infrastructure".

According to the paper, "no more than minor clarification and limited amendment" of the Copyright Act is necessary (IITF, 1995, p. 17). The proposed changes would strengthen the rights of the copyright owner, particularly by clarifying the concepts of "fixation", "distribution", "transmission" and "publication". The only major change that would be necessary is the introduction of a *sui generis* right to supplement copyright protection for databases (Lehman, 1995, p. 80).

Thus, the concepts of distribution, publication and transmission would be dematerialized in order to make clear that exclusive rights can be exercised with respect to the communication of works in a digital form and not necessarily in the form of tangible copies.

The Diplomatic Conference that established a Protocol to the Berne Convention adopted a proposal by the European Union and extended the right of communication to "any communication to the public..., by wire or wireless means, in such a way that members of the public may access these works from a place and at a time individually chosen by them" (WIPO Copyright Treaty, 1996, Article 8).

---

[20] Individual authors have, in fact, the unprecedented opportunity of becoming their own publishers and to distribute their works in digital form through computer networks (Dixon and Self, 1994, p. 466).

It should be noted that according to some domestic legislation and case law, fixation, including "reproduction" of a work, exists when any data or programs are temporarily copied in the computer's random access memory (RAM) (Dessemontet, 1996; Dixon and Self, 1994)[21]. Any unauthorized "copying" of any data or program constitutes, hence, an infringement. This concept, however, was not incorporated in the WIPO Copyright Treaty, despite a proposal to that effect of the European Union ("...the permanent or temporary storage of a protected work in any electronic medium constitutes a reproduction...This includes acts such as uploading and downloading of a work to or from the memory of a computer").

The narrowing of the "first-sale" exhaustion doctrine[22] has also been suggested, in order to avoid re-transmissions without the authorization of the rights-holder; there are also proposals to eliminate the "private-use" exception (Holleyman and Steinhardt, 1995, p. 65) and to consider that a "private copy" no longer constitutes, in an electronic age, an "honest use" (Antequera Parrilli, 1995, p. 187).

The "fair-use" doctrine, it is argued, is justified when the transaction costs are too high and prevent copyright owners and users from entering into a copyright licensing agreement, such as in the case of library photocopying or home videotaping. But technologies exist today that enable copyright owners and users to negotiate individual licences for electronically stored works at a low cost. This may be done, for instance, through a "Copyright Clearance Centre" that collects and administers royalties for each individual use (Goldstein, 1994, pp. 217, 223, 240).

The problem, according to the Commission of the European Union, is that the criterion of strictly private use is becoming more fluid and difficult to apply. Digital technology could make home copying a fully-fledged form of exploitation. A work can be reproduced systematically and any number of times without loss of quality.

---

[21] A work may be deemed "fixed" even if it only temporarily resides in the RAM of a computer linked to a network. This includes electronic network transmissions such as e-mail (IITF, 1995, p. 28).
[22] According to this doctrine, the rights of the title-holder with respect to a protected product are exhausted after the first sale thereof.

The danger of piracy and improper use without payment to the rights-holders will increase. There may be a growing need for arrangements at a community level to remunerate the rights-holder, and for the progressive introduction of techniques to limit copying of this kind (EU Commission, 1995, p. 28).

Based on its analysis, the EU Commission argues that while it was necessary to permit "private copying" when there were no means to prevent it, such copying is no longer justified since such means already exist (EU Commission, 1995, pp. 50 and 52).

b) Reconceptualizing copyright

On the other side, some authors consider that copyright, born in order to respond to the problems posed by printing, and adapted later to audiovisual works, needs to be reconceptualized in the digital era. The copyright subject matter has evolved over time from symbolic representations of sensual matter to the sensual matter itself, and from works passively received by the audience to works which interactively engage the audience (Christie, 1995, p. 523).

According to some views, the "right to prevent copying" (as conferred under copyright) should be replaced by a "right to prevent access" to a work (Olswang, 1995). This, of course, would imply the power to prevent **use**, in open contradiction to the still-in-force basic idea/expression dichotomy. Exclusive rights granted by copyright, which are becoming "outdated and irrelevant", could also be replaced by mere rights to obtain a remuneration (Ricketson, 1995, p. 898).

Others, more drastically, question the need for property rights at all, since online access to subject matter may be allowed only to those who agree to pay for it and comply with various restrictions regarding use of it. Payment for access could be guaranteed by way of automatic online debiting of a credit card account or a bank deposit account. Developments in the technology should make it possible to "lock" the digital data constituting the subject matter to which access is allowed, to prevent unauthorized use of it. In addition, it should be possible to detect and trace any subsequent unauthorized uses of the access subject matter, and to automatically debit an account by way of a contractually agreed right to compensation for the unauthorized use (Christie, 1995, p. 526).

IMPLICATIONS FOR DEVELOPING COUNTRIES

Access, Acquisition and Use

The implications of the described technological and legal trends for developing countries may be felt in a multiplicity of areas and forms. They may affect both innovation and diffusion, i.e., the adoption of ITs by potential users. Diffusion of ITs is dependent upon three main conditions:

- the **access** that potential users may have to certain hardware, software and digital information;

    Access may be limited by the lack of information on available options, commercial and governmental practices (e.g., restrictions on exports of technology due to security reasons), and legal impediments, such as those eventually stemming from IPRs.

- the **acquisition** of the necessary hardware/software;

    The acquisition of ITs is influenced by a number of "internal" and "external" factors. Internal factors refer to "who you are", "what you have done" in the past, and "what you want to be" (e.g., firm's characteristics, past experience and pursued strategies), while external factors refer to conditions which exist in the external environment and which may affect the adoption of decisions on technology acquisition and use (Lefebvre and Lefebvre, 1995, pp. 37 and 39).

    Table 2 summarizes different dimensions of external factors as they may influence adoption of ITs by firms. IPRs are one of the multiple factors that, as a part of "national policies", may affect adoption of ITs. The relative weight of IPRs *vis-à-vis* other relevant factors is unknown, though by their very nature (the fact that they confer rights to **exclude** competitors), they may in some cases have a definite and strong influence on adoption.

- the development of the capacity to **efficiently use** ITs.

The efficient use of ITs is dependent, on the one side, on general education, and particularly on the way in which it influences the "readiness" or "willingness" to use the technology. On the other side, training is a crucial aspect for proper use of ITs and to obtain access to digitized information[23].

Impact of IPRs

The impact of IPRs on the access to, and acquisition and use of ITs has not been systematically explored so far. Examining the impact of IPRs on access to, and acquisition and use of ITs (and digital information) in developing countries is a difficult theoretical and empirical endeavour.

Firstly, as mentioned above, it is extremely difficult to isolate the impact of legal factors from other social and economic considerations. There is no solid theoretical corpus to deal, in particular, with the impact of IPRs.

Secondly, ITs and the legal framework on IPRs are rapidly changing, and their likely impact in many areas is still uncertain.

Thirdly, major differences exist in the level of current diffusion and use of ITs among developing countries, in their capabilities to incorporate ITs, and in the level of protection of IPRs[24].

Fourthly, there is little empirical evidence on the conditions that affect the adoption of ITs in developing countries, and even less on IPRs-related factors.

Despite these limitations – but without ignoring them – the next section describes some of the possible implications of IPRs on IT adoption and use in developing countries.

---

[23] Based on the conclusions of Working Group 1, Information Technology (IT) and Development, United Nations Commission on Science and Technology for Development (UNCSTD), Cartagena, 30 January – 2 February 1996.

[24] The latter will become more harmonized once the transitional periods permitted by the TRIPS Agreement expire, provided that the necessary changes to comply with said Agreement have been made at the national level.

Table 2: External factors in the adoption of ITs		
I **Industry** **characteristics**	**II** **Macroeconomic** **environment**	**III** **National** **policies**

• overall competition
- type of competitors
- number of competitors
- proximity of
  competitors
	• availability of
	  capital
	
	• availability of
	  qualified manpower
		• trade policies
		
		• IPRs policies
		
		• industry regulation

• characteristics of
  demand
- type of customers
- number of customers
- sophistication of
  demand
- requirements imposed
  by major customers
	• quality of industrial
	  relations
	
	• inflation
	
	• business cycle
		• government buying
		  practices
		
		• technology adoption
		  tax credits
		
		• manpower training
		  policies and
		  programmes

• degree of diffusion of
  technologies
- by technology
- by type of competitors
 	
• availability of
  external know-how
- agencies
- institutes
- technology
  suppliers/vendors
- trade associations		

Source: Adapted from Lefebvre and Lefebvre (1995).

Software

Production

Developing countries have a marginal role in the production of computer software. The capacity to produce packaged software is one of the most important indicators of the degree of development of the software industry in a particular country.

Despite the progress made by some countries, such as India[25], developing countries account for little more than 1% of total software production (Göransson, 1994).

a) Impact of patents

Patents confer stronger rights than copyrights. They permit monopoly rents to be obtained by excluding competitors, totally or partially. If software patents are granted, several effects may be expected.

Firstly, a patented program cannot be used as a basis for further development without the authorization of the patent-holder. This may block a whole area of possible innovation. Unlike chemical patents, it may be difficult in some cases to "invent around" software patents, since mathematical rules are logical and precise, and in some cases there may be no alternative way for obtaining the same effect.

Secondly, if a licence is sought for and obtained on a piece of software, royalties may be too high – particularly for a small firm – to ensure the feasibility of the project.

Thirdly, even if patents may be "bypassed" and new technical solutions found, serious problems still remain. It may be impossible to design a program that at a certain point will not infringe an existing patent. Patent searches to establish whether patents would be infringed are extremely costly and difficult to undertake. What is even worse, a patent search does not guarantee that a patent would not be infringed; if this is the case, litigation costs may force a small firm out of business (Warshofsky, 1994, p. 168).

---

[25] A significant proportion of Indian software exports is, however, only "body shopping". See Correa (1996).

As a result, intimidated firms may opt for cancelling development projects. Thus, in a paper attributed to Bill Gates that highlights
the monopolistic power conferred by patents in this area, it is stated
that:

> "While this approach will allow companies like Microsoft, Apple
> and IBM to continue in business, it will shut new companies out
> of the field. A future start-up with no patents of its own will be
> forced to pay whatever price the giants choose to impose. That
> price might be high: Established companies have an interest in
> excluding future competitors" (quoted in Warshofsky, 1994, p.
> 171).

It should be noted that the patenting of software is not an
obligation under the TRIPS Agreement. The Agreement does not
include a definition of "invention"; therefore, any Member country
may consider that computer programs as such are not patentable. If
patentable, national legislation may apply compulsory licences in
different situations to be determined by the said legislation. Compulsory licences are permissible under Article 31 of the TRIPS Agreement.

b) Impact of copyright

Trends relating to copyright may have a significant impact on the
production of software, including multimedia products, in developing
countries.

The impact on production will be dependent on the modalities of
protection, particularly on the degree to which the idea/expression
dichotomy is recognized and enforced, and the extent to which "look
and feel" is deemed proprietary by domestic law.

The existence of protection against literal copying of software -
as required by the TRIPS Agreement – clearly benefits all parties
interested in the marketing of computer programs, whether local or
foreign producers. However, the main beneficiaries are those that sell
packaged software, since illegal reproduction of custom software may
be prevented even more efficiently by means of contractual stipula-
tions. Developing countries have made, as indicated above, little
progress in the production of packaged software so far.

If legitimate reverse engineering is limited, potential producers would have to pay royalties for the use of existing programs, or just remain outside the market. Allowing for reverse engineering will not, however, solve all problems. As mentioned before, it hardly works with large programs. In addition, decompilation and disassembly are complex, time-consuming and laborious tasks. As noted by the EC Commission in the Explanatory Memorandum accompanying its original proposal for the Software Protection Directive,

> "although it is technically possible to decompile a program in order to find out information concerning access protocols and interfaces, this is a lengthy, costly and inefficient procedure"[26].

The process requires considerable skill, and while executing it the programmers must supply information not available in the computer executable program. If the purpose of the process is to obtain a "clone" program, once the programmer has completed the analysis and determined the detailed specifications, he/she has to initiate the software engineering development in order to transform the specifications into new source code (Correa, 1993).

For these reasons, decompilation and disassembly are not used routinely. The Office of Technology Assessment did not find evidence indicating that decompilation is widely used by "pirates" to decompile entire programs and then rearrange the code in an attempt to hide copying (OTA, 1992, p.148).

On the other hand, access to user interfaces ("look and feel"), though also requiring skill and effort, makes it possible to develop competitive products. It will be extremely difficult for software start-ups to compete with companies selling established products if access to such interfaces is restricted. Users are uninterested in new products for which they must learn a new set of commands.

There are no internationally accepted rules on the extent of protection of user interfaces. Even in the United States, despite the decision in *Lotus vs Paperback* (which recognized protection of menu command structures), other cases have been resolved in a more

---

[26] O.J. Eur. Comm. (No. C 91) 8 (1989).

cautious and restrictive way.

In the case of multimedia products, the re-use of existing copyrighted materials from numerous rights-holders may pose a great burden and entail high transaction costs. The viability of a multimedia industry may be dependent upon a system of royalty collection based on a remuneration right or compulsory licences.

Compulsory licences allow the use of a protected work without the consent of the title-holder. They are common in patent as well as in copyright law. In the United States, for instance, once a song is recorded with the author's consent, anyone can record his/her own version, just by paying a fixed royalty (6.25 cents) (Goldstein, 1994, p. 20). The Appendix to the Berne Convention (1971) provides for compulsory licences for developing countries, which so far have been rarely used.

As indicated before, the TRIPS Agreement does incorporate the idea/expression dichotomy (Article 9.2). National legislation can, therefore, legitimately provide for reverse engineering of computer programs to develop either interoperative or substitute programs. Legislation also may or may not confer protection of input and output formats (user interfaces). Compulsory licensing may be implemented under the said Agreement in accordance with the Appendix to the Berne Convention (1971).

Developing countries may, however, be under pressure not to recognize the right to evaluate and reverse engineer. In South Korea, though an express "fair-use" exception in this regard was considered during the process of revision of the Computer Program Protection Act, the final approved reform eliminated such an exception (*World Intellectual Property Report*, Vol. 9, 1995, p. 349).

Use

Strict enforcement of IPRs may negatively affect the diffusion of computer programs. If, as generally assumed, such diffusion may foster increases in productivity and enhance firms' competitiveness, barriers to diffusion may in turn jeopardize economic performance.

Liberal copying would arguably reduce the cost of access to software. In the final analysis, suggests Wells, for a country which is not an innovator, it may be convenient, from an economic perspective, to facilitate the obtention of copies at low cost to stimulate rapid software diffusion and save foreign currency (Wells, 1987).

However, the advantages of unrestricted dissemination of non-authorized copies may be offset by some disadvantages (Correa, 1990c). Firstly, the lack of appropriate maintenance and after-sales support may hamper the efficient use of computer programs. Secondly, lack of or weak copyright protection may slow the diffusion of certain types of high-quality or complex software. Thirdly, all WTO Member countries will be obliged (by the year 2000 in the case of developing countries) to provide for protection of computer programs as "literary works", in accordance with the TRIPS Agreement. Non-complying countries may be subject to trade retaliation.

On the other side, the effect of unlimited or widespread copying on society's economic welfare is ambiguous. It depends upon a number of factors, including relative costs (of producing a copy versus another "original"), the degree to which copying affects the demand for originals, the production of new works, and the degree to which consumers value additional variety. Thus, copying may increase consumer welfare and producer profits in the short run – if private copying is efficient and the price of originals can be raised (OTA, 1992, p. 200).

Increases in prices may be required by producers in order to recover, from paying users, the income loss caused by copying. Suppliers may deliberately employ price discrimination according to the income levels of different countries or user groups, and charge some of them prices higher than the marginal cost (Gates, 1995, p. 266).

Copying may, however, cause producers to reduce prices in order to encourage the acquisition of legal copies. It may also reduce the number of originals produced and thereby "excessive" variety. This can increase welfare in the long run (OTA, 1992, p. 200).

Hardware

The impact of current IPRs trends on access to technology for the production of hardware in developing countries may also be significant.

The Washington Treaty, as supplemented by the TRIPS Agreement, may have significant implications for potential new entrants and for the diffusion of microelectronics technology on a global scale.

The highly concentrated structure of the industry and the growing reluctance of major firms to transfer their technology suggest that access to semiconductor technology is and will continue to be extremely difficult. Protection is likely to favour neither innovation nor technology transfer to developing countries, but rather reinforce the tendency of innovative firms not to part with their technology (Correa, 1990b).

Developing countries, in particular NICs, are likely to be the most affected by the new regulations. These countries are basically importers of integrated circuits and of informatics products (and, more generally, of manufactures that incorporate chips). They will be at a great disadvantage to determine whether chips imported or incorporated into imported products are infringing or not, especially if – as determined by the TRIPS Agreement – customs authorities are empowered to adopt measures at the border.

Title-holders are authorized, under the TRIPS Agreement, to stop the importation of industrial articles if they include an infringing chip (independent of its relevance in terms of both cost and function in the product). Trade flows may be significantly distorted. In addition, even an innocent infringer can be obliged to pay compensation to the design title-holder, or be forced to stop production or distribution.

Though the *sui generis* regime on integrated circuits' designs allows reverse engineering of protected layout designs, very few countries have the resources and skills necessary to undertake it. The process is extremely complex and costly, and even if successfully undertaken, the production and marketing of chips presents, as mentioned, formidable entry barriers.

In addition, patent protection in this area is very extensive. It is covered by literally thousands of patents and it is not possible, therefore, to license technology from a single firm. Moreover, a few large firms control substantial blocks of patents and hence exercise considerable power over the terms on which technology is available (Mody, 1989, p. 38)[27].

---

[27] According to Texas Instruments, for instance, "it is pretty impossible to make DRAM chips without using one of our patents" (*Financial Times*, 23 November 1988, p.26; quoted by Mody, 1989, p. 39).

The impact of IPRs, finally, may also extend from software to hardware. While PC producers were able to develop – quite successfully, indeed – IBM "clones" on the basis of reverse engineering the PC's BIOS (Basic Input-Output System)[28], attempts have been made to foreclose that possibility. Thus, IBM increased royalty rates (from 1% to 5%) on its AT machines, demanded retroactive payments and tried to prevent cloning of its PS/2 series of microcomputers by restricting access to the micro channel architecture (Mody, 1989, p. 36).

Information

Developments with respect to the protection of databases under a *sui generis* right against "extraction" will extend the appropriation of information well beyond the limits of copyright law. The impact of this expansion is difficult to predict. As mentioned before, it may become an international rule if approved by the WIPO Diplomatic Conference.

Like other IT industries, the "information industry" is largely controlled by firms in industrialized countries. Some developing countries have provided low-cost labour to "input" data, but they generally lack the organization and resources to distribute databases. On the other side, technological advances with CD-ROMs, which permit the distribution of copies of databases, are changing the online model of supply, by a mix of digital and material carriers.

A paradoxical implication of the new technological developments is that while they facilitate "almost unfettered access to protected works" (Dreier, 1993, p. 488) and the easy, rapid and inexpensive making of "perfect" copies, they also offer the technical means to control and manage such access.

Thus, devices can be implemented to allow access to but not the copying of a work (Quintanilla Madero, 1995, p. 43). Transmission is made by "pieces" and it is possible to prevent the full recomposition of the work. Already CD-ROMs can be encrypted, and many encryption and licence management technologies are under development or in use to prevent copying. For instance, within the EC ESPRIT II Program,

---

[28] Which is protected by copyright and hence susceptible of being legally accessed and reverse engineered.

a system of this type (see Box 7) was developed. Databases and other suppliers of digitized information have established terms and conditions for the transfer of information that restrict both access to and use of data. They condition access upon the payment of different fees (subscription, search-time, downloading, etc.) and are able to control and charge for each and every instance of access and use by the user of electronically processed information (who must log in and out). This control nullifies in practice the user's right – normally granted under copyright – to make copies for personal uses or for research purposes[29] (Reichman, 1993).

Many institutional users of digital information (such as libraries)

Box 7: Copyright in Transmitted Electronic Documents (CITED)

The model that the pan-European team has come up with is built around a tamper-proof software module which acts rather like indestructible tachometers installed on long-distance coaches and lorries, recording everything that happens to the copyrighted or commercially valuable material.

The basic idea is that the valuable material is linked to a specific piece of software. This software is required to gain access to the material, and it can only be converted into its usable form by someone in possession of the right key or password.

Thus, when the authorized user requests a piece of software or some pages of a report or journal, he or she will have to key in a password. From then on, each time a program is run or a print of a page is made, the associated software module sends a message back to the secure database stored on the computer. The database can then track every activity carried out by the organization's software modules, so providing an audit trail which shows whether any material is being printed or copied electronically. Eventually, it may be possible to forward this information to rights societies to help them determine how much artists, authors and publishers should be paid.

Source: Lawrence, Andy, *New Society*, Feb. 1995

---

[29] Other restrictions include, for instance, "one-at-a-time" use requirements that forbid networking by multiple users.

have already complained "about the difficulty of managing and complying with the variety of contract terms required by their large collections of data and software packages." Moreover, "because of uncertainties about users' rights to download or make copies of information, providers of digital information rely on contracts to limit customers' uses of information and do not sell information to customers, but merely authorize certain uses" (OTA, 1992, p. 26) [30]. According to Reichman, " aggressive licensing of electronic information tools could thus distort the public service mission of libraries by making them involuntary collection agents for publishers" (Reichman, 1993, p. 464).

Libraries, as document suppliers, are regarded as direct competitors to database providers and other commercial services. Libraries can not only receive and store information, but also repackage and electronically distribute it to an indefinite number of users.

Technical and legal developments, if combined, may result in growing barriers to the access to **all** types of information, which will be increasingly channelled through digital networks. Such barriers are likely to affect not only technology, but also general factual information as well as scientific knowledge. This may consolidate existing trends of not openly diffusing the results of scientific research (Correa, 1994b), and thereby restrict access by developing countries to the pool of scientific knowledge.

MAIN CONCLUSIONS

The following main conclusions may be drawn from the study made:

*   Important changes in the paradigm of IPRs regulation are taking place. The emphasis has shifted from protection of the author/ inventor to that of the investor, as epitomized by the recent EC Directive on databases. Moreover, new proposals are on the table to further expand appropriation so as to cover factual materials as such, i.e., non-copyrightable information.

---

[30] In some cases, data providers require librarians to waive contractually the privileges that copyright law otherwise affords (Reichman, 1993).

- A process of universalization of standards of IPRs protection has been fostered by the Uruguay Round. The TRIPS Agreement has clarified and reinforced IPRs protection in three key IT areas: computer programs, databases and layout designs of integrated circuits. Said Agreement leaves, however, some degree of flexibility to implement its standards in accordance with national legal systems and interests.

- The characteristics of software technology explain the key role played by IPRs in this field. Computer programs may be developed on the basis of knowledge in the public domain, and hence challenges to established firms may arise, in principle, from any place and at any time. Though market barriers are sufficiently high to limit that opportunity for newcomers, major software producers have actively sought to expand and increase protection. The easy and inexpensive production of "pirate" copies is another major reason behind this interest in IPRs.

- Trends with respect to the protection of computer programs show hesitation and conflict in applying copyright law and its inadequacies in protecting functional works. Despite some case law that extended copyright protection well beyond expression, the idea/expression dichotomy – explicitly incorporated by the TRIPS Agreement – limits the extent of exclusive rights and allows for (legitimate) reverse engineering. Countries are also free to decide on the scope and extent of protection of user interfaces.

- Given the essentially incremental nature of innovation in software, access to existing programs is crucial to maintaining a healthy environment for innovation and competition. Access to underlying ideas and concepts may be seriously restricted, however, by the patenting of computer programs. Patenting may lead to complete exclusion from certain market segments, and threaten potential competitors with costly litigation that may discourage firms or force them out of business.

- Current trends in IPRs relating to computer programs may impose even tougher conditions for the development of a software industry in developing countries. This shall be dependent, however, upon the way in which such countries frame their domestic laws while abiding by the TRIPS Agreement. It should be noted, in particular, that there is no obligation under existing international standards to confer patent protection on computer software.

•   Barriers to participation in the semiconductor industry are very high. The *sui generis* protection of the layout design of integrated circuits does not add too much to the fortress that the few chip producers have been able to build up. Unlike in the case of computer programs, such producers can survive and achieve progress (as happened in the past) without such protection. Patents on key semiconductor technologies permit the erection of even higher barriers for potential new entrants.

•   Strict enforcement of anti-piracy laws in the software area may lead to high prices and limit access by individuals and small firms. Such enforcement, however, is an unavoidable feature of the current IPRs regime. While in developing countries it mainly benefits (foreign) producers of packaged software, it can also help local industry to avoid illegal duplication and unfair competition. It may also open up opportunities – in some instances – to develop programs that are less expensive and better adapted to local conditions than imported packages.

•   Finally, with the development of computer networks and the possibility of providing a digital format to any piece of information, a major challenge has arisen. Technological and legal changes (such as the elimination of the exception for private copying or "fair use") may dramatically increase the barriers to access to and use of information of any kind, copyrightable or not. While the "information superhighway" is opening up enormous possibilities for low-cost communication on a global scale, legal developments may foreclose the prospect of an information society with equality of opportunities and free circulation of ideas and information.

References

Antequera Parrilli, Ricardo (1995), "Las 'Superautopistas Digitales' y las Reglas de Circulación (el ámbito de los derechos que se protegen)", WIPO Worldwide Symposium on Copyright in the Global Information Infrastructure, 22-24 May, México, D.F.

Bastos, Maria I. (1995), "State autonomy and capacity for S&T policy design and implementation in Brazil", in María Ines Bastos and Charles Cooper (Eds.), *Politics of Technology in Latin America*, UNU/INTECH, New York.

Buckner, Kathy (1995), "Educating the Multimedia Professional", *Managing Information*, January-February.

Cane, Alan (1992), "Information technology and competitive advantage: Lessons from developed countries", *World Development*, Vol. 20, No. 12.

Catalá, Pierre (1984), "Ebauche d' une théorie juridique de l'information", *Recueil Dalloz Sirey*, 16[0] Cahier, Paris.

Christie, Andrew (1995), "Reconceptualising Copyright in the Digital Era", *EIPR*, No. 11.

Cooter, Robert and Ulen, Thomas (1988), *Law and Economics*, Harper Collins Publishers, United States.

Correa, Carlos (1990a), "Protección del software: estudio de caso sobre el desarrollo del derecho económico", *Revista del Derecho Industrial*, Vol. 12, No. 36.

Correa, Carlos (1990b), "Intellectual Property in the Field of Integrated Circuits: Implications for Developing Countries", *World Competition*, Vol. 14, No. 2.

Correa, Carlos (1990c), *The Legal Protection of Software. Implications for Latecomer Strategies in Newly Industrialising Economies (NIEs) and Middle-Income Economies (MIEs)*, in OECD Development Centre, Technical Papers, No. 26, Paris.

Correa, Carlos (1993), "Legal protection and innovation in the software industry", *World Competition*, Vol. 17, No. 1.

Correa, Carlos (1994a), "Docencia e Investigación sobre Propiedad Intelectual en la RedPost", in *Impacto de los Programas de Postgrado en Planificación, Gestión y Estudios Sociales de la Ciencia y Tecnología en el Contexto Internacional*, Maracaibo.

Correa, Carlos (1994b), "Trends in technology transfer: Implications for developing countries", *Science and Public Policy*, Vol. 21, No. 6.

Correa, Carlos M. (Ed.) (1995), Special Issue on the Management of International Intellectual Property, *International Journal of Technology Management*, Vol. 10, No. 2/3.

Correa, Carlos (1996), "Strategies for Software Exports from Developing Countries", *World Development*, Vol. 24, No. 1.

Crucible Group, The (1994), *People, Plants and Patents. The Impact of Intellectual Property on Trade, Plant Biodiversity, and Rural Society*, International Development Research Centre , Ottawa.

David, Paul (1993), "Intellectual Property Institutions and the Panda's Thumb: Patents, Copyrights, and Trade Secrets in Economic Theory and History", in M. Wallestein; M. Mogee and R. Schoen (Eds.), *Global Dimension of Intellectual Property Rights in Science and Technology*, National Academy Press, Washington, D.C.

Dessemontet, Francois (1996), "Internet, le droit d'auteur et le droit international privé", *SJZ*, Vol. 92, No. 15.

Dixon, Allen and Self, Laurie (1994), "Copyright Protection for the Information Superhighway", *EIPR*, No. 11.

Dreier, Thomas (1993), "Copyright in the Age of Digital Technology", *IIC*, Vol. 24, No. 4.

Dreyfuss, Rochelle (1993), "A Wiseguy's Approach to Information Products: Muscling Copyright and Patent Into a Unitary Theory of Intellectual Property", *Supreme Court Review 1992*, University of Chicago.

EU Commission (Commission of the European Communities) (1995), *Green Paper. Copyright and Related Rights in the Information Society*, Brussels.

Fishman, Stephen (1994), *Software Development. A Legal Guide*, Nolo Press, Berkeley.

Foray, Dominique (1995), "Production and Distribution of Knowledge in the New Systems of Innovation: The Role of Intellectual Property Rights", *STI*, No. 16.

Frischtak, Claudio R. (1995), "Harmonization versus differentiation in international property rights regimes", *Technology Management*, Vol. 10, No. 2/3.

G-7 Ministerial Conference on the Information Society (1995), 26 February.

Gates, Bill (1995), *Camino al Futuro*, McGraw-Hill, Santafé de Bogotá.

Goldstein, Paul (1994), *Copyright's Highway. The law and lore of copyright from Gutenberg to the Celestial Jukebox*, Hill and Wang, New York.

Göransson, Bo (1994), *Trends in the Global Software Industry*, prepared for the United Nations Industrial Development Organization, Vienna.

Guglielmetti, Giovanni (1996), *L'nvenzione di Software. Brevetto e Diritto D'Autore*, Dott. A. Gioffré Editore, Milano.

Heker, Harald (1995), "The Publisher in the Electronic Age: Caught in the Area of Conflict of Copyright and Competition Law", *EIPR*, No. 2.

Holleyman, Robert and Steinhardt, Jeffrey (1995), "Multimedia Presentation on the Global Information Infrastructure", WIPO Worldwide Symposium on Copyright in the Global Information Infrastructure, Mexico, D.F.

IITF (Information Infrastructure Task Force) (1995), *Intellectual Property and the National Information Infrastructure: The Report of the Working Group on Intellectual Property Rights*, Washington, D.C.

Kitagawa, Zentaro (1994), "Comment on A Manifesto Concerning the Legal Protection of Computer Programs", *Columbia Law Review*, Vol. 94, No. 8.

Lefebvre, Elizabeth and Lefebvre, Louis (1995), *Methodologies for measuring the adoption and impact of information and communication technologies on the productivity and competitiveness of SMEs*, Université de Montréal.

Lehman, Bruce (1995), "Intellectual Property and the National and Global Information Structure", WIPO Worldwide Symposium on Copyright in the Global Information Infrastructure, Mexico, D.F.

Levin, Richard; Klovorick, Alvin; Nelson, Richard and Winter, Sidney (1987), "Appropriating the returns from industrial research and development", Brooking Papers on Economic Activity, 3.

Mansfield, E. (1993), "Unauthorised use of intellectual property: Effects on investment, technology transfer, and innovation", in M. Wallestein; M. Mogee and R. Schoen (Eds.), *Global Dimension of Intellectual Property Rights in Science and Technology*, National Academy Press, Washington, D.C.

Mansfield, E. (1994), "Intellectual Property Protection, Foreign Direct Investment and Technology Transfer", *IFC Discussion Paper 19*, International Finance Corporation, Washington, D.C.

Mody, Ashoka (1989), *New Environment for Intellectual Property*, Industry and Energy Department Working Paper, The World Bank Industry and Energy Department, Industry Series Paper No. 10.

Neff, Richard and Smallson, Fran (1994), *NAFTA. Protecting and Enforcing Intellectual Property Rights in North America*, Shepard's/McGraw-Hill, Colorado Springs.

Nelson, Richard (1994), "Intellectual Property Protection for Cumulative Systems Technology", *Columbia Law Review*, Vol. 94, No. 8.

OECD (1992), *Technology and the Economy. The Key Relationships*, Paris.

Olswang, H. (1995), "Accessright: An Evolutionary Path for Copyright into the Digital Era?", *EIPR*, Vol. 5, p. 215.

OTA (Office of Technology Assessment) (1992), *Finding a Balance: Computer Software, Intellectual Property and the Challenge of Technological Change,* Washington D.C.

Parliamentary Office of Science and Technology (1996), *Patents, Research and Technology*, London.

Pearson, Hilary E. (1996), "Information in a Digital Age – The Challenge to Copyright", *Net Law*, London.

Pérez, Carlota (1987), "Revoluciones tecnológicas y transformaciones socio-institucionales", in *Cuestiones de Política Científica y Tecnológica, Segundo Seminario "Jorge Sabato"*, Consejo Superior de Investigaciones Científicas, Madrid.

Quintanilla Madero, Carmen (1995), "La Tecnología Digital y el Derecho de Autor: lo que debe modificarse y lo que debe mantenerse", WIPO

Worldwide Symposium on Copyright in the Global Information Infrastructure, 22-24 May, México, D.F.

Reichman, Jerome (1993), "Electronic Information Tools – The Outer Edge of World Intellectual Property Law", *IIC*, Vol. 24, No. 4.

Ricketson, Sam (1995), "The Future of the Traditional Intellectual Property Conventions in the Brave New World of Trade-Related Intellectual Property Rights", *IIC*, Vol. 26, No. 6.

Rowley, Jennifer (1995), "Making the Internet Pay", *Managing Information*, 2-11.

Samuelson, Pamela; Davis, R.; Kapor, M.D. and Reichman, J.H. (1994), "A manifesto concerning the legal protection of computer programs", *Columbia Law Review*, Vol. 94, No. 8.

Siebeck, W. *et al.* (1990), *Strengthening protection of intellectual property rights in developing countries. A survey of the literature*,World Bank Discussion Paper, Washington, D.C.

Siegel, Daniel and Laurie, Ronald (1989), "Beyond Microcode: Alloy v. Ultrateck. The First Attempt to Extend Copyright Protection to Computer Hardware", *The Computer Lawyer*, Vol. 6, No. 4.

Stern, Richard (1993), "Is the Centre Beginning to Hold in US Software Copyright Law?", *EIPR*, Vol. 15, No. 2.

UNCTAD (1996), *Financial and Other Implications of the Implementation of the TRIPS Agreement for Developing Countries*, Geneva.

Warshofsky, Fred (1994), *The Patent Wars. The Battle to Own the World's Technology*, John Wiley & Sons, Inc., New York.

Wells, L. (1987), "US Pressures on Indonesia Intellectual Property, Investment, Trade and Immigration Policies" (mimeo), FR/117/87/13.

Zimmermann, Jean-Benoit (1993), "L' Industrie du logiciel: De la protection a la normalization" (mimeo), CNRS-Greqe, Marseille.

Chapter VI

Access to Plant Genetic Resources and Intellectual Property Rights[1]

INTRODUCTION

THE importance of the conservation and sustainable utilization of plant genetic resources (PGRs) for food and agriculture is broadly recognized today. The work of the FAO Commission on Genetic Resources for Food and Agriculture, and of many national and international institutions, experts and non-governmental organizations (NGOs), has contributed to the identification of a number of actions that are necessary and urgent at the national and international levels to prevent genetic erosion and to foster sustainable agriculture[2].

One of the areas for global action relates to farm conservation. Farmers not only use seeds; they are key players in the process of conservation and improvement of plant varieties. Their activities ensure crop evolution whereby new varieties arise through genetic recombinations, mutation and hybridization within and between cultivated and wild plant populations (Brush, 1994, p. 7).

The present and past contributions of farmers to plant diversity have been recognized by the International Undertaking on Plant Genetic Resources (IU). Current negotiations to define the content of "Farmers' Rights", in particular, have highlighted several areas in

---

[1] The author is thankful for the comments received on an early draft from J. Esquinas-Alcázar, G. Moore, A. Heitz and Clive Stannard. The content of this Chapter – based on a study prepared for FAO – was circulated as a background paper during the April 1999 meeting of the Commission on Genetic Resources for Food and Agriculture.

[2] See, in particular, the Report of the Leipzig Conference on Plant Genetic Resources.

which action would be required in order to preserve the process of on-farm conservation and integrate it with other forms of conservation. In addition, such negotiations have confirmed the importance of ensuring, at least for a number of crops, a regime that facilitates access to and exchange of PGRs, a key issue in the IU as originally adopted. Such access and exchange have so far been one of the bases of the continuous progress in agriculture worldwide. In every country, most of the germplasm used in agriculture comes from other countries and it is often very difficult or extremely costly, and sometimes practically impossible, to determine the country of origin. Every region of the world is dependent on genetic material which originated in other regions for over 50% of its basic food production, and for several regions of the world, such dependency is close to 100%.

The Convention on Biological Diversity (CBD), on the other hand, has stressed the importance of *in situ* conservation, and established rules on the access to genetic resources and on benefit-sharing, in the context of States' sovereignty over such resources[3].

In parallel with the recognition of the role of farmers, and of the relevance of the conservation and transborder flows of PGRs, the issue of protection of IPRs, including in plant materials, has become an important item in international negotiations. Article 27.3(b) of the TRIPS Agreement, in particular, requires Members to provide protection for "plant varieties" under IPRs.

The IU had recognized (FAO Resolution 4/89) that plant breeders' rights (PBRs) were not incompatible with its objectives of furthering the access to and sustainable use of PGRs for food and agriculture. At the time this declaration was made, the prevailing model of PBRs (as epitomized by the UPOV Convention, 1978 Act) clearly permitted the use of protected varieties as the source material for further variation and the re-use of saved seeds by farmers, both important mechanisms of diversity generation. Since then, however, the revision of the UPOV Convention in 1991 and, particularly, the growing acceptance of patents on plant materials, including genes, have changed the legal framework in which on-farm conservation and germplasm exchange are to take place.

---

[3] For an analysis of the CBD, see Lesser (1998).

The way in which those three instruments, the TRIPS Agreement, the UPOV Convention and the CBD, are implemented will influence the development and operation of a multilateral system on PGRs for food and agriculture. An important issue is, therefore, to what extent and how the objectives and principles of the said instruments may be compatibilized among themselves and with the objectives and principles of a revised IU.

This Chapter discusses how the granting of IPRs protection may affect the development of a multilateral system under a revised IU based on the principles of "shared access", that is, access given in the framework of a system that ensures the sharing of benefits. It will try to elucidate the extent to which IPRs affect the access to PGRs for research and breeding (R&B), and if and how the objectives of the CBD and the IU with regard to access to genetic resources may be compatibilized with IPRs legislation.

In particular, this Chapter examines the extent to which existing IPRs, particularly patents, PBRs and undisclosed information (trade secrets), may affect the principle of access as it is being developed in the framework of the IU and the CBD. It also briefly examines the main trends with respect to the protection of plants and PGRs, and discusses several elements of such regimes that may favour or block access to PGRs.

FROM "FREE" TO "SHARED" ACCESS

The development and sustainability of agriculture are strongly dependent on access to PGRs. Though there are important differences in the endowment of plant diversity, no country can claim self-sufficiency in this area. The global interdependency that prevails in respect of PGRs explains why access to PGRs is a cornerstone of international instruments dealing with PGRs, particularly the IU and the CBD.

Article 5 of the IU, as adopted in 1983, stated that:

> "It will be the policy of adhering Governments and institutions having plant genetic resources under their control to allow access to samples of such resources, and to permit their export, where the resources have been requested for the purposes of scientific research, plant breeding or genetic resource conservation. The

samples will be made available free of charge, on the basis of mutual exchange or on mutually agreed terms."

The CBD recognized sovereign rights on genetic resources and established new international rules on access, which is subject to the principles of prior informed consent and the sharing of benefits (Articles 3 and 15). One of the main objectives of the revision of the IU is to harmonize its provisions on access with the CBD principles. Though negotiations have yet to be concluded, current discussions[4] suggest that, given the peculiar nature and global distribution of PGRs, there is a basic agreement to develop a multilateral system of access and sharing of benefits for PGRs for food and agriculture. Under the proposed system, access to PGRs should be allowed to all parties participating therein, who shall benefit from such access and from other elements in the system (access to research results, international funding, etc.).

This process shows the shift from a concept of "unrestricted" or "free" access to a notion whereunder access is promoted and facilitated in the framework of a system for the sharing of benefits that are only available to those parties participating in the multilateral system. The emerging concept is, thus, one relying on a "shared-access" principle.

In the negotiation of the IU, one point seems to have remained clear: access to PGRs for food and agriculture is essential for sustainable agriculture and should be ensured by any multilateral system to be developed.

As reflected in the debates in the FAO Commission on Genetic Resources for Food and Agriculture, and in various contributions, studies and NGO statements, concerns have been growing with regard to the extent to which IPRs may jeopardize the exercise of sovereign rights over PGRs and make illusory the implementation of a balanced multilateral system based on a principle of shared access as defined above.

These concerns have been accentuated by the expansive application of IPRs, particularly patents, to living organisms, and by the

---

[4]   As reflected, in particular, in the reports of the FAO Commission on Genetic Resources for Food and Agriculture. See, in particular, the Report of the Fourth Extraordinary Session, Rome, 1-5 December 1997.

possibility available in most industrialized countries of obtaining exclusive rights of exploitation with regard to genes and any subcellular part of plants as well as of plant cells, plant varieties and species. According to the view of two researchers:

"Neither genes nor plant varieties will be available for further development without the previous consent from the holders of intellectual property rights. In addition, biotechnological processes of broad application in plant breeding, including techniques for screening, mapping and engineering genes, and methodologies for tissue culture, have been patented" (Miranda Santos and Lewontin, 1997, p. 5).

Diverging views on the likely impact of IPRs on the access to and use of PGRs for food and agriculture may jeopardize further advances in the development of a multilateral system on PGRs for food and agriculture. Some countries may find it difficult to agree on a system of shared access if the genetic resources maintained and developed by their farmers and communities may be appropriated under IPRs by foreign companies, especially if such IPRs may create barriers to access to and use of the protected material. This conflict has been described by Shiva and Holla-Bhar as follows:

"The Third World farmer has a three-fold relationship with the corporations that demand a monopoly of life forms and life processes. Firstly, the farmer is a supplier of germplasm to TNCs. Secondly, the farmer is a competitor in terms of innovation and rights to genetic resources. Finally, the Third World farmer is a consumer of the technological and industrial products of TNCs. Patent protection displaces farmers as competitors, transforms them into suppliers of free raw materials, and makes them totally dependent on industrial suppliers for vital inputs such as seeds" (Shiva and Holla-Bhar, 1996, p. 157).

Fears of a negative impact of IPRs on sovereignty over and access to PGRs have been exacerbated by current trends in the IPRs protection of genetic resources.

Firstly, a large number of patents have been granted on genetic resources obtained from developing countries, often without the knowledge and consent of the possessors of the resources. There has been extensive documentation of "biopiracy" involving resources protected "as is", that is, without further improvement (e.g., US patent No. 5,304,718 on quinoa granted to researchers of Colorado State University), and on products based on plant materials and knowledge developed and used by local/indigenous communities, such as the cases of the neem tree, kava, barbasco, endod and turmeric[5], among others (Mooney, 1998, pp. 152-154).

Secondly, some patents have been granted which have a broad scope, thus limiting access to a wide segment of germplasm. In some cases, claims described in functional – rather than in structural – terms[6] have been accepted with more or less latitude. In others, the claims cover the application of a technical solution to a wide range of undifferentiated germplasm, such as in the case of the "species-wide" patents. Examples of broad claims include an Agracetus patent refer-ring to any genetic manipulation of cotton regardless of the germplasm in use; a patent granted to Plant Genetic Systems covering the introduction of Bt into most field crops, and a patent obtained by Lubrizol covering sunflower seed with a high oleic acid and a low linoeic acid content.

Thirdly, some cases of protection by PBRs of materials deposited in genebanks and held in trust for the international community have been identified. This has led the Consultative Group on International Agricultural Research (CGIAR) Secretariat to call for a moratorium on the granting of IPRs on designated plant germplasm held in the collections of the CGIAR research centres around the world[7]. It is the CGIAR's stated policy that such germplasm is held in trust for the world community and should not be subject to IPRs by the centres and the recipients of the materials[8].

---

[5] A patent on turmeric granted to the University of Mississippi Medical Centre in December 1993 was recently invalidated by the US Patent Office upon the request of India's Council for Scientific and Industrial Research.

[6] This means that the invention is described on the basis of what **it does** rather than what **it consists of**.

[7] See CGIAR Press Release, 11 February 1998.

[8] See Guiding Principles for the CGIAR Centres on Intellectual Property and Genetic Resources, 1996.

Fourthly, the protection by IPRs of living materials, including plants, raises a number of ethical issues that, in the view of many authors and organizations, should be a sufficient basis to prevent any private party from obtaining exclusive rights on such materials[9]. The implications of IPRs on the access to and use of PGRs for food and agriculture are a preoccupation not only in developing countries. Thus, according to the Director of the AgBiotech Center of the State University of New Jersey, "in theory, the patent system is supposed to make material available for further research by protecting the interests of the patent-holder. In practice, the patent-holder can find many ways to block distribution of the patented material and to limit the uses made of it" (Day, 1995, p.83).

One of the conclusions of a workshop sponsored by several US organizations and the US Department of Agriculture in 1993 indicated that the patenting of plant materials may interfere with exchange of materials among researchers and among government, university and private laboratories (CSSA, 1993, p. 5). In a follow-up seminar held on the same issues four years later, one of the working groups recommended, more specifically, "full and open access to genetic materials" and that "the appropriate standards for utility patents be reconsidered...in light of the potential for serious impediments to effective research and genetic resource use, especially in the public sector in countries with limited economic resources" (CSSA, 1998, p. 109).

ACCESS TO PGRs UNDER PATENT LAWS

Plant Biotechnology Patents

The number of patents on biotechnological inventions has grown significantly since the first grants at the end of the seventies. Between 1990 and 1995, around 25,000 biotechnological patents were granted throughout the world. The annual grants on biotechnology represented about 1% of the total number of patents granted per year worldwide.

As indicated in Table 3, around 37% of biotechnology patents originated from the United States in 1990-1995, and a similar percent-

---

[9] For a discussion on ethical issues, see Macer (1990).

age from Japan.

The European Union accounted for about half that percentage (19%) in the said period. It is to be noted that the "rest of the world", where **all developing countries** are included, only accounted for less than 7% of the total number of patents granted in the said period. This is one indicator of the dramatic North-South asymmetry existing with regard to the innovative capabilities in modern biotechnology (Correa *et al.*, 1996).

Table 3: Origin of biotechnology patents, 1990-1995

Country of origin	Total per country No.	Total per country %
United States	5,775	37.5
Japan	5,706	37.1
EPO (European Patent Office) countries	2,903	18.9
Rest of Europe	268	1.7
Australia	181	1.2
Canada	94	0.6
China	173	1.1
Israel	70	0.5
Republic of Korea	119	0.8
Other countries	103	0.7
Total	15,392	100.0

Source: CEFI (1997).

Patents relating to agriculture represented 11% of the total for 1992-1995, and those specifically covering modified plants 6% of the total.

Table 4 contains a list of the most active enterprises and institutions in the field of plant patents. Out of the 16 listed, only five are of US origin, but they accounted for 44% of total plant patents, that is, about 7% more than the percentage for all biotechnology patents as indicated above.

Table 4: Most active applicants for plant patents, 1992-1995		
Applicant	**Country**	**Number**
Pioneer Hi-Bred International	United States	70
Zeneca/ICI	United Kingdom	50
Monsanto Co.	United States	28
Sandoz	Switzerland	24
Calgene	United States	23
Holden's Foundation Seeds	United States	23
Max Planck Gesellschaft	Germany	19
Ciba-Geigy AG	Switzerland	17
Hokko Chemical Industry	Japan	16
Dupont de Nemours	United States	15
Mitsui Toatsu Chemicals	Japan	14
Plant Genetic Systems	Belgium	14
Hoechst-Schering Agrevo	Germany	13
Japan Tobacco	Japan	13
Mitsubishi	Japan	12
Mogen International	Netherlands	12

Source: CEFI (1997)

The fact that the seventh most active applicant is a public research institution of Germany[10] suggests the special link existing between scientific and technological research in this field.

Do Patents Restrict Access?

If a crucial aspect of a multilateral system on PGRs for food and agriculture is, as mentioned, the possibility of accessing such re-

---

[10] When all biotechnology patents, and not only those relating to plants, are considered, among the 16 most active applicants are two US universities (California and Texas).

sources for R&B, it is essential to clarify the extent to which existing patent regimes may affect such access.

Access to existing genetic materials is necessary for the continuous adaptation and improvement of plants for food and agriculture. A new plant variety cannot be created from scratch. In the field of plant development, there is no actual "creation" (Vignoli, 1986, p. 205). The improvement of crops can only take place on the basis of the use and modification of what nature has created. Innovation in breeding activities is essentially of an "incremental" nature[11], in the sense that it progresses on the basis of successive changes on available varieties.

The granting of a patent entails a prohibition *(ius excluendi)* of use of the patented material in the countries where the rights have been recognized. According to Article 28.1(a) of the TRIPS Agreement, patents relating to products confer the right to prevent third parties not having the patentee's consent from "making, using, offering for sale, selling, or importing for these purposes" the product[12]. In the case of process patents, the patentee may prevent the use of the process as well as the commercialization of a product "obtained directly by that process". Thus, if a process to produce a plant (e.g., a transgenic plant) is patented, exclusive rights would also apply with respect to the plant obtained with the process.

Given the territoriality of patent rights, the title-holder cannot exercise his/her rights outside the jurisdiction where the patent has been registered. But he/she can prevent the importation of products made elsewhere containing the invention. This has been one of the main concerns, for instance, of Indian cotton producers in view of the patent on all transgenic cotton conferred on Agracetus (US patent No. 5,159,135), and of Andean farmers with respect to the already mentioned patent granted to Colorado State University (US patent No. 5,304,718). A similar concern has arisen more recently in regard to a

---

[11] The distinction made by innovation theory between "major" and "minor" or "incremental" innovations is relevant here. See, for instance, Freeman and Perez (1986).

[12] While this provision expressly refers to importation as one of the exclusive rights of the patent-holder, in a footnote to the same article a cross-reference is made to Article 6 of the Agreement, which allows Members to allow for "parallel imports" under the principle of international exhaustion of IPRs.

US patent relating to an allegedly improved form of "basmati" rice grown in sub-Himalayan India and Pakistan[13]. The existence of a patent thus prevents the production or commercialization of any product containing the invention. For instance, if a plant variety is protected, it may not be possible to use the propagating material of that variety for commercial purposes, including for breeding new varieties. Similarly, if modified plant cells are patented, any plant composed of those cells would infringe the patent.

In the framework of the International Undertaking and of the CBD, the key issue to be addressed is the use of a protected material for the purpose of improving it, for instance, by developing a new variety, rather than its use as such for production or reproduction. The first type of use is here called use for "research and breeding".

Patents on Biological Materials

Patent law has traditionally distinguished between "inventions", which are patentable, and "discoveries", which are not (Caforio, 1995, pp. 60-64). This distinction has been blurred in some countries, however, with the advent of genetic engineering.

In the United States, an isolated and purified form of a natural product is patentable. The concept of "new" under the novelty requirement does not mean "not preexisting" but "novel" in a prior art sense, "so that the unknown but natural existence of a product cannot preclude the product from the category of statutory subject matter" (Bent *et al.*, 1991, p. 123).

Under the rules of the European Patent Office, a patent can be granted when a substance found in nature can be characterized by its structure, by its process of obtention or by other criteria, if it is new in the sense that it was not previously available to the public. In the proposed European Directive on the matter, it is clarified that:

> "Biological material which is isolated from its natural environment or processed by means of a technical process may be the subject of an invention even if it already occurred in nature" (Article 3.2).

---

[13] See *SUNS (South-North Development Monitor)*, No. 4175, 19 March 1998.

Similarly, in Japan, the Enforcement Standards for Substance Patents stipulated that patents can be granted on chemical substances artificially isolated from natural materials, when the presence of the substance could not be detected without prior isolation with the aid of physical or chemical methods. The new Guidelines of the Japanese Patent Office on Biotechnological Inventions (February 1997) allowed freer expression formats in the description of claims than the 1993 Guidelines did, and removed some limitations on claims drafting, such as the obligation to restrict patent claims essentially to a single specific sequence (Okuyama, 1997, p. 8).

A recent comparative study on "Biotechnology Patent Practices"[14] by the Patent Offices of the US, the EU and Japan indicates that the differences with regard to patenting of biological materials have significantly narrowed down in those jurisdictions.

On the basis of these developments, numerous patents have been granted relating to biological materials taken from humans, animals and plants in industrialized countries. In particular, in many jurisdictions, the patenting of genes has become common practice. Claims in these cases normally refer to an isolated DNA sequence, DNA constructs and new transformed plants derived from it. Claims often include natural DNA sequences without limitations.

Patents covering genes are not generally confined to the sequence of a gene. The patent application typically claims: first, a gene or protein, standing alone, corresponding to that sequence; second, a vector or plasmid incorporating the sequence; and, possibly, third, an organism (e.g., a plant) that has been transformed by means of such a vector. Thus, the patent-holder gains effective control over use of the specified gene in genetic engineering (Barton, 1993, p. 14).

Some developing countries, however, have not gone so far with regard to the patentability of existing biological materials. Thus, the Mexican law excludes the patentability of all genetic materials. The Argentine patent law and the Andean Group Decision 344 do not allow the patentability of materials existing in nature. The Brazilian patent law (1996) stipulates that no patents shall be granted with respect to living beings or "biological materials found in nature", even if isolated, including the "genome or germplasm" of any living being.

---

[14] As a component of the Trilateral Project 24.1- Biotechnology.

Patents on Genes

Patent claims in the plant field may refer to a variety of materials and processes, such as:

* DNA sequences that code for a certain protein;
* isolated or purified proteins;
* plasmids and transformation vectors containing a gene sequence;
* seeds;
* plant cells and plants;
* plant varieties, including parent lines[15];
* hybrids;
* processes to genetically modify plants;
* processes to obtain hybrids.

Patents are normally granted with respect to isolated genes in some countries, where the mere fact that there has been isolation of a gene with a defined function is deemed sufficient ground to confer a patent, even if the protein that it codifies has been previously known[16]. The US Patent and Trademark Office, for instance, has issued numerous patents on isolated and purified forms of naturally-occurring DNA molecules as such. The only condition is that they must be claimed in a non-naturally-occurring form, e.g., as an isolated or purified molecule.

Processes involving the manipulation of genes may be based on the use of genomic DNA, a natural substance, or of cDNA, that is, a DNA copy of mRNA that does not exist as such in nature. Patentability may proceed in both cases. In the United States, the Court of Appeals for the Federal Circuit has affirmed the validity of claims to full-length DNA or genomic DNA molecules such as, in the pharmaceutical field, in the cases of erithropeietin, insulin and human growth factor (Tribble,

---

[15] Patents have been granted on the basis of claims relating to phenotypic characteristics, or to a combination of phenotypic and genotypic characteristics. Thus, a trait that has been identified or bred into plant lines may be claimed either phenotypically or genotypically.

[16] This is explained by the fact that a specific protein is not encoded by a single DNA sequence but by a large number of synonymous sequences (Vossius, 1997, p. 17).

1995, p. 100). The US Patent and Trademark Office issued a patent in favour of Plant Genetic Systems NV covering the full-length *cry1Ab Bacillus thuringiensis* (Bt) gene[17].

Claims relating to genes may be described by specifying their base sequence. Nevertheless, a description based on a combination of the gene's function, physical and chemical properties, origin, source or production process may be acceptable as well. Thus, in the US, the EU and Japan, claims that do not structurally describe the sequence of DNA, but the amino acid sequence of a protein encoded by the gene[18], are admitted.

Genes in plants, as mentioned, are often claimed in conjunction with a purified protein, plasmids and transforming vectors, and plants or seeds. The patenting of genes at the cell level extends the scope of protection to all plants which include a cell with the claimed gene. Box 8 provides some examples of patent claims relating to the use of *Bacillus thuringiensis* to generate plant resistance to certain insects.

Box 8: Examples of patent claims on Bt genes

The invention relates to a chimeric gene which, in the cells of cotton plants, expresses insecticidal compounds which essentially have the insect-toxic properties of the crystalline protein produced by *Bacillus thuringiensis*. The transformed cells are regenerated to complete plants which are toxic to the larvae of insects from the orders *Lepidoptera*, *Coleoptera* and *Diptera* (Ciba-Geigy AG, EP 0317511).

A DNA fragment, encoding all or an insecticidally-effective part of a Bt crystal protein, is modified by changing A and T sequences to corresponding G and C sequences encoding the same amino acids (Plant Genetic Systems NV, WO 9116432; EP 9100733).

A plant cell transformed with a *Bacillus thuringiensis* gene coding for a protein of at least 66 kDa that is toxic to *Coleoptera*. A plant containing the transformed cell is resistant to *Coleoptera*.

---

[17] *AgBiotech*, 1997, Vol. 9, No. 11, p. 252N.

[18] For instance, "a gene encoding a protein having an amino acid sequence of Met-Tyr...-Cys-Leu" (Japanese Guidelines for Biotechnological Inventions, February 1997).

In countries where the patenting of genes is admitted, an important issue is, therefore, the scope of the exclusive rights that the title-holder may exercise with regard to the use of the gene by third parties. In particular, a crucial issue in the plant field – relevant to the implementation of any instrument on access to plant genetic resources – is the extent to which the patentee may prevent the use of a recombinant gene as well as of the gene in its natural form.

According to one opinion, patents on genes protect the patent-holder "against use of the gene by another biotechnologist, but leave anyone free to use and breed with organisms containing the gene naturally" (Barton, 1997, p. 1). Thus, the patent would prevent a third party from crossing the inserted gene into a different variety and marketing it[19], but not from developing by conventional breeding methods a variety that includes and expresses the natural gene.

This would imply that if a gene is identified in a plant and subsequently patented in a country, breeders may still use the natural gene in breeding activities (Heitz, 1991, p. 21), but the use of the isolated gene to develop transgenic plants may be restricted by the patent-holder in that country, till the expiration of the patent. Hence, the conventional way of utilizing the natural gene may be unrestricted for R&B purposes.

This interpretation seems to find support, in principle, in the doctrines and legislation of some countries. In the United States, a natural DNA sequence has been deemed "free to all men and reserved exclusively to none", despite the fact that a "purified and isolated" DNA sequence was clearly considered as patentable subject matter (*Amgen Inc. vs Chugai Pharmaceutical Co.*)[20].

The previous UK patent law (Article 4.7) included a "disclaimer" according to which claims did not extend to a product "when found in nature". This was also the position of German courts in some decisions; however, some authors contend that the protection conferred by

---

[19] Prof. Day has documented the problems faced by his university team when they tried to use the **bar** gene in a turf grass species to confer herbicide resistance. The gene had been patented as a selective marker for the laboratory, for recovering products of transformation and for field use to confer herbicide resistance (Day, 1995, p. 81).

[20] 13 USPQ2d 1737, 1759 (D. Mass. 1989).

a patent should extend to the natural substances if covered by the claims (Bergmans, 1991, p. 278).

Patenting principles and practices on biotechnological inventions are still in a state of flux, including in those countries that have already gained experience in the patenting of genes. The extent to which a patent on an isolated gene may extend to genes existing in nature may be subject to different interpretations[21] under national laws and over time. Patent-holders may not quietly consent to breeders putting a (protected) gene into a variety that would ultimately compete with the patentee's own variety. As noted by a member of the plant biotechnology industry, "many patents are still pending...and represent an uncertainty. Indications from the first products being commercialized in cotton, corn and soybean suggest that patents are being aggressively enforced and are being used to establish competitive advantage in the marketplace" (Evans, 1996, p.75).

Even if courts may finally limit the patent rights to non-naturally-occurring substances [22], the threat of litigation[23] may deter innovation and effectively block or reduce the use of germplasm for R&B[24]. According to Miranda Santos and Lewontin, "patents on genes of wide utilization in agriculture can block the development of new varieties in clear contradiction to the objectives for which the (patent) system was designed" (Miranda Santos and Lewontin, 1997, p. 5).

---

[21] According to Crespi, for instance, patents on genes should "have the same legal effect as other patents for chemical compounds and should therefore extend to all compositions containing them and to all uses to which they are applied to exploit their properties" (Crespi, 1988, p. 114).

[22] In Europe, for instance, defendants may argue that natural genes are the result of "essentially biological processes", which are not patentable.

[23] The extension of patents to living materials has given rise to a large number of contradictory procedures before patent offices and to substantial litigation in courts, notably in the United States and Europe. Plant-related patents have been responsible for a good part of this turmoil (Barton, 1997, pp. 6-15).

[24] See also Plowman (1993), p. 35. On the use of "strategic litigation" to prevent competition, see Barton (1995), p. 163.

Patents on Varieties

Patents on plant varieties are accepted in some countries, such as the United States[25] and Australia[26]. There are several examples of patents granted with respect to plant varieties in the United States (see Box 9).

Box 9: Examples of patents on plant varieties

"An inbred corn line having the designation AI" (US Patent 4,594,810, Claim 1)

"Novel soybean varieties CX174" (US Patent 4,626,610, Claim 7)

"A new and distinct plant variety, Yensen 3a, of *Distichlis palmeri* ..." (US Patent 4,762,964, Claim 1)

"Inbred corn seed designated PHN73 having ATCC Accession No. 75205" (US Patent 5,157,208, Claim 1)

"Novel F1 generation hybrid corn seed DK672" (US Patent 4,607,453, Claim 2)

"F1 generation hybrid corn plant DK524" (US Patent 4,629,819, Claim 1)

Source: Seay (1993), p. 69.

The examples in the Box show that varietal protection is also available for F1 hybrid plants and for inbred plant lines. Hybrids may also be claimed simply by designation.

The UPOV Convention, as revised in 1978, banned the accumulation of PBRs with patent protection for one and the same botanical genus and species. This restriction was in line with the European Patent Convention, which prohibited the patenting of both "plant varieties" and "animal races" (Article 53 b).

---

[25] This form of patent has not yet been tested in courts in the United States (Barton, 1998, p. 25).

[26] Mexico admitted patents on plant varieties in its law of 1991, but their patentability was excluded in 1994, when the law was amended as part of the process of accession to the North American Free Trade Agreement.

Though the prohibition of the European Patent Convention remains in force, the proposed Directive on the Legal Protection of Biotechnological Inventions is likely to limit the scope of the exclusion. It stipulates that "inventions which concern plants or animals may be patented if the application of the invention is not confined to a particular plant or animal variety" (Article 4.2), and that "the protection conferred by a patent on a product containing or consisting of genetic information shall extend to all material...in which the product is incorporated and in which the genetic information is contained and expressed" (Article 9)[27].

The approach of the European Patent Convention has been followed in the legislation of many other countries as well. Thus, Brazil enacted PBRs legislation in 1997 that is reported to prohibit patents on plant varieties (Article 2)[28]. Patents on plant varieties are also excluded in Argentina (Decree 260/96).

While the requirements to obtain a patent are stricter than those for PBRs (in the latter case, it is not necessary to prove that the variety is novel and "non-obvious"), the legal powers conferred on the patentee are broader than those granted to the PBRs title-holder. Hence, though the number of patented plant varieties may be much less than those under PBRs, such varieties will be subject to more severe restrictions, particularly with respect to access for R&B.

In most patent laws, in effect, there is no exception similar to the "breeders' exemption" under PBRs. Hence, the patentee may, in principle, prevent a third party from using the patented variety for further R&B. He could prevent, for instance, multiplication of the variety, even experimentally, testing of crosses and any subsequent research and development with the crosses made (Roberts, 1996, p. 533), as well as the use of the material as the parent of another variety, unless the patent claims do not cover such use (Barton, 1998, p. 26).

---

[27] In one case, the Board of Appeals of the European Patent Office had held that patent claims on genetically modified plant cells could not extend to seeds and cells, since protecting the latter would amount to patenting a "plant variety" (Plant Genetic Systems/Glutamine synthetase inhibitors, T356/93).

[28] According to this article, PBRs are "the only form of protection on plants or their parts" available in Brazil.

Since a plant variety "is characterized by essentially all of its genes" (Roberts, 1996, p. 535), the patenting of plant varieties may restrict the access to and use of the whole combination of genes that constitutes a variety, and prevent the development of new combinations of such genes. Moreover, according to one view, such a restriction would not only apply to the overall genetic structure of the protected variety, but also include "isolated traits or genes embodied in it" (Miranda Santos and Lewontin, 1997, p. 5).

Patent laws may, however, provide for certain exceptions and mechanisms that limit the patentee's rights with regard to R&B, such as by allowing for experimental uses, as discussed below.

Can Patents and Access for R&B be Reconciled?

The previous section has indicated that patents, in principle, prevent third parties from accessing the protected materials for R&B purposes. This effect is particularly strong when patent claims are broadly drafted. The recognition of patents on plant materials may, therefore, frustrate one of the desired principles of a multilateral system of access to and exchange of PGRs.

This section examines whether, and to what extent, that incompatibility may be overcome, or attenuated, by designing a patent regime that specifically addresses the issues relating to the control and use of PGRs. This can be achieved in a straightforward way if patents are excluded in the plant field, totally or partially. As examined below, such exclusion is allowed under the TRIPS Agreement.

If such exclusion is not provided for, the extent to which the access to a patented material for R&B would be subject to the patent-holder's authorization would depend on: a) the scope of the claims; b) the interpretation given to the claims; c) the access to samples of the patented material; d) the exceptions to the exclusive rights recognized by the national law, particularly for experimentation; e) the availability of compulsory licences; and f) the possible revocation of a patent when the applicant fails to demonstrate the prior consent of the country of origin of patented materials. These issues are briefly examined below.

Exclusions from patentability

a) Substances existing in nature

Nothing in the TRIPS Agreement or in other international conventions on IPRs obliges WTO Member countries to follow an expansive approach in respect of the patenting of substances existing in nature, such as genes, cells or plants as such. In effect, the TRIPS Agreement specifies the requirements that an invention must meet in order to be patentable, but it does not provide a definition of what an invention is. This leaves WTO Member countries with the freedom to determine what should be deemed an invention. Many laws in developing countries (e.g., Argentina, Brazil, Andean Group) exclude the patentability of materials found in nature, even if isolated therefrom.

An exclusion of this type (for instance, on the entire range of sequence variation that occurs in nature for any gene[29]) would solve part of the access-related problems mentioned above. The exclusion may ban the patenting of genes, cells or any other subcellular part found in nature or isolated therefrom.

It should be noted that though the TRIPS Agreement requires that "microorganisms" be protected, nothing would prevent WTO Member countries from applying the scientific definition of "microorganism" (limited to viruses, algae, bacteria, fungi and protozoa) rather than a definition encompassing any microscopical life form which is accepted by institutions for the deposit of microorganisms.

b) Plants

The TRIPS Agreement specifically allows for the exclusion of the patentability of "plants" without referring to any specific classification thereof. Countries may exclude the patentability of plant species, varieties, including hybrids and transgenic plants, as well as their cells and seeds. It should be noted that if patents are granted on "plants", the protection may extend to a large number of plant varieties that incorporate the features on which protection is grounded.

---

[29] See Miranda Santos and Lewontin (1997), p. 7.

Clearly, though plant varieties need to be protected by IPRs, as discussed elsewhere in this Chapter, there is no obligation to implement such protection under patents.

c) Processes

Another possible exclusion relates to "essentially biological processes for the production of plants or animals". This concept, inspired by European law[30], has generated considerable debate (Bergmans, 1991, p. 96).

The notion of "essentially biological" has been defined by the European Patent Office according to the degree of "technical intervention"; if the latter plays an important role in the determination of or control over the results, the process may be patentable (Guidelines for Examination of the EPO, No. X-232.2).

Under this notion, classical breeding methods are not patentable[31]. In contrast, methods based on genetic engineering (e.g., the production of a "transgenic" plant) where the degree of technical intervention is significant would be patentable.

d) Exceptions based on morality/*ordre public*

Article 27.2 and 27.3 of the TRIPS Agreement specify the exclusions to patentability that any country may (but is not obliged to) establish in its domestic law. There are different hypotheses in which Member countries may not grant patents[32] based on this provision.

The exclusion of inventions which are contrary to *ordre public* or morality, or similar grounds, is provided for in most patent laws.

---

[30] More precisely, by Article 2b) of the Strasbourg Convention on European Patents.

[31] In the the Lubrizol case, however, the EPO admitted the patentability of a method to obtain hybrids.

[32] Article 27. 2 states that: "Members may exclude from patentability inventions, the prevention within their territory of the commercial exploitation of which is necessary to protect *ordre public* or morality, including to protect human, animal or plant life or health or to avoid serious prejudice to the environment, provided that such exclusion is not made merely because the exploitation is prohibited by domestic law".

Both concepts are relative to the values prevailing in a society. They vary in different cultures and countries, and change over time. Some important decisions relating to patentability may depend upon the judgment about morality, as illustrated by the case of the Harvard "oncomouse"[33].

The morality issue was addressed by the European Patent Office in relation to the patentability of a herbicide-resistant plant. The patent being opposed related to herbicide-resistant plants. The opponent argued that risks in connection with release of the plants into the environment were impossible to predict accurately and therefore a potential risk to mankind existed. "This argument was rejected," explained the Director of the European Patent Office, "because it was not considered appropriate to carry out the balancing exercise of the Harvard Oncomouse decision. The reasons given for this were manifold, but were primarily the lack of consensus in society on 'objective morality' and the inability not only of the opponents but of all experts to prove the extent of the risks" (Gugerell, 1996, p. 97).

Patentability requirements

An important issue is how "novelty" and "inventiveness" (or "non-obviousness") are interpreted. There are some important differences in national legislation in this regard. For instance, in the United States, the divulgation of an invention outside the country which has not been made in a written form is not admitted as destructive of novelty (Section 102.a, 35 U.S.C). This is one of the reasons why materials used by farmers and communities outside the United States have, in some cases, been declared eligible for patent protection.

There are often differences in the way different patent offices judge novelty requirements, particularly with regard to the extent that the previous knowledge of a substance may prevent the granting of subsequent patents relating to the same matter. For instance, the Australian Patent Office withdrew patent rights (conferred to Hoffman-LaRoche) on the thermostable enzyme tag DNA polymerase in its

---

[33] The patentability of the oncomouse was rejected by the examiner at the European Patent Office on morality grounds. This decision was reversed by the EPO Technical Board.

native form, based on precedents in "prior art" that had not been admitted by the EPO[34].

Similarly, how the existence of an "inventive step" is determined will define the scope of the possible protection. This is quite a difficult issue in the case of applications relating to plants. In one case (*Ex parte C*, 27 USPQ. 2d. 1492)[35], the Board of Patent Appeals and Interferences of the US Patent and Trademark Office did not accept the difference from previous varieties as sufficient to demonstrate non-obviousness. The court stated:

> "We have reviewed the data and the declaration but are unpersuaded of patentability because there is nothing of record which explains why the differences between the claimed variety and a rot resistant variety such as 'Pella 86' are so significant and unexpected that they should weigh more heavily than the numerous similarities between the claimed variety and the varieties of the cited prior art."

Scope of claims

If patents on plant materials are allowed, careful consideration should be given to the types of claims that are acceptable. This is an area where countries are not limited by international rules. For instance, till recently Japan only accepted claims that stated the purpose, constitution and effect of the invention. In the case of genes, only claims based on a description of a specific base sequence were admitted (Okuyama, 1997, p. 7).

As mentioned above, claims that describe function rather than structure have been widely accepted in some countries. The admission of functional claims broadens the scope of protection to any means that performs the claimed function. Functional language in patent claims is often the source of considerable controversy and litigation (Taylor, 1997).

In an intermediate position, the use of functional claims may be accepted, for instance, only in cases where the description of the

---

[34] See *Nature*, Vol. 390, 27 November 1997.
[35] Quoted by Barton (1998), p. 25.

invention is otherwise impossible, along the lines of the European practice on the matter[36].

Interpretation of claims

Another component of patent law that in practice determines the scope of the rights conferred on the patentee is how non-literal infringement is judged.

The extent to which a given product (or process) is infringing is generally judged literally by comparing the possible infringing product (or process) with the one claimed, as expressly described in the patent. In many cases, however, there may be no "literal" infringement (e.g., there may be differences in the means used by the patentee and the possible infringer), but a court may find that the alternative embodiment of the invention is "equivalent" to the protected invention.

Different versions of the "theory of equivalents" allow for more or less room to improve on and develop around a patented invention. A strict construction of claims and a narrow doctrine of equivalents expand the field available for competitors to work around, improve or adapt protected inventions (UNCTAD, 1996, p. 33).

At least one case has already been decided in which the "theory of equivalents" has been applied to a patent covering genetic materials. The Osaka High Court decided (in *Genetech vs Sumitomo Pharmaceuticals*, March 1996) that a change at only one position in a sequence of more than 500 amino acid residues of tissue plasminogen activator (TPA) was an "equivalent" to the patented invention.

Important questions arise with regard to the scope of the protection conferred by a (utility) patent on a plant variety. While under PBRs, varieties should be distinguishable at least by one clear feature, there are no specific rules with respect to patents. When may a variety be deemed an "equivalent" to another, protected variety?

The principles of the "theory of equivalents" may be inadequate to judge these cases, since the development of a new variety through breeding methods usually does not involve any "inventive step" and

---

[36] See Decision T 68/85 of the EPO Technical Board

may, hence, be considered an obvious variant of the patented variety[37]. A more narrow interpretation may thus be necessary in such cases, as illustrated by the decision in *Imazio Nursery Inc. vs Dania Greenhouses*, where the US Court of Appeal for the Federal Circuit established that in order to determine infringement of a plant patent[38], it was necessary to prove that the 'accused' plant had been derived from the patented plant, i.e., that the former is an actual copy of the latter (Gioia, 1997, p. 516).

Access to samples of patented materials

In order to comply with the disclosure requirement of patent law, the description of a biotechnological invention generally needs to be supported by the deposit of samples of the material that contains the relevant information.

Legal systems vary considerably on this topic. Under US law, access to the sample can only take place after the granting of the patent. Generally, commercial use of the sample will amount to an infringement of the patent, but experimental uses are allowed. Under European law, samples may be obtained after publication of the application through an independent expert and for experimental purposes only.

National legislation may determine how to deal with the conditions of access to the deposited samples and, particularly, when and under what circumstances samples may be obtained by third parties. The Budapest Treaty – which establishes an international system for the deposit of biological materials – is based on the assumption that access to the sample will be granted after publication of the relevant application (Rule 11.3 (a) of the Regulations of the Treaty). Access to samples after such publication may accelerate innovation based on improvements of the protected invention or the development of new inventions.

---

[37] For an interesting discussion on the application of the "theory of equivalents" and its implications on technical progress, see Merges and Nelson (1996), pp. 120-144.

[38] Plant patents are conferred in the United States under the Plant Patent Act of 1930 for asexually reproduced plant varieties (excluding tuber propagated plants). Different principles of interpretation might apply in the case of utility patents.

Access to deposited samples may, however, be problematic. As noted by a researcher, "even after the patent is filed and granted, access to the material can be denied by failure to answer requests. Such access as may be granted may not be meaningful since profitable use of the materials may be prohibited and, even if allowed, is subject to restrictions. The result is that the laws sometimes limit, or even prevent, beneficial applications" (Day, 1995, p. 83).

It should be noted that the failure to supply deposited samples or the lack of correspondence between the claimed and the deposited material may result in the invalidity of the granted patent (Correa, 1994a, p. 20).

Experimentation exception

A crucial issue that may affect access for R&B is the extent to which an invention may be used for experimentation purposes. Some patent laws admit exceptions to the title-holder's exclusive rights with regard to experimentation on the invention. However, the scope of the exception varies significantly in different countries.

In the United States, the exception is not a part of the patent statute. It has been created by case law but in rather narrow terms. Experimentation is admitted for "philosophical" (i.e., "scientific") purposes, and to create **other** products outside the scope of a patent (Wegner, 1994, p. 458). If restrictively interpreted, this exception is not likely to entitle a third party, for instance, to cross patented seeds to produce improved varieties.

In Japan, the research exception is expressly provided for under the patent law, Article 69(1) ("The effects of the patent right shall not extend to the working of the patent right for the purposes of experimentation or research."). In Europe, experimentation **on** the invention (as opposed to **with** the invention), even for commercial purposes, is generally considered legitimate.

Experimentation on the invention may be undertaken, for instance, to test an invention to determine its sufficiency or compare it to prior art; to determine how the invention works; to improve on or develop another invention; to "invent around" or to test the invention before requesting a licence.

The scope of the exception is particularly ambiguous in the

biotechnology field, for instance, with regard to the use of cDNA sequence information to produce a certain protein. Such use is likely to be deemed illegal in the United States, while it is unclear whether it would be acceptable under the "research exception" in Europe and Japan (Wegner, 1994, pp. 458-459).

Patent scholars have, however, supported the recognition of such an exception on broader terms, so as to further technological development on the basis of protected inventions (Wegner, 1994, p. 456). The need for an experimentation exception is particularly felt in sectors dominated by "incremental" innovation, i.e., by changes and additions to existing knowledge, rather than by discrete innovations.

The introduction of an explicit research exemption for patents on plants has been recommended by experts in the United States, where it has also been suggested that all biological materials required for IPRs protection become "part of the national germplasm system" (CSSA, 1993, p. 9).

In Mexico, the 1991 patent law (revised in 1994) provides for an explicit exception with regard to patents "relating to living materials". It states that the title-holder cannot prevent a third party from making use of the patented product "as an initial source of variation or propagation to obtain other products, except where such use was made previously" (Article 22,V).

Compulsory licences

A compulsory licence is an authorization conferred by a relevant national body to use a patent without the consent of the patent owner. Most countries provide some modalities of compulsory licensing, which is explicitly allowed by the TRIPS Agreement. The Agreement does not limit the grounds for the granting of compulsory licences, but establishes the conditions under which the grant may take place (Correa, 1994b, p. 331).

Access to a patented material, and its use for R&B, if not otherwise ensured, may be obtained by means of compulsory licences, if provided for by national legislation. Such licences may be granted on grounds related to public interest, lack of exploitation of the invention, anti-competitive practices of the patentee, emergency, or other reasons, including conservation or protection of the environment.

A very detailed provision on compulsory licences grounded on the dependency of patents is contained in Article 31(l) of the TRIPS Agreement. It contains a number of conditions for the granting of compulsory licences relating to the technical and economic importance of the "second patent" (it shall involve "an important technical advance of considerable economic significance"), the granting of "a cross-licence on reasonable terms" to the owner of the "first patent", and the non-assignability of the licence (except with the assignment of the "second patent").

Dependent patents are particularly relevant in those areas in which innovation proceeds by incremental steps, by adaptation or improvement of preexisting knowledge, rather than in a discrete form. Plant breeding, as mentioned above, clearly falls within this category. Starting from a patented plant variety, an improvement thereon made by a third party may (if the patentability requirements are met) give rise to a dependent patent.

The problem, however, is that in order to improve a variety, the third party should be able to have legitimate access to the protected material, a possibility that the patent-holder may restrict. Unauthorized use of the protected material, in the absence of an exception, as indicated above, may constitute infringement and entail civil and criminal sanctions.

Since, as mentioned, the TRIPS Agreement does not limit the grounds for conferring compulsory licences, national legislation may provide for such licences as specifically required to ensure access to a patented material in order to attain specific agricultural objectives (e.g., availability of a given material for farmers) or food security, against a remuneration to be determined by the national authority.

Such licences may also be available whenever the patent-holder has not voluntarily assented to a request to grant a licence on reasonable commercial terms for the use of the patented plant material for improvement or development of a new variety.

It should be recalled, finally, that Chapter 34 of Agenda 21, provision 34.18, unanimously adopted at the Rio Conference, recommended the provision of compulsory licences to facilitate access to and use of environmentally sound technologies.

Revocation of patents

The grounds for revocation/forfeiture of a patent have not been dealt with in the TRIPS Agreement. The single provision on this matter only obliges Members to ensure the availability of a judicial review of a decision to revoke a patent, but does not limit the grounds on which such a decision may be adopted.

Patent applicants may be requested to declare the country of origin of biological materials related to the invention (what many applicants normally do in practice) (UNEP, 1996, p. 13). This requirement may help in identifying the country of origin of a given material and in the implementation of the obligation imposed by the CBD to share benefits.

If a patent, as determined by most laws, may be revoked due to the lack of payment of annual maintenance fees, among other reasons, nothing should prevent a WTO Member from cancelling a patent if the applicant has not complied with or has violated other rules, such as obtaining the prior consent of the country of origin of a material[39]. A patent law cannot be viewed in isolation from the rest of the legal system. There is a need, in particular, to better articulate IPRs legislation with the legal regimes that implement the CBD provisions.

ACCESS UNDER PLANT BREEDERS' RIGHTS

This section examines the extent to which PBRs, as generally granted under UPOV-like legislation, affect the access to plant genetic resources for R&B. As examined elsewhere[40], there are important differences between the nature and modalities of patents and PBRs protection, which help explain why the access issue is substantially different under each regime. Though such differences are not addressed here in detail, they should be borne in mind while analyzing how PBRs affect access for R&B.

---

[39] A provision of this type is contained in Decision 391 (1996), which establishes the Andean Group regime on access to genetic materials.

[40] See, for instance, Heitz (1991), pp. 19-22.

The compatibility of PBRs legislation with a multilateral system based on free access to PGRs was stated in FAO Resolution 4/89, which adopted an "agreed interpretation" of the IU:

> "Plant Breeders' Rights, as provided for under UPOV (International Union for the Protection of New Varieties of Plants), are not incompatible with the International Undertaking."

At the time of this Resolution, UPOV 1978 was in force. The question arises as to whether changes in legislation, particularly the adoption of UPOV 1991, entail any substantial change with respect to the declared compatibility.

Scope of Protection

PBRs are exercised in respect of the propagating materials of the protected varieties[41]; such rights do not cover the "process technology for the production of new varieties even where this is applicable to a wider range of plant materials than the individual variety of a particular species" (Crespi, 1988, p. 112).

By definition, PBRs prevent third parties from using those materials for production or reproduction (multiplication) and related acts (conditioning for propagation, offering for sale, selling, importing/exporting, stocking), but do not protect the germplasm as such. Thus, PBRs on a variety do not confer any specific rights with respect to certain genes or a combination of genes, which remain in the public domain for further R&B.

The PBRs regime has traditionally included an exception for the use of a protected variety for the purposes of R&B, clearly including the commercial breeding of a new variety. This feature is common in PBRs laws in developed and developing countries, including the most recent legislation on the matter (such as the legislation approved in the Andean Group in 1993, Mexico in 1996, and Brazil in 1997).

The "breeders' exemption" has also been recognized in the

---

[41] UPOV 1991 requires national legislation to extend the exercise of rights in respect of the harvested materials produced through unauthorized use of propagating material, if the title-holder had not had the possibility of exercising them with respect to the propagating materials.

UPOV Convention, including the 1991 Act. In line with the Convention, the UPOV Model Law suggests a provision stating that the breeder's rights shall not extend to acts done for "experimental purposes" and for "the purpose of breeding other varieties" (Article 14 (ii) and (iii)).

Infringement

The subject matter protected under PBRs is a new "plant variety" which meets the DSU (distinctness, stability, uniformity) requirements. The criterion of distinctness can be seen not only as a condition for protection, but also as defining the borders of protection. A variety that is distinct from a protected variety cannot infringe the latter; moreover, it may (if the other conditions are also met) obtain protection on its own right.

Infringement will only exist[42] when any of the acts subject to the exclusive rights of the title-holder is performed without his/her authorization with respect to:

• protected varieties;

• varieties which are not clearly distinguishable from the protected variety; and

• varieties whose production requires the repeated use of the protected variety.

As mentioned, under UPOV 1991, it is also an infringement to produce/reproduce and perform related acts with respect to "essentially derived varieties". The introduction of this concept broadens the scope of protection conferred on the title-holder, and may limit the diffusion of varieties improved by farmers, though (if the farmers' privilege is recognized) it would not prevent them from using the derived varieties in their own exploitations.

In sum, unlike patents, PBRs do not restrict the access to plant materials for R&B. National laws and the UPOV Convention specifi-

---

[42] See the UPOV Model Law, 1996.

cally exclude R&B activities from the scope of the title-holder's rights. Though the concept of "essentially derived varieties" broadens the "distance" required to be outside the scope of protection conferred with respect to a protected variety, the basic principle of free access to germplasm for developing **new** varieties remains as an essential feature of the PBRs regime.

Deposited Materials

Under PBRs laws, protected materials become available for R&B when commercialized by the title-holder or with his/her consent. UPOV-like legislation protects varieties on the market and generally does not allow access by third parties to any non-marketed deposited material. Non-marketed materials thus accumulate PBRs and trade secrets protection. In this case, access is often granted under "material transfer agreements" for non-commercial purposes, subject to grant-back provisions (Houser, 1993, p. 109).

The accumulation of PBRs and trade secrets does not, however, seem to be a necessary requirement in UPOV-type laws. As noted in a recent seminar sponsored by the US Department of Agriculture and other entities, "there is no reason why a country adopting a UPOV-type system could not require that the deposits could be open, and this would give the choice to the plant breeder" (CSSA, 1998, p. 108).

ACCESS UNDER THE REGIME ON UNDISCLOSED INFORMATION

Material that is held as confidential information by its legitimate possessor is not accessible to third parties without his/her consent. This is particularly relevant in the case of hybrids. Since hybrid seeds need to be replaced for each cycle of production because they do not breed true, such seeds are protected by their very nature against unauthorized reproduction. Hybrid seed producers tend to keep secret the corresponding parent lines[43] and have been slow in adopting formal protec-

---

[43] The protection of inbred lines as a trade secret was explicitly recognized in the United States in the case of Pioneer Hi-Bred against Holden, in which the former was awarded $47 million as damages arising from the misappropriation of the said lines by the latter.

tion under PBRs, especially in the United States. However, the general tendency today is to protect the hybrids and the parent lines themselves under PBRs.

The TRIPS Agreement obliges Member countries to protect undisclosed information of commercial value, provided that other specified requirements are met (Article 39). Hence, parent lines may be kept secret and should, as a minimum, deserve the protection accorded under the Agreement. To the extent that access to the said lines is effectively restricted by secrecy, it will not be possible for third parties to undertake improvement activities without the authorization of the possessor of the secret lines.

Unlike patents and other IPRs, however, the protection of undisclosed information does not confer an exclusive right, but only the faculty to act in cases of dishonest commercial practices. The distinction is important, since it means that information and materials protected because they are secret may be used and reproduced by a third party, if such acts do not imply an unfair commercial practice: trade secrets law does not protect against discovery and use through independent development, or accidental or wilful disclosure.

Moreover, under many laws (including in the United States), the **reverse engineering** of trade secrets is legitimate (Neff and Smallson, 1994, p. 102; Barton, 1998, p. 26). The same approach seems to have been followed by the TRIPS Agreement. According to its Article 39.2(b), in order to be protected, the "undisclosed information" must be "secret in the sense that it is not ... readily accessible to persons within the circles that normally deal with the kind of information in question". Hence, to the extent that the secret can be discerned through evaluation of a product that "incorporates" it, no protection would be available.

Contractual clauses applied by seed companies in some countries have been reported to aim at preventing reverse engineering. Conditions of sale and label licences on bags of seeds ("shrink wrap" licences) are often very restrictive on the use of seeds (CSSA, 1998, p. 115), imposing restrictions beyond those determined by the applicable substantive laws.

In sum, the extent to which trade secrets protection may restrict access for R&B will depend on the rights conferred on the possessor in respect of acts of reverse engineering when the information is "embodied" in and obtainable from the products and, possibly, on the terms and conditions of the particular sales contract. In the case of parent lines, if they are used to produce hybrids and are not commercialized as such, the legal protection creates a barrier against the unauthorized access to and use of the said lines for further R&B.

CONCLUSIONS

Access to PGRs for food and agriculture for R&B is an essential element in any possible multilateral system on the conservation and exchange, including benefit-sharing, of such resources. Concerns have been voiced both in developing and in developed countries with regard to the extent to which IPRs may restrict such access.

The analysis made has shown the implications of three types of IPRs (patents, PBRs, undisclosed information) on access to protected materials for R&B. Patents are currently granted in some countries in respect of genes, plant varieties and other plant materials, as well as processes for their manipulation.

Patents on isolated genes, generally claimed jointly with vectors, and modified cells and plants, permit control over the use of the genes in genetic engineering, but should not, in principle, block the use of the original gene in its natural form in conventional breeding. The acceptance of broad claims, the uncertainty about the limits of the patentee's rights, and the aggressive enforcement of patent rights may, however, limit R&B activities. Clear rules establishing, at the national and international levels, that despite the patenting of isolated genes, they remain "free to all men and reserved exclusively to none"[44], may contribute to dissipating current concerns over the implications of this type of patents for R&B.

In some jurisdictions, plant varieties are also eligible as patent subject matter. Protection of this sort, in the absence of adequate exceptions for experimentation, may effectively block access to the patented material as a source of further variation.

In the framework of the international standards in force on patent protection, as determined by the TRIPS Agreement, different types of provisions and exceptions may be introduced in national laws in order

---

[44] A provision on this issue may be considered in an eventual revision of the TRIPS Agreement (Article 27.3(b)).

to ensure access to patented plant materials for R&B. Patent grants on any classification of plants and of parts thereof may be excluded by national laws. Moreover, several options exist to deal with issues such as the admissible scope and the interpretation of claims, access to the deposited material, the "experimentation" exception, the granting of compulsory licences and the revocation of patents. Adequate provisions on these issues may also contribute to ensuring access to PGRs for R&B.

Unlike patents, PBRs contain a clear exception for R&B. Though the scope of the exception may be limited by the notion of "essentially derived varieties", the PBRs system does not seem to create barriers to access to protected materials for R&B and, in this regard, seems compatible with the objectives of a multilateral system for shared access to PGRs for food and agriculture.

Finally, the protection of plant materials as undisclosed information may limit access, but it neither creates exclusive rights nor prevents, in principle, the reverse engineering of products legitimately put on the market. The compatibility of this form of protection with a multilateral system on PGRs for food and agriculture has been acknowledged in the framework of the IU.

In sum, the extension of IPRs on plant materials does give rise to a number of issues relating to access to PGRs for R&B, which may be addressed at the national level as well as by means of clarification of some of the international rules applicable on the matter, notably on the effects of patents on genes and on the admissibility of an "experimentation" exception in respect of patented plant materials.

Based on the previous analysis, and having in view the development and future implementation of a multilateral system on PGRs for food and agriculture under a revised IU, a number of conclusions for action at the international level may be drawn, namely to:

a)   preserve the right of any country, as currently recognized under the TRIPS Agreement, to exclude plants and any parts thereof, including DNA sequences, from patentability;

b)   adopt clear rules indicating that naturally-occurring plant materials, including genes, are and shall remain outside the scope of any form of IPRs protection in any country;

c) define the novelty requirement in a manner that excludes the patentability of any subject matter which was made available to the public by means of a written description, by use or in any other way[45] in any country before the date of filing, including use by local and indigenous communities and deposit of a material in a germplasm bank or other deposit institutions where the said material is publicly available;

d) establish commitments by governments not to grant, or to cancel *ex officio* or upon request, IPRs on plant materials obtained: i)from collections held in international germplasm banks and other deposit institutions where such materials are publicly available; ii)without the prior consent of the country of origin or otherwise inconsistently with the principles of Article 15 of the CBD;

e) specifically provide for the right of any country to allow for an experimentation exception (including research and breeding) in case patents were granted on plant materials, including plant varieties.

References

Barton, John (1993), "Introduction: Intellectual property rights workshop", in Crop Science Society of America, American Society of Agronomy, Soil Science Society of America, *Intellectual Property Rights: Protection of Plant Materials*, CSSA Special Publication No. 21, Madison.

Barton, John (1995), "Adapting the intellectual property system to new technologies", *International Journal of Technology Management,* Special Issue on the Management of International Intellectual Property edited by C. Correa, Vol. 10, Nos. 2/3.

Barton, John (1997), *The Impact of Contemporary Patent Law on Plant Biotechnology Research* (mimeo).

Barton, John (1998), "Acquiring Protection for Improved Germplasm and Inbred Lines", in F.H. Erbisch and K.M. Maredia (Eds.), *Intellectual Property Rights in Agriculture Biotechnology*, Biotechnology in Agriculture Series, No. 20, Cab International, Wallingford-New York.

---

[45] See Article 54.2 of the European Patent Convention.

Bent, S.; Schwab, R.; Conlin, D. and Jeffrey, D. (1991), *Intellectual property rights in biotechnology worldwide*, Stockton Press, New York.

Bergmans, Bernhard (1991), *La Protection des Innovations Biologiques. Une étude de Droit comparé*, Maison Larcier S.A., Bruxelles.

Brush, Stephen (1994), *Providing Farmers' Rights Through In Situ Conservation of Crop Genetic Resources*, report to the Commission on Plant Genetic Resources, University of California.

Caforio, Giuseppe (1995), *Le Invenzioni Biotecnologiche. Nell'Unitá del Sistema Brevettuale*, G.Giappichelli Editore, Torino.

CEFI (1997), *The Challenges of Biotechnology*, Madrid.

Correa, Carlos (1994a), *Sovereign and Property Rights Over Plant Genetic Resources*, Commission on Plant Genetic Resources, FAO, Paper 2, Rome.

Correa, Carlos (1994b), "The GATT Agreement on Trade-Related Aspects of Intellectual Property Rights: New Standards for Patent Protection", *EIPR*, Vol.16, No. 8.

Correa, Carlos; Díaz, A.; Burachik, M.; Jeppesen, C.; Gil, L.; Moreno Posada, F.; Sorj, B. and Sutz, J. (1996), *Biotecnología: Innovación y Producción en América Latina*, Colección CEA-UBA, Buenos Aires.

Crespi, R. (1988), *Patents: A basic guide to patenting in biotechnology*, Cambridge University Press, Cambridge.

CSSA (Crop Science Society of America) (1993), *Intellectual Property Rights: Protection of Plant Materials*, Special Publication Number 21, Madison.

CSSA (1998), *Intellectual property rights III. Global genetic resources: access and property rights*, Madison.

Day, Peter (1995), "The Impact of Patents on Plant Breeding Using Biotechnology", *NABC Report 7. Genes for the Future: Discovery, Ownership, Access*, New York.

Evans, David (1996), "Genetic Engineering of Flavor and Shelf Life in Fruits and Vegetables", *NABC Report 8. Agricultural Biotechnology: Novel Products and New Partnerships*, New York.

Freeman, C. and Perez, C. (1986), "The diffusion of technical innovations and changes of techno-economic paradigm", *Conference on Innovation Diffusion. Ca' Dolfin, Dorsoduro 3825/E*, 17-22 March, Venice.

Gioia, Vincent (1997), "Plant Patents – R.I.P.", *Journal of the Patent & Trademark Office Society (JPOS)*, July.

Gugerell, Christian (1996), "The European experience", in Perret *et al.* (Eds.), *Le génie génétique. Biotechnology and patent law*, CEDIDAC, Lausanne.

Heitz, Andre (1991), "Genetic Resources and Plant Breeders' Rights", *Seminar on the Nature of and Rationale for the Protection of Plant Varieties under the UPOV Convention*, Buenos Aires.

Houser, David (1993), "Exemptions under patents and certificates covering plants and comments on material transfer agreements", in CSSA (1993).

Lesser, W. (1998), *Sustainable Use of Genetic Resources under the Convention on Biological Diversity*, Cab International, Wallingford-New York.

Macer, Darryl (1990), *Shaping Genes. Ethics, Law and Science of Using Genetic Technology in Medicine and Agriculture*, Eubios Ethics Institute, New Zealand.

Merges, Robert and Nelson, Robert (1996), "The Complex Economies of Patent Scope", in *The sources of economic growth*, Harvard University Press, Cambridge.

Miranda Santos, M. and Lewontin, R. (1997), "Genetics, plant breeding and patents : Conceptual contradictions and practical problems in protecting biological innovations", *Plant Genetic Resources Newsletter*, No. 112.

Mooney, Pat Roy (1998), "The Parts of Life. Agricultural Biodiversity, Indigenous Knowledge, and the Role of the Third System", *Development Dialogue*, Special Issue.

Neff, Richard and Smallson, Fran (1994), *NAFTA. Protecting and Enforcing Intellectual Property Rights in North America*, Shepard's/McGraw-Hill, Colorado Springs.

Okuyama, Shoichi (1997), "New JPO Guidelines for Biotech Inventions – Focus on Disclosure Required and Claims Allowed", *Patents & Licensing*, June.

Plowman, R.D. (1993), "Intellectual Property Protection of Plants – The Agricultural Research Service Perspective", in CSSA (1993).

Roberts, Tim (1996), "Patenting Plants Around the World", *EIPR*, No. 10.

Seay, Nicholas (1993), "Intellectual Property Rights in Plants", in CSSA (1993).

Shiva, Vandana and Holla-Bhar, Radha (1996), "Piracy by Patent: The Case of the Neem Tree", in Jerry Mander and Edward Goldsmith (Eds.), *The Case Against the Global Economy and For a Turn Toward the Local*, Sierra Club Books, San Francisco.

Taylor, Roger (1997), "The pitfalls of functional claims", *Managing Intellectual Property*, June.

Tribble, Jack (1995), "Gene Ownership versus Access: Meeting the Needs", *NABC Report 7. Genes for the Future: Discovery, Ownership, Access*, New York.

UNCTAD (1996), *The TRIPS Agreement and Developing Countries*, New York and Geneva.

UNEP (1996), *The impact of intellectual property rights systems on the conservation and sustainable use of biological diversity and on the equitable sharing of benefits from its use*, UNEP/CBD/COP/3/24, Conference of the Parties to the Convention on Biological Diversity, Third meeting, Buenos Aires, 4-15 November 1996.

UPOV (1996), *Model Law on the Protection of New Varieties of Plants*, Geneva.

Vignoli, Giulio (1986), *Aspetti giuridici delle attivita genetiche in agricoltura*, Universitá Degli Studi di Genova, No. 9, Milano.

Vossius, Volker (1997), "Patenting Inventions in the Field of Biology and Chemistry: Case Law", *BSLR*, No. 1.

Wegner, Harold (1994), *Patent Law in Biotechnology, Chemicals and Pharmaceuticals,* Stockolm, Basingstoke (UK).

Chapter VII

Upcoming Review of the TRIPS Agreement

INTRODUCTION

AS discussed in previous chapters, the TRIPS Agreement brought about a "signal change" in the protection of intellectual property rights (UNCTAD, 1996, p. 18). This Agreement is, by its coverage, the most comprehensive international instrument on IPRs.

The Agreement establishes minimum standards on almost all areas of IPRs in terms of both the availability of rights and their enforcement. The inclusion of this latter type of provisions – one of the main innovations of the Agreement with respect to preexisting conventions on IPRs – means that whenever the Agreement enters into force, the particular Member country must have in place the legal procedures and the administrative and legal infrastructure necessary to actually enforce the conferred rights.

Any deviation from the standards set forth by the Agreement may lead to a dispute settlement procedure within the WTO, in accordance with the Dispute Settlement Understanding. If the existence of a violation is determined, the affected country can apply trade retaliation against the non-complying country in any area covered by the WTO Agreement.

As a result of its broad coverage and the nature of its provisions, the implementation of the TRIPS Agreement requires dealing with a significant body of national legislation in terms of both substantive as well as procedural rules. In many developing and least developed countries, such implementation calls for massive changes in preexisting laws.

The Agreement provides a framework for legislation and not

operative provisions that may be directly imported into national laws. In some cases, there is considerable room for interpretation. For instance, the concept of "exclusive marketing rights" as contained in Article 70.9 is undefined. Article 27.3(b) allows Members to develop an "effective *sui generis* regime" for plant varieties that may be designed without following any specific model. In other cases, the provisions explicitly determine options for legislation, such as Article 34 on the reversal of the burden of proof.

Even in those cases where the standard of protection is clearly stated, Member countries must decide how to implement it according to their own legal system (Article 1).

The implementation of the TRIPS standards, in sum, requires considerable elaboration at the national level.

IDENTIFYING NATIONAL INTERESTS

In order to comply with the Agreement, there is a need to assume a wide range of obligations in almost all areas of IPRs. In many areas, the pre-TRIPS laws of developing countries require very substantial change, particularly in order to handle new issues, such as the protection under copyright law of computer programs and databases.

There are also areas in which no previous legislation existed at all, such as in the case of undisclosed information, integrated circuits and plant varieties.

As mentioned, the TRIPS Agreement includes enforcement rules and not just substantive provisions. Member countries do not only face the task of drafting and obtaining parliamentary approval of new legislation. Compliance with the Agreement also calls for the revision of national laws in respect of civil, criminal and administrative procedures, as well as redefining the role of the police and customs authorities. As illustrated by the UNCTAD study on TRIPS (1996), the costs of developing the institutional infrastructure to implement the TRIPS Agreement standards may be substantial.

Amending or developing new legislation on IPRs requires legal expertise in a number of fields, which is often lacking in developing countries and LDCs. The drafting of legislation needs the active involvement and cooperation of different State organizations, and also interaction with the private sector and society at large.

The adoption of new IPRs rules may affect different industrial and commercial activities in the country. Given the flexibility left by the TRIPS Agreement to deal with some issues (e.g., parallel imports, compulsory licences) and the likely impact of different solutions, the appropriate involvement of the local private sector in the discussion of new legislation seems essential. Similarly, the strengthening of IPRs may affect consumers and other groups (e.g., local communities).

Concerns have been voiced in many developing countries, for instance, with regard to the possible impact of the introduction of product patent protection in the pharmaceutical sector[1]. Though the estimates vary significantly, several studies indicate that an increase in the prices of new medicines (as compared to a situation of open competition) will be the probable outcome of such an introduction, with a possible welfare loss for the particular country (Scherer, 1999). Likewise, stronger protection of computer programs might reduce access to information technology systems by small and medium enterprises and educational institutions.

The TRIPS Agreement aims at balancing the interests of producers and users of technology (Article 7). Developing the appropriate mechanisms to do so is quite a difficult task, for which adequate consultation processes, reliable data and deep knowledge of each particular area are required.

The process of drafting legislation to implement the TRIPS Agreement is, therefore, not only a complex technical problem. It also raises a number of public policy issues that need to be properly addressed.

TRANSITIONAL PERIODS

Developing countries and LDCs were accorded transitional periods (Article 65) to implement the Agreement. Application of the Agreement will become obligatory for the former countries by 1 January 2000. Products that are not patentable at that date need to be protected from the year 2005.

The provision of such periods was an important element in the delicate balance reached as the outcome of negotiations. They were

---

[1] For a more general discussion, see Chapter II.

included to allow developing countries time to elaborate and adopt the required legislation, and to design any other policies necessary to minimize the possible negative effects of new IPRs rules. This was particularly the case with regard to products which were not patentable (such as pharmaceuticals, agrochemicals and food).

Despite the automatic nature of the transitional periods, many developing countries have been under pressure by some developed countries to accelerate the pace of reforms, so as to give immediate application to the TRIPS Agreement standards. These pressures have complicated rather than facilitated the process of legislative change.

Though so far only one case relating to TRIPS has been decided under the WTO dispute settlement mechanism (USA-India on implementation of Article 70.8), several complaints and requests for consultations have been filed during the last few months, including by the EU against Canada relating to the "early-working" exception for patents on pharmaceuticals (also known as the "Bolar" exception), Canada against the EU relating to the extension of the patent term for agrochemical and pharmaceutical patents, the US against Argentina on the recognition of "exclusive marketing rights", and the US against Canada relating to the extension of patents issued before 1989.

A significant number of developing countries have not been able to adapt their legislation to the Agreement's minimum standards yet, and are unlikely to do so before the end of the general transitional period on 31 December 1999. Even some developing countries that have made substantial steps to implement the Agreement have not been able to cover all areas (particularly those in which they had no legislation previously), or have not been able still to reform enforcement-related rules.

This situation may put such countries in a situation of violation on 1 January 2000, which may lead to a large number of actions under the WTO dispute settlement mechanism against them. In fact, the US Trade Representative (USTR) has already announced that it will assess the situation at the end of 1999 in order to take action as of January 2000.

In view of this situation, a possible approach may be to negotiate an extension of the transitional period as contained in Article 65.2. Alternatively, proposals could be made in order to reach a consensus

for non-action in cases of non-compliance with the TRIPS Agreement
by developing countries, for a certain agreed period.

BUILT-IN AGENDA

Article 27.3(b) is the only provision in the TRIPS Agreement subject
to an early review, in 1999. So far, there has been no agreement in the
Council for TRIPS on the meaning of "review". Developed countries
hold that it is a "review of implementation" which is called for, while
for developing countries a "review" should open the possibility of
revising the text.

Several proposals have been made, particularly by IPRs-con-
cerned NGOs, for the revision of Article 27.3(b), for instance, in order
to ensure that naturally occurring materials are not patentable, and to
recognize some form of protection for the "traditional knowledge" of
local and indigenous communities. The aim of some developed
countries, if a revision takes place, would seem to include the elimination of the exception for plants and animals, and establishing that plant
varieties should be protected in accordance with the UPOV Convention as revised in 1991.

The outcome of a possible revision of this Article is unclear. For
developing countries, it would be important to ensure that the exception for plants and animals is maintained, as is the flexibility to develop
sui generis regimes on plant varieties which are suited to the seed
supply systems of the countries concerned.

In the revision of this provision, the following elements may be
considered:

a)   to preserve the right of any Member country to exclude from
      patentability plants and animals and to develop a *sui generis*
      regime for the protection of plant varieties[2];

---

[2]   See the position submitted by the government of Egypt in document WT/
CG/W/136. In contrast, the United States has already indicated that the
Council for TRIPS should inititate work "to consider whether it is desirable to
modify the TRIPS Agreement by eliminating the exclusion from patentability
of plants and animals and incorporating key provisions of the UPOV agreement regarding plant variety protection" (document WT/CG/W/115).

b) to clarify that naturally occurring substances, including genes, shall remain outside the scope of any IPRs protection;

c) to determine the novelty requirement in a manner that excludes the patentability of any subject matter which was made available to the public by means of a written description, by use or in any other way in any country before the date of filing, including use by local and indigenous communities, or by deposit of a material in a germplasm bank or other deposit institutions where the said material is publicly available;

d) to establish commitments by governments not to grant, or to cancel *ex officio* or upon request, IPRs on biological materials obtained: i) from collections held in international germplasm banks and other deposit institutions where such materials are publicly available; ii) without the prior consent, where applicable, of the country of origin;

e) to ensure, as appropriate, compliance with the obligation to share benefits with the country of origin of a patented biological material.

A possible revision of Article 27.3(b) may also include – though this would not be strictly necessary – a provision specifically allowing for an experimentation exception (including the breeding of new plant varieties).

Another issue to be dealt with by the Council for TRIPS is the treatment of "non-violation" complaints, which are not subject to the dispute settlement mechanism till the end of 1999 (Article 64.2 and 64.3). A decision should be taken – by consensus – on whether to extend this period or to determine the disciplines to be applied. An extension of the transitional period seems advisable.

Moreover, a deeper examination of the implications of this clause in the IPRs field may be undertaken. IPRs are generally defined in a precise manner since they imply the stipulation of a right to prohibit third parties from using, producing or commercializing a product or service. Non-violation would open a window for challeng-

ing on discretionary grounds national regulations[3] and domestic policies in different areas beyond IPRs, such as price controls and regulations on royalty remittances. Hence, the application of the non-violation clause may create a gray area and provide a basis for challenging national policies beyond the scope of IPRs.
It should be noted that according to Article 19.2 of the Dispute Settlement Understanding, the WTO adjudication process "cannot add to or diminish the rights and obligations provided in the covered agreements", and that in the US-India panel on Article 70.8[4] the Appellate Body rejected the "legitimate-expectations" test derived from GATT jurisprudence on non-violation acts, thereby confirming that

> "the developing countries are free to adopt their own laws and policies with respect to all intellectual property issues that were not expressly harmonized in TRIPS standards themselves" (Reichman, 1998, p. 597).

Finally, work has been undertaken in the Council for TRIPS for the establishment of a registration system for geographical indications for wines, in accordance with Article 23.4 of the TRIPS Agreement. The European Union has proposed that geographical indications registered under the international system be automatically protected in participating Member countries, subject to a procedure for dealing with oppositions from each Member which considers that a geographical indication is not eligible for protection in its territory. In contrast, the United States and Japan have suggested the compilation of an international database of geographical indications to which Members would be expected to have reference in the operation of their national systems. In the context of the review provided for under Article 24.2, proposals have also been made for the expansion of the product areas that must benefit from the higher level of protection (see "Other issues" below).

---

[3] See South Centre (1998), p. 26.
[4] See Panel Report USA vs India, WT/DS50/R, 5 September 1997 (WTO 97-3496) and WT/DS550/AB/R, 19 December 1997 (97-5539).

REVIEW OF THE AGREEMENT

Article 71.1 provides for a review of the implementation of the TRIPS Agreement after the year 2000, and for possible reviews "in the light of any relevant new developments which might warrant modification or amendment".

There are already several proposals, some formally submitted, to revise the TRIPS Agreement in a future round of multilateral trade negotiations. A preliminary question, however, is what should be the developing countries' strategy on this matter.

Negotiating Strategies

A first strategy may aim at a comprehensive revision, in order to effectively implement through specific provisions Articles 7 and 8 of the Agreement and strike a balance between the interests of producers and users of technology. The rationale behind this strategy would be that the Agreement, as it stands, primarily reflects patterns of IPRs protection suitable for developed countries, but which largely disregard the "development dimension".

A component of this strategy may be to **clarify** various elements of flexibility which are present in the text, but which are or may be contested, such as the right to allow parallel imports (Article 6) including when originating from a compulsory licensee, the non-patentability of uses of known products (interpretation of Articles 27.1 and 28), and the right to grant compulsory licences on different grounds to be determined by each national law (Article 31). In addition, certain obligations may be clarified, such as developed countries' obligations under Article 66.2 with respect to LDCs and Article 67 relating to technical assistance.

This strategy may lead to an improvement of the present text from the perspective of developing countries. There is, of course, the risk that, depending on such countries' level of preparation and bargaining power, the revision of many provisions may lead instead to texts which are more restrictive than the existing ones. A careful political evaluation of possible scenarios is, therefore, needed.

A second strategy may, in contrast, be based on a *de minimis* approach, that is, opening for renegotiation as few provisions as possible. The rationale for this position would be that the TRIPS Agreement is not a uniform law, and that it leaves developing countries some room for manoeuvre that may be lost if the text is broadly revised. This position also assumes that the chances for developing countries to obtain favourable amendments are slim, given the sensitive nature of IPRs issues and the pressures exerted on developed countries' governments by powerful industrial lobbies.

Under this approach, only a few key provisions should be subject to re-examination, such as Article 31(g) (termination of a compulsory licence), which seriously undermines the compulsory licensing system.

Finally, a third strategy may be based on a "policy" or "issues approach", that is, on a systematic review of the Agreement in the light of a particular objective. This strategy would be most effective if the review systematically covers **all** WTO agreements that may affect the attainment of a certain objective, and not only the TRIPS Agreement. For instance, when dealing with technology transfer, in addition to particular provisions in the said Agreement, relevant provisions in the Agreements on the Application of Sanitary and Phytosanitary Measures (Article 9), Technical Barriers to Trade (e.g., Articles 11 and 12), and Subsidies and Countervailing Measures (SCM) (e.g., Article 8), and in the General Agreement on Trade in Services (GATS) (Articles IV and XIX), may be considered.

Policy-oriented Approaches

It is possible to identify different approaches for a systematic review as proposed:

1) Transfer of technology

Several developing countries have stressed[5] the need to develop particular provisions in the TRIPS Agreement so as to ensure that the objective of fostering the transfer and dissemination of technology (Article 7) is effectively realized. In fact, developing countries and

---

[5] See the submissions by the Dominican Republic and Honduras (WT/GC/W/119), Egypt (WT/CG/W/136) and, notably, India (WT/GC/W/147).

LDCs face growing constraints in getting access to up-to-date technologies (Correa, 1994a). Given that the issues at stake are complex, the development of a multifaceted and comprehensive approach is needed (Roffe, 1999).

The enhancement of technology flows to developing countries may require the revision of several articles of the TRIPS Agreement, such as Article 27.1 (working obligations), Article 31(b) (broader application of "refusal to deal" as an autonomous ground for compulsory licences), Article 40 (specification of illegal restrictive business practices in voluntary licences) and Article 66.2 (further specification of measures to be adopted to encourage the transfer of technology to LDCs).

This approach may be supplemented, as mentioned, by an analysis of the amendments or new provisions that may be needed in other WTO agreements, such as GATS and the SCM Agreement. For instance, consideration could be given to the exemption under the SCM Agreement of subsidies related to the export of technology and associated equipment to developing countries.

2) Environment

Within the WTO Committee on Trade and Environment, India has already indicated the need to amend the TRIPS Agreement in order to facilitate the access to and use of environmentally sound technologies. The proposal requires the amendment of Articles 31 (compulsory licences) and 33 (duration of patents), and suggests that patent-holders should be subjected to an obligation to transfer environmentally sound technologies on fair terms and most favourable conditions. It also proposes a financial compensatory mechanism[6].

3) Biodiversity

The reconciliation of the TRIPS Agreement with the CBD may be one of the main objectives of possible negotiations[7]. This may include the

---

[6] See WTO/CTE/1, 12 November 1996.

[7] For a justification and proposals on this issue, see the Indian submission as contained in WT/GC/W/147. See also Chapter VI above.

amendment of Article 27.1 (requirement of universal novelty as a condition for patentability) and Article 29 (obligation to prove that prior informed consent has been obtained with regard to claimed biological materials). A new provision on "traditional knowledge" may also be considered, though the complexity of this issue would justify the establishment of a working group to study and clarify possible options (see below).

4) Health

The implementation of public health policies may be restrained by the implementation of IPRs protection, if the latter is not designed in a manner that effectively takes into account the objectives of such policies. The TRIPS Agreement leaves some room therefor (Correa, 1997; Velásquez and Boulet, 1999).

Under an approach focused on public health, however, some articles may require revision, for instance, Article 27.1 in order to exclude the patentability of "essential medicines" listed by the World Health Organization (WHO); Article 30 so as to incorporate an explicit recognition of an "early-working" exception for the approval of generic products before the expiration of a patent; and Article 31 in order to clarify the right to grant and the scope of compulsory licences for public health reasons[8].

5) Competition

The expansion and strengthening of IPRs in developed countries has taken place *pari passu* with an effective application of competition law. Illustrative of this linkage is the large number of compulsory licences granted in the United States in order to remedy anti-competitive practices[9].

In developing countries, in contrast, IPRs protection is being enhanced in consistency with the TRIPS Agreement, but competition

---

[8] It should be noted that the WHO Assembly approved in May 1999 a resolution giving WHO the mandate to work on issues relating to the implementation of the WTO agreements as they may affect public health.
[9] See Chapter III.

law is non-existent or weak in many countries.

Revision of the Agreement could be made with a view to strengthening the competition-related provisions thereof (such as Article 40) and incorporating new disciplines, for instance, those relating to measures to prevent and remedy abuses of IPRs. Specific work could be undertaken on vertical restraints, such as tying arrangements and restrictive practices in licensing agreements, as well as on horizontal restraints, such as pooling and cross-licensing and industry standardization.

Other Issues

Some proposals have been made by developing countries to revise the TRIPS Agreement in order to expand the special protection of geographical indications under Article 23 (now limited to wines and spirits) so as to cover other products of export interest, such as basmati rice[10]. Such increased protection, if admitted and not subject to special and differential treatment, could benefit all Members; therefore, its net impact in developing countries would depend on the economic importance of such countries' indications *vis-à-vis* those of other Members.

Both the United States and the European Union have suggested[11] that a possible amendment to the TRIPS Agreement should incorporate the two conventions approved under the auspices of WIPO in 1996, that is, the WIPO Copyright Treaty and the WIPO Performance and Phonograms Treaty[12]. The WIPO Copyright Treaty reconfirms the pertinent provisions of the TRIPS Agreement on copyright. It also contains provisions particularly relevant to the use of works in a digital environment, like the "right of distribution" (Article 6)[13] and the "right of communication to the public", including when "members of the public may access these works from a place and at a time individually chosen by them" (Article 8).

---

[10] See Indian submission WT/GC/W/147.
[11] See WT/GC/W/115 and WT/GC/W/193.
[12] For an analysis of these treaties, see Vinje (1997).
[13] This right may be subject to the principle of exhaustion (Article 6.1).

Possible amendments that developing countries may consider include the establishment of the first-to-file principle[14] for patent applications[15], and clarifying Article 70.9 relating to "exclusive marketing rights". The application of these rights – which do not constitute a category of intellectual property[16] – has given rise to certain abuses[17] that may be partially corrected by clarifying that they should only be conferred in respect of new chemical entities, and that only patents granted in another WTO Member with a serious examination system may be considered as a basis for granting those rights (Velásquez and Boulet, 1999, pp. 29-30).

Another important issue is the possible development of some form of protection for traditional knowledge. The adoption of the Convention on Biological Diversity has given impetus to this idea by establishing the obligation to "respect, preserve and maintain knowledge, innovations and practices of indigenous and local communities embodying traditional lifestyles relevant for the conservation and sustainable use of biological diversity..." (Article 8 j).

Many approaches and proposals have been developed to deal with communities' knowledge[18], ranging from the creation of new types of IPRs to the simple option of legally excluding all forms of appropriation, be it under patents, breeders' rights or other modalities of IPRs. Only a few countries have so far started to address the complex conceptual and operational problems involved in the recognition of communities' rights on their knowledge. For instance, "collective" IPRs have been recognized by the Constitution of Ecuador (1998). The Biodiversity law of Costa Rica (1998) protects "*sui generis* community rights" (Article 82), and a draft law in Brazil (Bill No. 306, 1995) recognizes the rights of local communities to collectively benefit from

---

[14] According to this principle, applied by most countries in the world, the right to a patent corresponds to the first applicant. In the United States, a patent is granted to the "first inventor", a principle that allegedly leads to complex controversies and an unnecessary burden on inventors.

[15] This is also proposed by the European Union (WT/GC/W/193).

[16] According to Article 1.2 of the TRIPS Agreement, intellectual property rights are only those referred to in Sections 1 through 7 of Part II of the Agreement.

[17] See Chapter III.

[18] For an analysis of different approaches, see Correa (1994b); Posey and Dutfield (1996).

their traditions and knowledge and to be compensated by means of IPRs or other measures. The creation of a new, *sui generis* form of protection has also been proposed in a draft bill in Thailand, which would recognize rights of traditional healers and on medicinal genetic resources.

At least some aspects of communities' knowledge – the artistic components – may be protected as "works of folklore", in accordance with the UNESCO (UN Educational, Scientific and Cultural Organization)/WIPO "Model Provisions for National Laws for the Protection of Expressions of Folklore against Illicit Exploitation and other Prejudicial Actions" developed by a Committee of Governmental Experts in 1982. An interesting element of this proposal is that unauthorized utilization of expressions of folklore with gainful intent and outside the traditional or customary context of folklore, can be prevented by the community concerned or a competent authority. Indigenous communities are not prevented from using their expressions or from developing them by continuous reproduction, recitation or performance[19].

Any WTO Member may provide protection beyond the TRIPS Agreement standards (Article 1), and is fully empowered to create new titles of IPRs or new forms of protection to the extent that this does not diminish or neutralize the protection to be granted in the areas covered by the Agreement. If such a new title or form of protection were established and a WTO Member does not apply the principle of national treatment, there would be no violation of the TRIPS Agreement or of any other international instrument. A good illustration of this possibility is the European Union Directive 96/9/EC on the Legal Protection of Data Bases, which created a new *sui generis* right for databases, subject to the principle of reciprocity.

Developing countries may keep their right to deal with communities' rights at the national level, without submitting them to international rules. In order to get recognition of such rights in other countries, however, some form of pluri- or multilateral agreement would be necessary.

---

[19] Several countries (e.g., Tunisia, Bolivia, Chile, Iran, Morocco, Algeria, Senegal, Kenya, Indonesia, Niger, Panama) protect such works under national copyright law .

A review of the TRIPS Agreement could explicitly recognize the Members' right to legislate on communities' rights, for instance, by indicating – like in Article 6 of the said Agreement – that no Member can be submitted to a WTO panel based on the adoption of protection for traditional knowledge. A further step would be to develop in the Agreement itself certain elements of such protection in order to get international recognition of such rights. This would imply, however, the application thereon of the TRIPS Agreement's principles of national treatment and most favoured nation. Given the status of the debates on the matter, this latter approach seems unlikely to succeed, but discussions could be started by the setting up of a working group.

References

Correa, Carlos (1994a), "Trends in technology transfer: Implications for Developing Countries", *Science and Public Policy*, Vol. 21, No. 6.

Correa, Carlos (1994b), *Sovereign and Property Rights over Plant Genetic Resources*, FAO, Commission on Plant Genetic Resources, First Extraordinary Session, Rome.

Correa, Carlos (1997), *The Uruguay Round and drugs*, WHO, Geneva.

Posey, Darrell A. and Dutfield, Graham (1996), *Beyond Intellectual Property. Toward Traditional Resource Rights for Indigenous Peoples and Local Communities*, International Development Research Centre, Ottawa.

Reichman, Jerome (1998), "Securing compliance with the TRIPS Agreement after US vs India", *Journal of International Economic Law*, Vol.1, No. 4, pp. 585-601.

Roffe, Pedro (1999), "The implementation of the TRIPS Agreement and transfer of technology to developing countries" (mimeo), Geneva.

Scherer, F. (1999), "The patent system and innovation in pharmaceuticals", presented at the AIDE Conference on Pharmaceutical Patents, Innovation and Public Health, 28-30 January, Toulouse, France.

South Centre (1998), *The WTO multilateral trade agenda and the South*, Geneva.

UNCTAD (1996), *The TRIPS Agreement and Developing Countries*, New York and Geneva.

Velásquez, G. and Boulet, P. (1999), *Globalization and access to drugs*, DAP Series No. 7 Revised.

Vinje, Thomas (1997), "The new WIPO Copyright Treaty: A happy result in Geneva", *EIPR*, No. 5.

Annex

Options for Implementing the TRIPS Agreement in Developing Countries
Updated and revised report of an Expert Group on the TRIPS Agreement and Developing Countries

NOTE: This is an updated and revised version of a report prepared by an independent Expert Group on the TRIPS Agreement and Developing Countries in order to provide suggestions and proposals to developing countries for the national implementation of the TRIPS Agreement.

The Expert Group was convened by the Third World Network with the objective of getting together a team of individuals with in-depth knowledge of intellectual property rights (and, in particular, of the TRIPS Agreement) in order to provide guidelines and proposals to policy-makers and the public in developing countries on the options available to them during the process of implementing the TRIPS Agreement.

The aim of the Expert Group was to review the Agreement and point out the options available in various aspects of the Agreement, as well as to propose recommendations on options which would be more appropriate to and consistent with the interests of the developing countries.

This was done in the understanding that the way in which the Agreement is implemented is likely to have significant implications for the developing countries' access to and use of technology and for their economic and social development.

The report was the result of the work of the Expert Group, which convened in Geneva in July 1997 to discuss an initial draft prepared by Dr Carlos Correa. Following extensive discussions to review and amend the draft, the members of the Group subsequently continued to work on the document through correspondence. A revised draft was

*presented to participants of a Workshop on "Some Current Issues in
the WTO" that the Third World Network organized in Geneva in 1997.
Their comments were also taken into account in the preparation of the
final report.*

*The main author of the report is Dr Carlos Correa, Director of
the Masters Programme on Science and Technology in the University
of Buenos Aires, Argentina.* Comments on the report were made by
*Bernard Remiche (Professor, Law Faculty, Université Catholique de
Louvain et Avocat, Brussels, Belgium), Chakravarthi Raghavan (Chief
Editor,* South-North Development Monitor, *Geneva) and Bhagirath
Lal Das (former Director of International Trade Programmes in the
United Nations Conference on Trade and Development) in their
personal capacity. The views expressed in the report are those of the
members of the Group, and do not necessarily reflect those of the
organizations to which they are affiliated.*

*Besides the members of the Expert Group, several other persons
who provided valuable comments on the draft report included
Abdulqawi A Yusuf (who also attended the July 1997 meeting) and the
diplomats and individuals who took part in the October 1997 Workshop.*

INTRODUCTION

DEVELOPING countries have undertaken, as a result of the agreement reached during the Uruguay Round, to introduce substantive
changes in their legislation on intellectual property rights (IPRs).

The adoption of new international rules on the matter has been
actively promoted by industrialized countries in order to obtain
worldwide protection for the innovations they generate. The expansion and strengthening of such rules are bound to take place in a
scenario of deep North-South asymmetry. Only a small fraction of
world research and development (R&D) expenditure is made in
developing countries, which are overwhelmingly dependent upon
innovations made in the industrialized world.

The Agreement on Trade-Related Aspects of Intellectual Property Rights (or the TRIPS Agreement) provides minimum standards
for the protection of IPRs in all countries. Though such standards are
considerably detailed, particularly in the patent field, they leave

different degrees of freedom for legislation at the national level. The TRIPS Agreement does not create a "uniform law", but preserves a certain degree of freedom to legislate at the national or regional level. The way in which the Agreement is implemented may have important implications for developing countries regarding the conditions for their access to and use of technology and their economic and social development. It is crucial for these countries, therefore, to clearly identify the options left by the Agreement to implement its provisions in a manner that is consistent with their interests and strategies.

The granting of IPRs may create several conflicts of interest, namely, between the IPRs-holders and the consumers. While the enjoyment of exclusive rights may permit the former to obtain greater benefits than in a competitive situation, these benefits are normally made at the expense of consumers who have to pay higher prices. The IPRs legislation should aim at balancing those interests in a manner that ensures adequate protection of the public.

Developing countries are obliged to comply with the Agreement by the year 2000; those that do not now provide product patents in certain fields may delay the introduction of such patents till 2005. Least developed countries may delay compliance until 2006, and request an extension of this period.

The implementation of the TRIPS Agreement is a very complex task, due to the Agreement's broad coverage and the need to reform many, if not all, national statutes on the matter in the short periods mentioned above.

This Guide has been devised in the framework of Articles 7 and 8 of the TRIPS Agreement, which provide the basic elements that should be considered in the implementation of the Agreement[1].

Purpose and Scope

The purpose of this document is to provide some orientation with regard to available options for implementing the Agreement in areas of particular relevance for the access to and development of technology in developing countries. This document focuses on provisions

---

[1] See Chapter I.

relating to patents and undisclosed information as well as to computer programs and databases. It also briefly addresses the issue of restrictive practices in voluntary licences.

One of the underlying concepts in the preparation of this document is that governments in developing countries should implement the TRIPS Agreement in a fully informed, democratic and specific manner. The Agreement requires them to make several critical decisions that may affect, *inter alia*, the appropriation of natural resources, the access to technology, and the consumers' welfare. Implementing legislation should be as specific as possible on certain crucial issues – identified below – in order to give precise orientation to the administration and the judges, who will be in charge of the application of the relevant legislation.

This document only addresses a selected number of topics related to those issues. There is no attempt to be exhaustive. Instead the aim is to highlight and offer possible approaches and options to deal with those areas considered most relevant in terms of possible implications for the use and diffusion of technologies.

The options offered in this document are clearly consistent with the TRIPS Agreement. Indications are given in the few instances where the ambiguity of the text may allow for different, controversial interpretations.

It seems unnecessary to indicate that the suitability of the suggestions made in this document for a particular country depends upon that country's relative level of development, and on its peculiar strengths and weaknesses in the area of science and technology. The appropriateness of the proposals made, therefore, should be judged in each case against the particular situation and policy objectives pursued.

Since developing and least developed countries have a limited period to implement the Agreement, and there is no conclusive evidence on how it may affect innovation, development and trade in these countries, it seems advisable for them to take a cautious approach in the implementation process, and to adopt the minimum standards of protection allowed by the Agreement.

It should be noted that the innovative path prevailing in developing countries is mostly based on minor innovations, as well as on the use of local/indigenous knowledge. Though these issues are not specifically addressed in this document, the particular case of the "small inventor" and of local and indigenous communities should be taken into account in these countries' legislation on IPRs.

With regard to the "small inventor", legislation may provide for "improvement patents", as well as for "utility models" (or "petty patents") – a modality of protection currently recognized in many developed and developing countries. Since utility models are not covered by the TRIPS Agreement, countries have ample room to design their legislation on this matter. This is in order to promote local innovation through the use of IPRs adapted to the types of technological development actually taking place. A similar consideration applies to the case of communities' rights, for which different proposals are currently under discussion at the national level, based on the recognition of such rights by the Convention on Biological Diversity (Article 8 j)[2].

As countries or certain sectors develop, it may be possible to consider changes in the legislation in order to adapt it to the new circumstances. For example, if the still weak capabilities of most developing countries in R&D improve, there may be grounds for expanding the IPRs protection granted in the future. While this will always remain a possibility, the reverse is not true. Once a country has increased its level of protection for IPRs during the transitional periods, it may be blocked from going back to diminish protection by the "freezing clause" contained in Article 65.5 of the TRIPS Agreement.

PATENT PROVISIONS

The Concept of "Invention"

Article 27.1 of the TRIPS Agreement stipulates that:

• patents shall be available for any inventions, whether products or processes, in all fields of technology; and

---

[2] See, in this regard, Nijar, G.S. (1996), *In Defence of Local Community Knowledge and Biodiversity*, TWN, Paper 1, Penang; and Posey, D. and Dutfield, G. (1996), *Beyond Intellectual Property. Toward traditional resource rights for indigenous peoples and local communities*, IDRC, Ottawa.

• patent rights shall be enjoyable without discrimination as to the field of technology.

The TRIPS Agreement does not specify, however, what an "invention" is; national laws may define this concept according to standards generally applied to the matter.

The concept of invention has been broadened in many developed countries since the 1980s, particularly in order to encompass developments in the field of biotechnology and, in some countries, of computer technology. The extension of patents to living matter, in particular, raises fundamental ethical and legal issues that need to be addressed in the implementation of the Agreement.

Since the concept of "invention" is not defined in the Agreement, and there is no "universal" concept thereof, developing countries can, within certain limits, opt for various alternatives. The scope of the concept can be determined by national legislation, in a broad or narrow manner.

Thus, there is no obligation under the TRIPS Agreement to adopt an expansive concept of "invention", as is currently done by many developed countries. In particular, nothing in the Agreement obliges Members to consider that substances existing in nature, biological or not, are patentable, even if isolated and claimed in a purified form.

While implementing Article 27.1, developing countries should carefully consider the economic, legal and ethical aspects involved in the patenting of living materials or certain types thereof. As a matter of principle, it is recommended not to grant patents on living materials as such.

Some countries may also decide not to confer protection on new uses of plants, such as for medicinal purposes.

The exclusion may also encompass "second uses" of known medicinal products, the patentability of which has been accepted in most industrialized countries but on the basis of a legal fiction.

Likewise, computer programs should be deemed not patentable, as in most countries in the world. Patentability in this field – which is not required by the TRIPS Agreement and has been resisted by programmers and scientists in developed countries – may hinder innovation and the development of a software industry in countries with good capabilities in information technologies.[3]

Some countries may feel that – given their wealth in natural resources – it is precisely in developing innovations related to such resources (e.g., new uses of plants) that local researchers may be able to generate results worthwhile protecting under patent rights. Similarly, the identification of new uses of known products may be more accessible than the development of completely new products.

However, countries that adopt this former approach should note that, due to the "national treatment" principle, broadening the concept of "invention" would benefit foreign as well as national inventors – and that the former are generally better equipped than the latter to take advantage of a broad concept of invention.

Recommended option

The following are not considered inventions[4]:

a)   *discoveries, scientific theories and mathematical methods;*
b)   *aesthetic creations;*
c)   *rules and methods of, and schemes for performing mental acts, playing games or doing business, and programs for computers;*
d)   *presentations of information;*
e)   *the whole or part of natural living beings and biological materials found in nature, even if isolated from it or purified, including the genome or germplasm of any natural living being;*
f)   *essentially biological processes*[5] *for the production of plants and animals other than non-biological and microbiological processes;*
g)   *new uses of a known product or process, including the second use of a medicine.*

---

[3] Computer programs are protectable in most countries under copyright law. This is also the approach adopted by Article 10.1 of the TRIPS Agreement.
[4] Items (a) to (d) are based on the text of the European Patent Convention; item (e) is partially based on Article 10.IX of the Brazilian Industrial Property Code, Law 9,279, 1996.
[5] These processes, if deemed an invention, may be considered as non-patentable (see the European Patent Convention, Article 53.b).

Exceptions to Patentability

In addition to defining what is not an invention[6], national laws can establish exceptions to the patentability of inventions that would otherwise be protectable. Article 27.2 and .3 of the Agreement specifies the exclusions from patentability that any country may provide for. Based on these provisions, several exclusions from patentability that are consistent with the Agreement may be provided for.

This is an area where developing countries also enjoy some room for manoeuvre. The ethical, economic and legal implications of allowing the patenting of plants and animals (as well as parts thereof), even if genetically altered, strongly indicate that these should be subject to a clear exclusion from patentability. The same applies to therapeutic and surgical methods[7] and, more generally, to inventions the use of which may be contrary to *ordre public* or morality.

If, however, the patentability of plants or animals were allowed, the national legislation should incorporate specific provisions in order to limit the extent of the exclusive rights, particularly with regard to the multiplication of the protected material. Thus, in line with the concept of the "farmers' privilege", as allowed under the plant breeders' legislation, it is possible to establish that the patent owner should not be able to prevent the replanting of patented seed nor the exploitation for agricultural purposes of the progeny of patented animals[8].

There is an obligation, under the TRIPS Agreement, to grant patents on microorganisms (Article 27.3). However, this obligation may be interpreted as applicable only to genetically modified microorganisms, and not to those existing in nature. In some jurisdictions, the concept of "microorganism" has been extensively interpreted. However, in accordance with the scientific concept that may be

---

[6] Note that a positive definition of "invention" is not indispensable. Most laws only define it in a negative manner (by exclusion).

[7] These methods may be considered not only as not patentable, but also as not constituting an "invention", as prescribed, for instance, by the European Patent Convention (Article 52.4).

[8] The replanting of patented seeds is allowed (for small farmers) in accordance with the Directive on biotechnological patents approved by the Parliament and the Council of the European Union in July 1998. The use of protected livestock is also permitted for agricultural activity but not sale.

adopted by national legislation, a "microorganism" is a member of any of the following classes: bacteria, fungi, algae, protozoa or viruses[9].

World Trade Organization (WTO) Members are obliged to provide for the protection of plant varieties either by patents or by an effective *sui generis* system or by a combination thereof[10]. This obligation shall be reviewed in 1999.

The patentability of plant varieties is a possible option. However, Members are strongly recommended not to follow this option, since it may hinder plant breeding and farming practices. The advisable approach is to develop a *sui generis* regime. WTO Members may but are not obliged to follow the standards set forth by the Union for the Protection of New Varieties of Plants (UPOV). If such is the case, it should be noted that UPOV, as revised in 1978, provided a more flexible framework for regulating the matter than the new version of the Convention, as adopted in 1991[11]. Currently, however, UPOV 1991 is the only Act open for adhesion.

Possible elements of a *sui generis* regime include the following:

• the protection conferred should not accumulate with other forms of protection, notably patents[12];

• the obligation to declare the origin of the materials used and to demonstrate the prior consent of the country of origin and, if applicable, of the respective indigenous or farming communities;

• compensation for the communities that provided the material used in the development of a new variety, in the form of a general

[9] See Coombs, J. (1986), *Macmillan Dictionary of Biotechnology*, The Macmillan Press, London and Basingstoke, p. 198.
[10] The possible content and scope of a *sui generis* regime shall be dealt with in a separate document. As background material, see The Crucible Group (1994), *People, Plants and Patents*, IDRC, Ottawa.
[11] It should be noted that most developing countries that recently adhered to UPOV (e.g., Argentina, Uruguay, Mexico, Brazil) opted for the 1978 Act.
[12] Article 2 of UPOV 1978 forbade the cumulative protection of plant varieties through different regimes.

contribution to a fund or specific compensation to the community/ies concerned.

Recommended option

The following inventions shall not be patentable:

a)   *inventions whose use would be contrary to* ordre public *or morality, or injurious to human, animal or plant life or health or to the environment;*

b)   *diagnostic, therapeutic and surgical methods for the treatment of humans or animals;*

c)   *plants and animals[13] in whole or any part thereof, including DNA, cells, seeds, varieties and species;*

d)   *the human body and all its elements in whole or in part.*

Criteria of Patentability

Article 27.1 establishes that patents shall be granted to protect inventions which are "new, involve an inventive step and are capable of industrial application". In a footnote, the Agreement allows Member countries to interpret "inventive step" as synonymous with "non-obvious" (the equivalent concept applied in the United States).

Similarly, a country can consider that "capable of industrial application" is synonymous with "useful". However, the latter concept is broader, since it would allow even the patentability of purely experimental inventions.

Other options to be considered relate to the concept of "prior art" which may be defined more or less broadly, and to the treatment of processes which are not novel but which use or produce a novel product[14].

---

[13] The TRIPS Agreement refers to "plants and animals" and not to a certain classification thereof ("varieties", "races" or "species"). Thus, the exception is broader than under European law, whereunder only plant *varieties* and animal *races* are not patentable.

[14] The patentability of such processes, denied by case law in the US (notably in re *Durden*, 1985), has been allowed by an amendment to the US law in order to expand the protection of biotechnological processes (see the Biotechnology Process Patent Protection Act, 1995).

The advised approach is to apply a broad concept of "prior art" in order to ensure that patents are granted to actually "new" inventions, and to stick to the need for novelty of the process itself as a condition for granting a patent.

In accordance with the generally accepted concept of novelty, it may be destroyed by any prior disclosure, written or not[15], of the invention in any part of the world. However, nothing prevents national legislation from providing a less stringent concept of novelty in other areas of IPRs, for instance, in order to protect "minor" innovations under utility models or similar forms of protection.

Prior art may also be deemed to include any material deposited in a gene bank or other deposit institutions. This provision would be advisable if the patenting of biological materials is permitted.

Likewise, prior art may be deemed to include knowledge (e.g., of the use of medicinal plants) diffused within a local or indigenous community. An express rule of this type may prevent the patenting of knowledge or materials developed by and diffused within local or indigenous communities.

An option that national legislation may also adopt is to allow for a grace period – as in the case of the US, Mexico and Argentina – during which disclosure by the inventor does not destroy novelty. This may prove useful for the protection of research results obtained in universities and other public research institutions, where researchers are usually under pressure to promptly publish the findings of their research.

Recommended option

Patents shall be granted to inventions that are new, involve an inventive step and are capable of industrial application.

An invention shall be deemed to be new when it does not form part of the state of the art. The state of the art shall comprise everything made available to the public in any country by means of a written or

---

[15] Under European law and the law of many other countries, novelty is destroyed by an oral communication or by the use of the invention. The text on this issue recommended below is based on Article 54 of the European Patent Convention.

oral description, by use or in any other way, including by publication of a patent application.

The state of the art shall include knowledge made available within a local or indigenous community in any country.

A process shall not be patentable if it is not new and if it does not imply an inventive step, even if it uses or produces a new product.

The communication to the public of the results of research undertaken by universities and public institutions, within one year before the date of application, shall not preclude the granting of a patent on part or the whole of such results.

Rights Conferred

Article 28 sets forth the rights that a patent should confer on its title-holder by referring to the two traditional categories of inventions: products and processes. Such rights must be defined in a negative way, i.e., as the faculty to prevent certain acts relating to the invention.

While defining the rights conferred in the case of process patents, an option which is open is to exclude the extension of protection to the product when the latter is excluded from patentability (e.g., plants or animals, inventions contrary to *ordre public*, etc.). This is to avoid an indirect "product-by-process" protection that would nullify the exclusion from protection.

According to Article 6, nothing in the TRIPS Agreement shall be used to address the issue of exhaustion for the purposes of dispute settlement. This means that a Member cannot request the constitution of a panel, in accordance with the WTO Dispute Settlement Understanding, on the basis that another Member provides for international exhaustion of a patent (or other IPRs).

An important option that developing countries can consider is to provide for an international exhaustion of rights[16], in order to allow "parallel imports" of legitimate products from any country and ensure access to the said products on a competitive basis.

---

[16] The basic concept behind this principle is that once a product has been legitimately put on the market, the rights of the patentee are exhausted, since he/she has already exercised his/her rights thereon.

The possibility, recognized by Article 6, of legally admitting parallel imports is of particular importance. The principle of exhaustion was extensively developed by the European Community in order to avoid the partitioning of the market and the exercise of discriminatory policies by IPRs title-holders within the Community. The doctrine of exhaustion has been applied in recent cases in Europe (relating to exports of pharmaceutical products from Spain) and by the Japanese Supreme Court[17].

The recognition of the principle of international exhaustion in the TRIPS Agreement may be seen to logically reflect the globalization of the economy. At the national level, this solution is necessary to ensure the competitiveness of local companies, which may be jeopardized if they are bound to buy exclusively from a local distributor that charges higher prices than elsewhere. Likewise, the recognition of this principle acknowledges the consumer's right to buy legitimate products from foreign sources at lower prices, if available.

Recommended option

Patents relating to products shall confer the right to prevent third parties not having the patentee's consent from making, using or offering for sale the product.

The protection conferred by process patents shall extend to the product obtained directly by that process, provided that the said product is not excluded from patentability in accordance with the law.

The rights conferred shall not extend to the importation of a product legitimately put on the market in any foreign country.

Disclosure

The full disclosure of the invention is one of the basic principles of patent law. The public's full access to the knowledge developed by the inventor provides a partial justification of the costs that society must

---

[17] In the Aluminium Wheels case, where the Court stressed the principle of independence of patents. In accordance with this decision, parallel imports may also originate in a country where the patent is subject to a compulsory licence.

incur by granting patent rights. Patents and trade secrets are, thus, mutually exclusive.

The obligation to disclose the invention is reflected in Article 29 of the TRIPS Agreement. Its implementation should be in a manner that ensures that the invention can be understood and executed by an expert with average skills in the relevant field. This test should be applied at the national level, i.e., the description should be sufficient to teach the invention to a local expert.

WTO Members may require the applicant "to indicate the best mode for carrying out the invention known to the inventor" at the filing or priority date (Article 29). This requirement[18] aims not only at ensuring the reproducibility of the invention by a person of ordinary skill, but also at preventing inventors from obtaining protection while concealing from the public the preferred embodiments of their inventions.

Disclosure should be complete and precise. It should describe the invention in its technical features. One option that developing countries may implement is not to admit a purely functional description, since actual disclosure requires knowledge about the technical features of the invention as such. They may also require the full definition of a product in order to confer a patent thereon[19].

Further, legislation may limit protection to the embodiments of the invention for which the applicant has provided sufficient information to enable the reproduction of the invention. If several embodiments are claimed, the enablement requirement should apply to the whole range thereof[20]. This would prevent excessively broad claims, for instance, covering methods or products that have not been described by the applicant in a form that allows their reproduction by a third party.

One important issue – which is not dealt with by the TRIPS Agreement – concerns the disclosure of inventions relating to micro-

---

[18] The "best-mode" requirement is contained in US law and in the law of many other countries.

[19] This would exclude the so-called "product-by-process claims" admitted in some jurisdictions when no information is available in the application to define the product satisfactorily.

[20] This is what a British High Court decided, in 1995, in re *Biogen vs Medeva* (relating to a product for preventing hepatitis B).

organisms, since access to the relevant knowledge is only possible through access to the material itself. Access to the material should be available starting from the publication of the application – as provided under European law – as in the case of other inventions. With regard to the interpretation of patent claims relating to biological materials, it is important to ensure that the scope of protection is limited to the material actually deposited. If there is no full correspondence between the description and the deposited material, the patent (or claim) should be deemed void.

Finally, national laws may require that applicants inform the country of origin of any biological material covered by a patent, and that it is demonstrated that they have complied with the relevant rules regarding access to the said material.

This requirement[21] will ensure that the pertinent provisions of the Convention on Biological Diversity and of national implementing legislation are observed and enforced.

Recommended option

The invention shall be disclosed in a manner sufficiently clear and complete for the invention to be carried out by a local person having ordinary skill in the art to which the invention pertains.

The applicant shall disclose the best mode known at the date of the application or priority for the execution of the invention.

The description and claims of a patent shall define the invention for which protection is sought in terms of its purpose, constitution and effects. A claim which only recites the operation and effects of an invention shall not be accepted. A product claim shall not be admitted if the product is not sufficiently defined as such.

The description shall enable the execution of all the embodiments of the invention.

In the case of inventions related to microorganism(s), the applicant shall deposit a culture thereof not later than the date of filing of the application. After the publication of the application, any interested

---

[21] An obligation of this type was incorporated in the draft EU Directive on patents on biotechnology, as approved by the European Parliament in July 1997.

party shall have access to a sample of the deposited culture, subject to the obligation by the said party to use the said sample for experimental purposes only until such time the patent application is refused or withdrawn, or up to the date of granting of the patent.

In the case where the description is supplemented by the deposit of a microorganism, the scope of the claim shall be determined on the basis of the material deposited by the patentee.

The applicant shall disclose the place of origin of any biological material and shall demonstrate compliance with the applicable rules on access, export and use of the said material.

Interpretation of Claims

The TRIPS Agreement does not specify how claims are to be interpreted. This is an important issue left to national legislation, since the actual scope of the rights conferred by a patent is determined by the interpretation of the respective claims under the so-called "theory of equivalents". Legislation should define in which cases inventions that are not literally described in a claim may be deemed "equivalent" and therefore to be infringing the patent rights.

There are different approaches to deal with this issue. Under one approach, equivalence may be found if the allegedly infringing process or product performs substantially the same function as the invention. For a second approach[22], which is recommended here, equivalence should not be merely based on a functional analysis, but on a comparison of the elements that constitute the invention. While the application of this solution permits adequate protection of the inventor's interests, it also facilitates improvements and further innovation in the field covered by the patent.

With regard to the date at which the equivalence should be considered, if the equivalence was not evident to a skilled person when the invention was first claimed, there is no justified reason to consider that there is an infringement. If the evaluation were made at the time

---

[22] As developed in Germany, on the basis of an objective evaluation of equivalence.

of the alleged infringement, the room for incremental or alternative innovation may be limited[23].

Recommended option

The scope of protection of a patent shall be determined by the statements of the patent claim(s). Protection shall not encompass subject matter that is disclosed but not claimed[24].

An element outside the wording of a claim may be deemed to be covered by a claim if for a person skilled in the art it was evident, at the time of the application, that the said element could achieve the same result as that achieved by the element expressed in the claim. The simple fact that an equivalent effect may be achieved shall not be deemed to be evidence of infringement.

Foreign Applications and Grants

Article 29 of the TRIPS Agreement authorizes Members to request information from applicants/patentees concerning the corresponding foreign applications and grants. This may facilitate the examination of applications as well as eventual decisions on the invalidation or revocation of patents.

Recommended option

The applicant of a patent shall provide the national authority, upon request, with the result of the examination made in one or more foreign countries. The patent-holder shall promptly inform the national authority about any decision adopted in a foreign country relating to the validity of a foreign grant.

---

[23] The WIPO draft Treaty Supplementing the Paris Convention as far as Patents are Concerned suggested that the evaluation of the equivalence should be at the time of the alleged infringement (Article 21).

[24] This limitation has been expressly admitted by a Federal Court in the United States in *Maxwell vs J. Baker Inc.* (1996).

Exceptions to Exclusive Rights

Though some of the proposals made during the TRIPS negotiations included specific wording on the exceptions that Members might allow[25], Article 30 of the TRIPS Agreement defines them in very general terms. Under this provision, there is considerable freedom for national legislation to define the kind and extent of exceptions to be granted. Based on comparative law, different types of exceptions may be provided for within the scope of Article 30.

Among them[26], it is important to provide for exceptions relating to research and experimentation on the invention. This exception is admitted in European[27] and other countries for scientific as well as commercial purposes. It is particularly important to facilitate innovation based on the improvement of protected inventions. The extemporaneous preparation of medicines in accordance with a medical prescription is also allowed in many laws[28].

In addition, the US Drug Price Competition and Patent Term Restoration Act permits testing to be carried out to establish the bioequivalency of generic products before the expiration of the relevant patent. The purpose of this exception (known in US law as the "Bolar exemption") is to help generic drug producers to place their products on the market as soon as a patent expires, and thereby allow consumers to obtain the medicines at the much lower prices that generally follow after such expiration.

Another common exception[29] relates to the prior use of an invention, i.e., with regard to a person who in good faith used the invention prior to the filing of a patent by a third party.

---

[25] See the EEC submission as contained in MTN.GNG/NG11/W/26 of 7.7.88.

[26] For examples of exceptions to the exclusive rights generally admitted in patent law, see the WIPO draft Treaty Supplementing the Paris Convention as far as Patents are Concerned (Article 20).

[27] See, for instance, Article L.613-15 b of French Law No. 92-597 (Intellectual Property Code).

[28] See also as an illustration the referred French law, Article L.613-5 c.

[29] Suggested also in the WIPO draft Treaty Supplementing the Paris Convention as far as Patents are Concerned (Article 20).

Parallel imports, permissible under the principle of exhaustion of rights, may also be listed as an exception to the exclusive rights[30].

Recommended option

The following acts shall not be subject to the authorization of the patentee:

- *acts done privately and on a non-commercial scale, or for a non-commercial purpose;*
- *use of the invention for scientific research;*
- *use of the invention for teaching purposes;*
- *experimentation on the invention for commercial purposes, for instance to test it or improve on it;*
- *preparation of medicines under individual prescriptions;*
- *experiments made for the purpose of seeking regulatory approval for marketing of a product after the expiration of a patent;*
- *use of the invention by a third party that had used it* bona fide *before the date of application for the patent.*

Compulsory Licences

Grounds for granting compulsory licences

Article 31 of the TRIPS Agreement on "Other use without the authorization of the right holder" contains a detailed set of conditions for the granting of compulsory licences. Article 31 should be considered in the light of the Preamble and Part I (particularly Articles 7 and 8) of the TRIPS Agreement.

The TRIPS Agreement refers to five possible specific grounds for the granting of compulsory licences (refusal to deal; emergency and extreme urgency; anti-competitive practices; non-commercial use; dependent patents).

Member countries, however, can determine other grounds, since the TRIPS Agreement does not limit the Members' right to establish

---

[30] This is the approach followed, for instance, by Decision 344 of the Andean Group (1993) and by the Argentine patent law (1995).

compulsory licences on grounds not explicitly mentioned therein[31]. The Agreement only sets out the conditions to be met for such a granting.

It should be noted that in some cases, for instance, in emergency and public non-commercial use, there is no need to have previously requested a voluntary licence, as required by Article 31b of the Agreement. Moreover, in the case of public non-commercial use, the patent-holder may be informed after the use of the invention has taken place, as soon as it is reasonably practicable (Article 31b)[32].

The licences to remedy anti-competitive practices are subject to a special treatment with regard to the remuneration to be paid to the patent-holder. Article 31k may be interpreted as allowing for a reduced remuneration or even for a "free-royalty" licence.

The TRIPS Agreement also allows for compulsory licences in cases of lack of or insufficient working. Article 27.1 of the Agreement stipulates that "patent rights shall be enjoyable without discrimination ... whether the products are imported or locally produced".

Though Article 27.1 has been interpreted as a prohibition of any obligation to locally execute a patented invention, this interpretation is not unanimous[33].

A possible option is to provide – in line with Article 8.1 of the TRIPS Agreement – for qualified cases of lack of working, for instance, when such a lack affects sectors of vital interest to the country.

Recommended option

Compulsory licences shall be granted in the following cases:

a)   *when an interested party demonstrates that the patentee has rejected or not replied to, within 150 days, a request for a voluntary licence under reasonable commercial terms and conditions;*

---

[31] Except for "semi-conductor technology".
[32] This type of compulsory licence is authorized, for instance, under US law for the benefit of public agencies such as NASA.
[33] For instance, the Brazilian patent law (1996) has included an obligation to locally exploit the patented inventions. See Chapter III above.

b)   *in cases of emergency;*
c)   *when required by public health;*
d)   *when required for security reasons;*
e)   *when necessary for environmental reasons, such as to preserve plants or animals or avoid prejudice to the environment;*
f)   *as a remedy against anti-competitive practices such as abusive pricing;*
g)   *when required for a public non-commercial use;*
h)   *when required to use a dependent patent, provided that it involves an important technical advance of considerable economic significance. In this case, a cross-licence on reasonable terms shall be granted, upon request, in favour of the owner of the first patent and the licence shall not be assignable except with the assignment of the second patent;*
i)   *lack or insufficiency of local working of the patent when necessary to promote a sector of vital interest to socioeconomic or technological development.*

Conditions for granting compulsory licences

As mentioned above, the TRIPS Agreement does not limit the grounds for the concession of compulsory licences. Instead, it is quite detailed with respect to the *conditions* under which a compulsory licence can be granted. In fact, most countries in the world (including the industrialized countries such as the UK, Germany, France and the US) provide for different types of compulsory licences.

The conditions for granting such licences include the following:

•   Case-by-case evaluation and decision

•   Prior request to the patentee for a voluntary licence

•   Determination of scope and duration of the compulsory licence

•   Non-exclusivity

•   Non-assignability

- Preference for the domestic market

- Remuneration

- Possibility of requesting the revision of decisions (on validity and remuneration) and the revocation of the licence.

The conditions that govern the granting of compulsory licences will determine the extent of the system's effectiveness in promoting local innovation and the transfer of technology. It should be noted that, as reported in the case of the United Kingdom[34], the fact that the number of applications for such licences may be low does not necessarily mean that the system is ineffective: the existence of a statutory provision itself may persuade rights-holders of the need to act reasonably in cases of requests for voluntary licences, while strengthening the bargaining position of potential licensees.

The following conditions for granting compulsory licences need careful consideration:

a) Scope and duration

According to the Agreement, the scope and duration of the authorization "shall be limited to the purpose for which it was authorized" (Article 31 c).

Among the options that developing countries may consider, one is about whether to grant the compulsory licence for the manufacture and/or the importation of the protected products. In many cases (such as where large investments are required, where there exist barriers to accessing operative technology, or where there is a need to remedy anti-competitive practices or to address emergency situations), the only effective way of using a compulsory licence would be through importation.

In addition, in order to be effective, a compulsory licence should in most cases be granted for the lifetime of the patent since a shorter period may not permit the amortization of required investments.

---

[34] See Cornish, W. (1989), *Intellectual Property: Patents, Copyright, Trademarks and Allied Rights*, Sweet & Maxwell, London, p.205.

Recommended option

A compulsory licence may be conferred to import or to locally produce the patented product or a product directly made with a patented process.

The licences shall be granted for the remaining lifetime of the patent, unless a shorter term is justified in the public interest.

b) Termination

According to the TRIPS Agreement, a compulsory licence is liable to be terminated when the circumstances which led to it cease to exist and are unlikely to recur (Article 31 g).

If literally applied, this provision may undermine the effectiveness of the compulsory licensing system.

Recommended option

The competent authority shall have the authority to review, upon motivated request, the continued existence of the circumstances that led to the granting of a licence, and may admit or refuse a request to terminate the licence. The eventual termination is subject to the adequate protection of the legitimate interests of the persons authorized to use the invention, particularly when the licensee has made serious preparations or established facilities to execute the invention.

c) Remuneration

The title-holder shall be paid "adequate remuneration in the circumstances of each case, taking into account the economic value of the authorization" (Article 31 h). As mentioned, special criteria to determine the remuneration may be applied in cases of licences to remedy anti-competitive practices (Article 31 k).

Considerable room is left for interpretation at the national level of the criteria to determine when remuneration is to be deemed "adequate". It must be determined in each individual case, taking into account the circumstances of the licensee and of the market where it operates, as well as the purpose of the licence. A standard that may be used to determine the applicable royalty rate is the average rate paid in voluntary licences in a given industry or branch.

Recommended option

The remuneration for a compulsory licence shall be determined as a percentage of net sales taking into account the value of the licence in the relevant domestic market and the average royalty rates usually paid in the sector or branch to which the invention belongs. The remuneration shall be reduced or excluded when the licence is necessary to remedy anti-competitive practices.

d) Review

The title-holder should be given the possibility of review, by a judicial or another higher authority, of the "legal validity" of any decision relating to the granting of a licence as well as of the determined remuneration (Article 31 i and g). This does not prevent a Member from giving immediate effect to a decision conferring a licence, pending a final decision on the review.

Recommended option

The patentee shall have the right to request a judicial review of any decision relating to the validity of a compulsory licence or to the remuneration determined by the national authority. An application for review shall not suspend the effects of a granted licence.

Reversal of the Burden of Proof

Article 34 provides for the reversal of the burden of proof in *civil* litigation involving *process* patents. The judicial authorities should have the authority "to order the defendant to prove that the process to obtain an identical product is different from the patented process". A similar faculty is provided for under Article 43 of the Agreement, in its Part III relating to "enforcement".

There is a *juris tantum* presumption according to which"any identical product when produced without the consent of the patent owner shall, in the absence of proof to the contrary, be deemed to have been obtained by the patented process." The Agreement specifies two options for the implementation of this presumption. It may be applied in either of the following cases:

* when the product obtained by the patented process is "new"; or

* when there is "a substantial likelihood that the identical product was made by the process and the owner of the patent has been unable through reasonable efforts to determine the process actually used".

The first alternative is the recommended option, since it limits the scope of the reversal of burden of proof to "new" products, while the second one applies to any product independent of its novelty, and is likely to create considerable uncertainty.

In addition, the reversal of burden of proof should only apply if the plaintiff has previously proved that the allegedly infringing product is identical to the product directly produced by his or her process (see Article 28 of the TRIPS Agreement).

Recommended option

The judicial authorities shall have the authority in civil procedures to order the defendant to prove that the process to obtain an identical product is different from the patented process. An identical product when produced without the consent of the patent owner shall, in the absence of proof to the contrary, be deemed to have been obtained by the patented process when it is new. For the purposes of this provision, a product is new if it has not been put on the market for more than one year before the date of the initiation of the judicial action by the patentee.

This provision shall apply subject to the prior proof by the plaintiff that the allegedly infringing product is identical to the product directly produced by the patented process.

Transitional Periods and Provisions

As mentioned earlier, developing countries can delay until 1 January 2000 the implementation of the Agreement, except for obligations concerning national treatment and most-favoured-nation treatment. In addition, a further period of five years is contemplated for developing countries that did not grant product patent protection in certain areas of technology on the general date of application of the Agreement for those countries (i.e., 1 January 2000). In the case of least developed countries, the transitional period is 11 years. An extension of this period can be granted by the Council for TRIPS (Article 66.1).

All these transitional periods are automatically applicable. However, in some countries, foreign patent-holders have attempted to obtain an anticipated application of the Agreement. In order to avoid this situation, a specific clause in the law to this effect may be included.

According to Article 70.7, if there is a patent application pending approval at the time the Agreement becomes enforceable in a Member country (i.e., 1 January 2000 for developing countries), it will be possible to amend the application to claim "any enhanced protection under the provisions of this Agreement".

Such a conversion cannot include "new matter". Hence, a process claim cannot be transformed into a product claim.

Despite the transitional periods, Members have been obliged to receive applications for pharmaceutical and agricultural chemical products since the date of entry into force of the Agreement, i.e., 1 January 1995 (Article 70.8). Patents are to be granted after the expiration of the transitional period, and for the remaining patent term.

"Exclusive marketing rights" (EMRs) must be granted during the transitional period under Article 70.9 of the Agreement. Such rights can be claimed if the following conditions are met:

a)   a patent application has been filed in a Member after the entry into force of the Agreement;

b)   a patent application has been filed in another Member after the entry into force of the Agreement and a patent has been granted;

c)   marketing approval for the protected product has been obtained in the said other Member;

d)   marketing approval has been obtained in the Member mentioned in (a) above.

EMRs should be conferred for five years after marketing approval has been obtained. These rights will be terminated if: i) the corresponding patent is finally granted, or ii) the patent application is rejected.

Since the effects of EMRs are not specified in the Agreement, different options for implementing them are open to developing countries.

If EMRs were interpreted as the provision of a right to exclude third parties from marketing the relevant product, the EMRs should be subject to the exceptions that apply to the exclusive rights granted by patents, as well as to compulsory licences. However, a reasonable interpretation of EMRs, in the light of the negotiations and general context of the Agreement, is that they are meant to confer fewer rights than a patent. It is thus clear that EMRs cannot be used to prevent production for export to third countries (since EMRs only refer to "marketing" in the domestic market).

A possible option is to interpret that the EMRs confer the right to receive compensation from those that commercialize the invention, rather than a right to forbid their activities. The infringement of EMRs would only allow a claim for compensation (that may be equivalent to a reasonable royalty rate or one based on actual damages). But infringement would not prevent commercialization by third parties[35].

Recommended option

The provisions implementing the TRIPS Agreement shall be effective as of 1 January 2000 (developing countries)/1 January 2006 (least developed countries). The provisions relating to products not previously patentable shall be effective as of 1 January 2005.

---

[35] The final interpretation of the scope of EMRs shall be given by relevant WTO bodies, if the issue is brought to their consideration.

A process patent application pending at the time of entry into force of the Agreement shall not be converted into a product application.

The exclusive marketing rights (granted in accordance with Article 70.9 of the TRIPS Agreement) shall confer the right to request a just compensation from third parties that commercialize the invention during the transitional period in the domestic market.

UNDISCLOSED INFORMATION

Article 39.1 of the TRIPS Agreement stipulates that Members shall protect undisclosed information and the "data submitted to governments or governmental agencies" as a condition for approving the marketing of pharmaceutical and agrochemical products.

It is important to note that the Agreement subjects the legal treatment of "undisclosed information" to the discipline of unfair competition, as regulated by Article 10 *bis* of the Paris Convention. This means that there is no obligation to confer exclusive rights on undisclosed information, but just to protect it against unfair commercial practices.

While implementing this part of the Agreement, a balance should be established between the interests of the possessor of secret information and society's interests in the mobility of personnel and diffusion of technologies.

Although Article 39.1 refers to "undisclosed information" and to "undisclosed test" or other "data submitted" to governments as two separate issues, the latter also needs to be "undisclosed" in order to be covered under the terms of the Agreement. Further, the obligation of Article 39.3 only applies to "new" chemical entities and the origination of the data should have involved a "considerable effort".

The protection to be granted is against "unfair commercial use" of the relevant protected information. This means that a third party cannot be prevented from obtaining the registration of a similar product through an abbreviated procedure on the basis of bioequivalence and bioavailability studies; or if it has independently developed the relevant data and information or obtained them from other sources; or if registration does not imply the use of the undisclosed information by the applicant.

Recommended option

Undisclosed information, including data submitted to the government for the approval of pharmaceutical and agrochemical products consisting of new chemical entities, shall be protected against unfair commercial practices, provided that such information

- *is secret in the sense that it is not, as a body or in the precise configuration and assembly of its components, generally known among or readily accessible to persons within the circles that normally deal with the kind of information in question;*
- *has commercial value because it is secret; and*
- *has been subject to reasonable steps under the circumstances, by the person lawfully in control of the information, to keep it secret.*

In the case of data submitted to governments, this protection shall be conferred on data, the development of which implied a considerable technical and economic effort. However, this protection shall not prevent the approval of a similar pharmaceutical or agrochemical product at the request of a third party, subject to the submission of bioequivalence and bioavailability studies.

COMPUTER PROGRAMS

Article 10.1 provides that "computer programs, whether in source or object code, shall be protected as literary works under the Berne Convention (1971)." This means that they are subject to the term of protection and other norms established for literary works. National laws may determine the number and the type of permitted copies and adaptations for a legitimate user, since there are no provisions on the matter in the Agreement.

Another important aspect left to national legislation is the regulation of reverse engineering, i.e., the study of a product to understand its functional aspects and underlying ideas. Reverse engineering may lead to the development of an interoperable program, or to a product which is competitive with the evaluated program. Though there is no specific rule in the Agreement on this topic, Article 9.2 clearly states that "copyright protection shall extend to expressions and not to ideas, procedures, methods of operation or mathematical concepts as such." Article 11 of the TRIPS Agreement introduces as a minimum standard the recognition of "rental rights" in respect of the "commercial" rental of "at least computer programs and cinematographic works". Article 11 *in fine* provides that rental rights in respect of computer programs do not apply "to rentals where the program itself is not the essential object of the rental".

Recommended option

Computer programs shall be protected as literary works. The legitimate user shall be authorized to make two back-up copies and adaptations necessary for the personal use of the program.

The title-holder of a computer program shall have the right to authorize or to prohibit the commercial rental to the public of the original or copies of his or her work.

The author of a computer program shall not be authorized to prevent a third party from evaluating and reverse engineering such a program in order to develop an interoperable or substitute program.

DATABASES

According to Article 10.2 of the TRIPS Agreement, compilations of data or other material, whether in machine-readable or other form, which – by reason of the selection or arrangement of their contents – constitute intellectual creations shall be protected as such. Such protection, which shall not extend to the data or material itself, shall be without prejudice to any copyright subsisting in the data or material itself.

On this basis, the TRIPS Agreement requires protection of databases to the extent that they are original. It neither obliges Members to protect databases which are not original, nor to confer a "right to prevent unfair extraction" of data, as required under the European Union Directive on the Protection of Databases. Moreover, it is clear that under the Agreement protection shall not extend to the data or material itself.

Recommended option

Databases which are original by reason of the selection or arrangement of their contents shall be protected as intellectual creations. Such protection shall not extend to the data or material itself, and shall be without prejudice to any copyright subsisting in the data or material itself.

RESTRICTIVE PRACTICES IN CONTRACTUAL LICENCES

Section 8 of the TRIPS Agreement contains a set of rules aimed at the control of "anti-competitive practices" in voluntary licences. They constitute an application of the general principle stated in Article 8.2 of the Agreement.

Article 40.1 recognizes that some licensing practices pertaining to intellectual property rights which restrain competition "may have adverse effects on trade and impede the transfer and dissemination of technology". Article 40.2 expressly allows Member countries to adopt measures to control or prevent certain licensing practices. The test to assess the practices to be prevented should be based on a case-by-case analysis of whether the practices constitute an "abuse" of intellectual property rights with an "adverse effect on competition in the relevant market".

Article 40.2 also provides a few examples of practices which may be deemed restrictive, but this list is not exhaustive. In some cases (e.g., non-challenge clause), where a practice will always constitute an abuse with adverse effects on competition, they may be defined as restrictive *per se*.[36]

Recommended option

The licensing agreement shall not contain terms and conditions that adversely affect competition. In particular, the following may be deemed null and void:

---

[36] See UNCTAD (1996), *The TRIPS Agreement and Developing Countries*, New York and Geneva, p.55.

a)   *to oblige the licensee to transfer the improvements made on the licensed technology exclusively to the licenser;*

b)   *to oblige the licensee not to challenge the validity of licensed rights;*

c)   *to impose the obligation to acquire from the licenser other technologies or inputs the licensee does not need or desire;*

d)   *to restrict the use of the technology after the expiration or invalidation of the patent;*

e)   *to restrict research and experimentation on the licensed technology;*

f)   *to determine the price or volume of production.*